A VHDL Synthesis Primer

Second Edition

"Where there is a will, there is a way."

"If at first you fail, try, try, try again"

- My Mom

This book is dedicated to her for all the hard work she has done in raising five children.

A VHDL Synthesis Primer

Second Edition

J. BHASKER

Bell Laboratories, Lucent Technologies

BSP BS Publications

An Imprint of **BSP Books Pvt. Ltd.**

4-4-309/316, Giriraj Lane,

Sultan Bazar, Hyderabad - 500 095

A VHDL Synthesis Primer, Second Edition *by* J. Bhasker

First Indian Ed. 2001

Sixth Reprint 2025

Published by:

BSP BS Publications
An Imprint of **BSP Books Pvt. Ltd.**
4-4-309/316, Giriraj Lane, Sultan Bazar,
Hyderabad - 500 095
Phone: 040 - 234456688
e-mail: info@bspbooks.net
website: www.bspublications.net

In arrangement with
Star Galaxy Publishing
1058 Treeline Drive, Allentown, PA 18103
Phone : 610-391-7296

For sale in India, Pakistan, Srilanka, Bangladesh, Nepal, Maldivies and Maynmar only.

Price: Rs. 695.00

ISBN: 978-81-7800-014-5 (Paperback)

Contents

Preface

Here is a practical and useful guide to VHDL synthesis. To many, synthesis appears like a black-box; a design described in VHDL goes in, and out comes a gate-level netlist. Designers are not comfortable with this black-box approach. To take full advantage and usefulness of a synthesis system, it is important to understand the transformations that occur during the synthesis process. The purpose of this book is to expose the black-box myth by describing the transformations that occur during the synthesis process from a hardware description language model to a netlist; VHDL is used as the modeling language.

VHDL is one of the dominant hardware description languages that is used for synthesis. VHDL was originally developed for the Department of Defense, but subsequently it also became an IEEE and an ANSI standard. Its flexibility lies in the fact that it is a very broad language containing constructs that can be used to describe sequential behavior, concurrent behavior, and structure, including data abstraction, all using one modeling language. The language provides support for modeling the system hierarchically and also supports top-down and bottom-up design methodologies. A digital system and its sub-systems can be described at any level of abstraction ranging from the architecture level to the gate level. Precise simulation semantics are associated with all the language constructs and therefore models written in this language can be verified using a VHDL simulator.

Synthesis, in general, has a different meaning to different people. In this book, I refer to synthesis of a design described in VHDL; this design describes combinational logic and or sequential logic. In case of sequential logic, the clocked behavior of the design is expressly described. This precludes talking about logic synthesis (a design described in terms of primitive gates) and about high-level synthesis (behavior specified with no clocking information). The synthesis process transforms this VHDL model into a gate-level netlist. The target netlist is assumed to be a technology-independent representation of the modeled logic. The target technology contains technology-independent generic blocks such as logic gates and register-transfer level (RTL) blocks, such as arithmetic-logic-units and comparators. The succeeding phases of a synthesis process, which are technology translation (that is, mapping of generic gates to specific parts in a library) and module binding (that is, building RTL blocks using primitive gates) are not described in this book.

It is difficult to write a book on synthesis due to its rapidly evolving nature. In this book, I have therefore tried to provide the basic information that will hold true by and large. I have tried to stay clear of ambiguous topics including implementation-specific issues. Because of the richness of the VHDL language, there may be more than one way to describe a certain behavior. This book suggests one or two such modeling styles that are synthesizable. Again, not all constructs in the language can be synthesized since VHDL was designed to be a simulation language. Therefore, in this book, I have tried to show constructs that would be supported by a majority of synthesis systems.

I have also tried to avoid mentioning the various features of vendor-specific synthesis tools. However, there are certain cases when it becomes necessary to show an example of an implementation. In such a case, I have showed how the feature is implemented in the ArchSyn (version 14.0) synthesis system developed at AT&T Bell Laboratories.

CAUTION: Not all available synthesis systems may support the VHDL constructs described in this book. The ArchSyn-specific features described in this book are for illustrative purposes only. For more details on specific features of the ArchSyn system, or on any other synthesis system, the reader is urged to consult the respective vendors' documentation.

This book assumes that the reader knows the basics about the VHDL language. The book is targeted to electrical engineers, specifically circuit and system designers, who are interested in understanding the art of synthesis. The book does not try to explain any of the synthesis algorithms. My belief is that by understanding what results to expect from synthesis, a designer will be able to control the quality of the synthesized designs by writing optimized behavioral models. This is because the synthesized structure is very sensitive to the way in which a certain model is written.

The VHDL used in this book is based on IEEE Std 1076-1993. The IEEE standard package for model interoperability, STD_LOGIC_1164 (IEEE Std 1164-1993) is also used in many examples in this book.

Book Organization

Chapter 1 gives a brief overview of the VHDL language. It is not intended to be a tutorial or a complete description of the language. The reader is urged to read any other text book on VHDL for further details (such as "A VHDL Primer, Revised Edition", J. Bhasker, Prentice Hall, ISBN 0-13-181447-8) or refer to the VHDL Language Reference Manual (LRM), the official bible for VHDL.

The basics of the synthesis process are described in Chapter 2. The basics include topics such as what is a wire, a flip-flop or a state, how are the sizes of objects determined, and so on.

Chapter 3 describes the mapping of VHDL constructs to logic gates. It gives examples of how combinational logic is inferred and how these get transformed into basic gates and interconnections. Styles for modeling synchronous designs are also described along with examples for modeling asynchronous preset and clear, synchronous preset and clear, multiple clocks, and multiple-phase clocks.

Occasionally it becomes necessary to use predesigned blocks in a design. Chapter 3 further describes how to model structure, including the capability to model partial structure in a behavior model.

Chapter 4 describes powerful techniques that can be applied to a VHDL model to provide quality synthesized netlists. The optimizations described in this chapter may be performed automatically by a synthesis system; if not, it may have to be performed manually by the designer to achieve quality results.

Having synthesized a VHDL model, it is often necessary to validate the synthesized netlist with the input model. Chapter 5 provides testbench writing strategies that can be used to verify the synthesis results. Because VHDL is not specifically designed to be used as a synthesis language, differences do arise between pre- and post-synthesis simulation results. This chapter explains the cause of many such discrepancies.

Chapter 6 describes how VHDL constructs are collectively used to model hardware elements. While Chapter 3 describes the mapping of VHDL to logic gates, this chapter describes the opposite scenario, which is, how to model a hardware element for synthesis using VHDL. Elaborate examples are provided for many common hardware elements, such as multiplexers, counters, decoders and arithmetic-logic-units.

In order to illustrate a subset of VHDL supported for synthesis by a typical synthesis system, Appendix A gives a construct by construct description of what is supported by the ArchSyn synthesis system. However, such a subset may vary between different synthesis systems.

Appendix B gives a listing of an arithmetic package, *STD_LOGIC_ARITH*, that is based on the IEEE standard package *STD_LOGIC_1164*. The *STD_LOGIC_ARITH* package was used in many of the examples described in the first edition of the book.

Appendix C describes the logic gates in a generic library that are used in the synthesized circuits described in this book.

Appendix D contains a listing of the IEEE standard arithmetic packages, *NUMERIC_BIT* and *NUMERIC_STD*. These packages are used in many examples in this edition of the book.

The synthesized netlists shown in this book are NOT optimized netlists; thus the logic shown in some cases may be suboptimal. This is acceptable since the purpose of this book is to show the transformation of VHDL to gates and not that of demonstrating logic optimization techniques. Some of the netlists have been optimized purposely so that the netlist could be captured as a figure in the book.

In all the VHDL descriptions that appear in this book, reserved words are in **boldface**. Occasionally ellipsis (. . .) is used in VHDL source to indicate code that is not relevant to that discussion. All examples that are described in this book have been synthesized using the ArchSyn synthesis system and validated using a native VHDL simulator.

Certain words in the text have been written using `Courier` font, such as `if` statement and `wait` statement; this was done so as not to confuse these with their normal English meaning. This convention is applied only for words that cause confusion with the English language. Words such as "variable" in variable assignment and "report" in report statement are not set in a separate font.

Acknowledgments

I would like to thank and acknowledge the following individuals for providing invaluable comments and constructive suggestions that has resulted in a much improved book:

- Doug Smith, Kevin Duke, Brett Graves from Intergraph Electronics.
- Jim Vellenga from Viewlogic Systems.
- Rob Anderson from VLSI Technology.
- J. Vijay Kumar from Hong Kong University of Science and Technology.
- Mourad Takla, Daniel Johnson, Kanchan Mhatre, Carlos Roman, John Jansen, Sriram Tyagarajan from AT&T Bell Laboratories.
- Rich Hatcher from Texas Instruments.

I am very grateful to these individuals for their help.

I would also like to acknowledge Hao Nham, Jean Dussault and Mike Tong for their constant encouragement and in providing a flexible and conducive atmosphere at AT&T Bell Laboratories for making this book possible.

My wife, Geetha, and my two rajahs, Arvind and Vinay, deserve a very special thanks for their continued support, understanding and encouragement throughout the development of this book. The motivation and driving force for this book also comes from my family, especially from my two rajahs who are very proud to have a Dad whose book is sold at a local bookstore.

J. Bhasker

January, 1996

Preface to Second Edition

In the rapidly developing synthesis technology domain, it is important to provide the latest state of the art which is why this second edition has become inevitable. Many changes have occurred in this technology domain since the first edition. The IEEE standard package, *STD_LOGIC_1164* (IEEE Std 1164-1993), has become the default logic package used in almost all models and the synthesis interpretations of the values of type *STD_ULOGIC* are built-in into many synthesis systems. In addition, two arithmetic packages - *NUMERIC_BIT* and *NUMERIC_STD*, have become an IEEE standard (IEEE Std 1076.3-1997). At the time of this publication, the IEEE VHDL Synthesis Interoperability Working Group, of which I'm the Chair, is actively trying to standardize a subset of VHDL for RTL synthesis.

This edition of the book is based on the IEEE standard arithmetic packages - *NUMERIC_BIT* and *NUMERIC_STD*. Also, all examples in the book are based on the dominant logic type package *STD_LOGIC_1164*. A new appendix has been added that describes the IEEE standard arithmetic packages. In addition, more examples have been added. The size and format of the book have been changed to make it more readable.

I feel very exhilarated to note that my first edition was a big success. This edition is an effort to keep up with the latest state of the art so that its usefulness continues to increase. I hope that you will find this edition more useful.

It gives me great pleasure to acknowledge Egbert Molenkamp of University of Twente, the Netherlands, for doing a thorough review of a draft manuscript of this edition; his critical remarks and constructive suggestions have lead to significant improvements. My personal thanks to all others who have provided corrections and suggested improvements to the first edition. I sincerely appreciate their efforts in making this a useful and practical book for all designers to use.

If you have any comments on this book or any suggestions to help improve the quality of this book, please feel free to contact me at jbhasker@lucent.com or through my publisher.

J. Bhasker

June, 1998

Chapter 1

Language Basics

This chapter provides a very brief introduction to the VHDL language. It is intended to act as a refresher on VHDL and is not intended to be a comprehensive description of the language and does not describe all its features. The reader is urged to read a text on VHDL or the VHDL Language Reference Manual for further details. Details of a synthesizable subset of VHDL is given in Appendix A.

1.1 About VHDL

VHDL is a hardware description language intended for documenting and modeling digital systems ranging from a small chip to a large system. It can be used to model a digital system at any level of abstraction ranging from the architectural level down to the gate level.

The language was initially developed specifically for Department of Defense VHSIC (Very High Speed Integrated Circuits) contractors. However, due to an overwhelming need in the industry for a standard hardware description language, the VHSIC Hardware Description Language (VHDL) was selected and later approved to become an IEEE standard called the IEEE Std 1076-1987. The language was updated again in 1993 to include a number of clarifications in addition to a number of new features like report statement and pulse rejection limit. The examples in this book are based on this version of the language called the IEEE Std 1076-1993.

1.2 Design Units

There are five kinds of design units provided in VHDL.

a. *Entity declaration*: An entity declaration describes the interface of the design to its external environment, that is, it describes the ports (inputs, outputs, etc.) through which the design communicates with other designs.

```
library IEEE;
  -- Library clause declares the design library IEEE.
use IEEE.STD_LOGIC_1164.all;
use IEEE.NUMERIC_STD.all;
  -- The use clauses import all declarations in the packages
  -- STD_LOGIC_1164 and NUMERIC_STD into the design
  -- unit (entity declaration) that follows it.
entity FILTER4 is
  port (XIN, XD1, XD2, XD3: in UNSIGNED (3 downto 0);
      YOUT: out UNSIGNED (7 downto 0));
  -- Declarations may also be present here.
end FILTER4;
-- The entity FILTER4 has four input ports and one output port.
```

b. *Architecture body*: An architecture body describes the composition or functionality of a design. This could be described as a mix of sequential behavior (behavioral style), concurrent behavior (dataflow style), and connected components (structural style). A design may have more than one architecture body, each describing a different composition, that is, using a different style of design. An architecture body is always associated with an entity declaration that provides its interface.

```
architecture A1 of FILTER4 is
  -- This is the declarative part:
  constant K0: UNSIGNED (3 downto 0) := "0111";
  constant K1: UNSIGNED (3 downto 0) := "0101";
```

```
    constant K2: UNSIGNED (3 downto 0) := "0011";
    constant K3: UNSIGNED (3 downto 0) := "0100";
  begin
    -- This part contains concurrent statements:
    YOUT <= (K0 * XIN + K1 * XD1) + (K2 * XD2 + K3 * XD3);
      -- The overloaded definitions for the "* " and the "+ " operators are
      -- defined in package NUMERIC_STD.
  end A1;
  -- Architecture name is A1, and its interface is defined by the
  -- entity declaration FILTER4.
  -- All declarations visible in the entity declaration (including those
  -- made visible by the use clauses) are also visible in the
  -- architecture body.
```

c. *Configuration declaration*: A configuration declaration is used to specify the bindings of components present in an architecture body to other design entities. An entire hierarchy of a design, that is, the bindings that link all the design entities in a hierarchy, can also be specified using the configuration declaration.

```
configuration COMB of FILTER4 is
  for A1
  end for;
end COMB;
-- Configuration COMB selects entity FILTER4 with architecture A1.
```

d. *Package declaration*: A package declaration is a repository to store commonly used declarations.

```
library IEEE;
use IEEE.NUMERIC_BIT.all;
package OVERLOAD is
  function "and" (L, R: UNSIGNED) return UNSIGNED;
end OVERLOAD;
-- Package OVERLOAD contains one function declaration.
```

e. *Package body*: A package body is always associated with a package declaration and contains subprogram bodies, along with other declarations.

```
package body OVERLOAD is
  function "and" (L, R: UNSIGNED) return UNSIGNED is
    alias LOT: UNSIGNED (1 to L'LENGTH) is L;
    alias ROT: UNSIGNED (1 to R'LENGTH) is R;
    variable RES: UNSIGNED (1 to L'LENGTH);
  begin
    assert L'LENGTH = R'LENGTH;
```

```
      for J in LOT'RANGE loop
        RES(J) := LOT(J) and ROT(J);
      end loop;

      return RES;
    end "and";
  end OVERLOAD;
  -- Package body for package OVERLOAD contains
  -- the function's body.
```

The minimum design units required to model a design is an entity declaration and one architecture body.

1.3 Data Objects

A data object holds a value or a sequence of values of a certain type. There are four classes of data objects.

a. *Constant*: A constant holds a value of a specified type. It is set once in a constant declaration, and its value cannot be changed later.

```
constant LINELENGTH: NATURAL := 132;
-- Constant LINELENGTH is of the predefined integer subtype
-- NATURAL and its value is 132.
```

b. *Variable*: A variable also holds a value of a specified type. It can be assigned a value using a variable assignment statement.

```
-- Example of a variable declaration:
variable RES: UNSIGNED (1 to L'LENGTH) := (others => '0');
-- Variable RES is of type UNSIGNED with size L'LENGTH and has a
-- default value of all zeros.
```

c. *Signal*: A signal has a current value and a set of future projected values. A future value can be assigned to a signal using a signal assignment statement.

```
-- Example of a signal declaration:
signal SBOX, ABOX: INTEGER := 5;
-- Two signals ABOX and SBOX are of type INTEGER and their
-- initial values are 5.
```

d. *File*: A file contains a sequence of values of a specified type. Values can be written to or read from using procedures.

```
-- Example of a file declaration:
file STROBE: TEXT open WRITE_MODE is "./strobe.dat";
-- File STROBE is to be opened in write-only mode and is associated
-- with the physical file "./strobe.dat".
```

1.4 Data Types

A data type represents a collection of values. The following data types are available in VHDL.

a. *Enumeration type*: Values of this type are defined by the user.

```
type FDS is (ADD, SUB, GT, EQ);
-- The enumeration type FDS contains four user-defined values.
```

b. *Integer type*: Values of this type are integer numbers.

```
type SBOX_TYPE is range 0 to 31;
-- SBOX_TYPE is an integer type with values in the
-- range 0 through 31.
```

c. *Physical type*: Values of this type represent measurement of some physical quantity.

```
type TV_TIME is 0 to 20_000
  units
    hours;
    days = 24 hours;
  end units TV_TIME;
-- TV_TIME is a physical type that can have units of hours and days.
```

d. *Floating point type*: Values of this type are real numbers.

```
type SWING is range –30.0 to +30.0;
-- Type SWING is a floating point type with real numbers
-- in the range –30.0 through +30.0
```

e. *Array type*: An object of this type represents a collection of elements of the same element type.

```
type UNSIGNED is array (NATURAL range <>) of BIT;
-- UNSIGNED is an unconstrained array type, each element
-- is of type BIT.
```

f. *Record type*: An object of this type represents a collection of elements, possibly of different types.

```
type CHECKING is
  record
    DATE: STRING (1 to 6);
    DOLLARS: NATURAL;
  end record CHECKING;
-- CHECKING is a record type with two elements, DATE
-- and DOLLARS.
```

g. *Access type*: Values of this type represent pointers to other objects.

```
type FDS_PTR is access FDS;
-- FDS_PTR is an access type that contain addresses that point to
-- objects of type FDS.
```

h. *File type*: Contains a sequence of values of a specific type.

```
file BIT_PAT is file of BIT;
-- BIT_PAT is a file type that contains a sequence of values of type BIT.
```

Subtypes

A *subtype* is a type with possibly a constraint.

```
subtype BOX_ARR is UNSIGNED (0 to 15);
-- BOX_ARR is a subtype of the type UNSIGNED with an index
-- constraint of 0 to 15.
```

1.5 Design Description

A design is described using one or more concurrent statements in an architecture body. The execution of a concurrent statement is based on events on the signals in its input list, and thus the order of concurrent statements within an architecture body is not important. The following concurrent statements are available.

a. *Block statement*: A block statement is used to represent a partition of a design.

```
BLAB: block (HANDLE)
begin
  TOG <= guarded BOG after 5 ns;
end block BLAB;
-- Block statement has a label BLAB. A guard expression,
-- HANDLE, is present. Whenever HANDLE is true, BOG is
```

```
-- assigned to signal TOG after 5 ns. If HANDLE is false, signal
-- TOG retains its previous value.
```

b. *Concurrent procedure call statement*: The specified procedure is called whenever an event occurs on an input signal parameter.

```
ADDER (FIRST => GUMP, SECOND => HUMP, RESULT => LUMP);
-- Procedure ADDER is called when there is an event on signal GUMP
-- or HUMP, assuming that FIRST and SECOND are input
-- signal parameters.
```

c. *Concurrent assertion statement*: The assertion is checked whenever an event occurs on a signal used in the assert expression.

```
assert (CLK = '0' and PCK = '1') or (CLK = '1' and PCK = '0')
  report "CLK and PCK are overlapping."
  severity ERROR;
-- Assertion is checked on every event that occurs on
-- signals CLK and PCK.
```

d. *Concurrent signal assignment statement*: The signal assignment statement executes whenever there is an event on a signal that is used in the right-hand-side expression. The value of the right-hand-side expression is then assigned to the left-hand-side signal or aggregate after the specified delay. If no delay is specified, a delta delay is assumed. A delta delay is an infinitesimally small delay that is used for ordering events that occur at the same time.

```
RX_LINK_CODE(0 to 5) <= "011001" after 3 ns;
```

e. *Component instantiation statement*: A component instantiation represents a child component of a design. The component is evaluated whenever an event occurs on any of the signals connected to its input ports.

```
L0: NOR2 port map (A => S1, B => S2, Z => SET);
-- L0 is the component label, NOR2 is the component. Assuming
-- component ports A and B are input ports, this component is
-- executed whenever an event occurs on signals S1 or S2.
```

f. *Generate statement*: This statement is executed at elaboration time. The execution either causes replication of concurrent statements or causes conditional selection of concurrent statements.

```
GEN_BANK: if NEED_FF generate
  process
  begin
    wait until CLK = '1';
    Q <= DATA_IN;
```

```
end process;
end generate GEN_BANK;
-- GEN_BANK is the label for the generate statement. If NEED_FF
-- is true, the process statement is included in the description. If value
-- is false, the process statement is not included in the description.
```

g. *Process statement*: A process statement is used to describe the behavior of a design using sequential statements. These statements execute sequentially. The following sequential statements are available.

1. *Wait statement*: The wait statement causes the process, or the calling process, to suspend.

```
wait for 15 ns;
```

2. *Report statement*: The report statement prints a message and reports a severity level to the simulator.

```
report "This branch of code is executed"
  severity WARNING;
```

3. *Assertion statement*: If assertion is false, a message is printed and a severity level is reported to the simulator.

```
assert TOG > 15
  report "TOG is less than or equal to 15"
  severity NOTE;          -- NOTE is the severity level.
```

4. *Signal assignment statement*: The value of the expression on the right-hand-side is assigned to the left-hand-side signal or an aggregate after the specified delay (if no `after` clause is present, delta delay is assumed. A delta delay is an infinitesimally small delay).

```
PAR <= A xor (B xor C) after 2.1 ns;
```

5. *Variable assignment statement*: The value of the expression on the right-hand-side is computed and immediately assigned to the left-hand-side variable or an aggregate.

```
RESULT := A(K) or A(J);
```

6. *Procedure call statement*: The specified procedure is called.

```
PROPAGATE_DELAY (IN_SIG => Q, OUT_SIG => PROP_Q,
                 DELAY => DLY);
```

7. *If statement*: If condition is true, the corresponding set of sequential statements are executed.

```
if DOLLARS < 20 then
  DOLLARS := DOLLARS + FEES;
end if;
```

8. *Case statement*: Depending on the value of the branch expression, the corresponding set of sequential statements are executed.

```
case FDS_VAR is
  when ADD =>
    Z <= A + B;
  when SUB =>
    Z <= A – B;
  when GT =>
    Z <= A > B;
  when EQ =>
    Z <= A = B;
end case;
```

9. *Loop statement*: The execution of the loop statement causes the statements within the loop to be iterated the specified number of times. A loop statement can be a for-loop, a while-loop or a repeat-forever-loop.

```
-- This is an example of a for-loop:
for K in 1 to L loop
  SUM := SUM + K;
end loop;
```

10. *Next statement*: Causes the next iteration of the specified loop to be executed. This statement can only be present within a loop statement.

```
next LAB1 when SUM > 10;
-- Executes the next iteration of loop LAB1 if specified
-- condition is true.
```

11. *Exit statement*: Causes the specified loop to be exited. This statement can only be present within a loop statement.

```
exit when SUM = TOG – 2;
-- Exits innermost loop if specified condition is true.
```

12. *Return statement*: Causes the subprogram that contains this return statement to terminate.

```
return TO_BITVECTOR(46, 6);
-- Returns the value of the expression to the calling
-- process or subprogram.
```

13. *Null statement*: Does not perform any action.

```
null;
```

1.6 Design Libraries

A *design library* is a place in the host environment (*host environment* is the system that provides for VHDL compilation and simulation) where compiled descriptions of design units are stored. A *design file* may contain one or more design units. After successful compilation, compiled design units are stored in a design library that is designated as a working library. Each design library is assigned a logical name (a logical name is a name by which the design library will be referenced in VHDL models) and one of the libraries must be designated as the working library. The design library designated as the working library also has the logical name *WORK*.

In addition, a predefined design library *STD* is always present in a host environment. The design library *STD* contains the predefined packages *STANDARD* and *TEXTIO*. The host environment may also provide a design library *IEEE* that stores the IEEE standardized packages, for example, *STD_LOGIC_1164*, *NUMERIC_BIT* and *NUMERIC_STD*.

1.7 Simulating a Model

Once all design units related to a complete design have been compiled, the top-level design entity or its configuration is selected for simulation. A simulator then proceeds through the following three stages:

a. Elaboration: Expands the hierarchy down to a set of behavioral models.

b. Initialization: Signals are initialized and processes are executed until they all wait.

c. Event-based simulation: Simulation starts from time 0 and simulation progresses based on events, until no more events are present, or *TIME'HIGH* is reached (*TIME'HIGH* is the maximum value for type *TIME* as defined in the predefined package *STANDARD*).

1.8 Synthesizing a Model

This is the topic for the rest of this book.

❑

Chapter 2

Synthesis Basics

VHDL is a hardware description language that can not only describe hardware at the gate level and the register-transfer level (RTL), but also at the behavioral level using abstract data types. This makes translating a design described in VHDL to logic gates a non-trivial process.

This chapter explains the basics involved in the mapping of the VHDL model to logic gates. It shows what VHDL objects become the value carriers in hardware. VHDL types play an important role in determining the bit-width of a particular object; the mechanics of how bit-widths are computed is explained in this chapter. This chapter also shows that a mapping mechanism i necessary to map the literals in VHDL to values necessary to represent harc ware.

2.1 What is Synthesis?

Synthesis is the process of constructing a gate-level netlist from a model of a circuit described in VHDL.[1] Figure 2-1 shows such a process. A synthesis program may alternately generate a RTL netlist, which is comprised of register-transfer level blocks such as flip-flops, arithmetic-logic-units, and multiplexers, interconnected by wires. In such a case, a second program called the RTL module builder is necessary. The purpose of this builder is to build, or acquire from a library of predefined components, each of the required RTL blocks in the user-specified target technology.

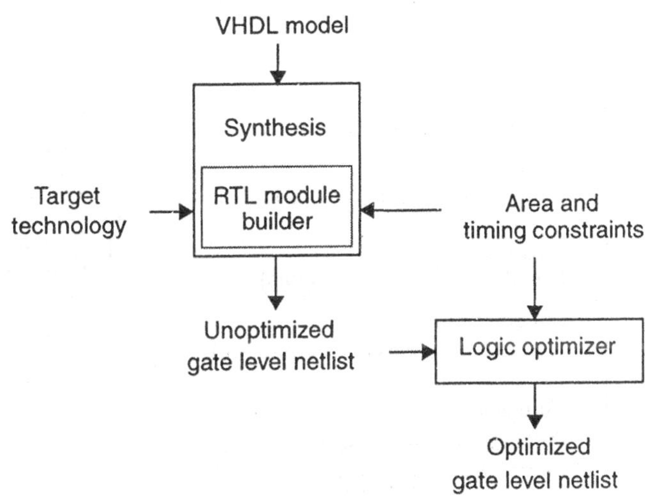

Figure 2-1 The synthesis process.

Having produced a gate-level netlist, a logic optimizer reads in this netlist and optimizes the circuit for the user-specified area and timing constraints. These area and timing constraints may also be used by the module builder for appropriate selection or generation of RTL blocks.

1. This is the definition used in this book.

In this book, we assume that the target netlist is at the gate level. The logic gates used in the synthesized netlists are described in Appendix C. The module building and logic optimization phases are not described in this book.

Figure 2-2 shows the basic elements of VHDL and the elements used in hardware. A mapping mechanism or a construction mechanism has to be provided that translates the VHDL elements into their corresponding hardware elements. Questions to ask are:

- How does a data type translate to hardware?
- How are literals mapped to logic values?
- How do data objects map to hardware?
- How are statements translated to hardware?

The following sections discuss these mappings in more detail.

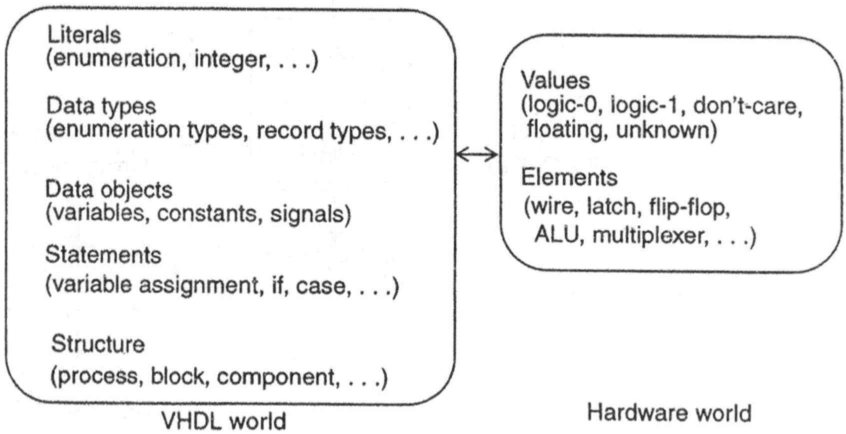

Figure 2-2 The two worlds of synthesis.

2.2 Synthesis in a Design Process

VHDL is a hardware description language that allows a designer to model a circuit at different levels of abstraction, ranging from the gate level, RTL level, behavioral level to the algorithmic level. Thus a circuit can be described in many different ways, not all of which may be synthesizable. Confounding this is the fact that VHDL was designed primarily as a simulation language and not as a language for synthesis. Consequently, there are many constructs in VHDL that have no hardware counterpart, for example, an assertion statement. Also there is no standardized subset of VHDL for synthesis.

Because of these problems, different synthesis systems support different VHDL subsets for synthesis. Since there is no direct object in VHDL that means a latch or a flip-flop, each synthesis system may provide different mechanisms to model a flip-flop or a latch. Each synthesis system therefore defines its own subset of VHDL language including its own personalized modeling style.

Figure 2-3 shows a circuit that is described in many different ways using VHDL. A synthesis system that supports synthesis of styles A and B may not support that of style C. This implies that typically synthesis models are non-portable across different synthesis systems. Style D may not be synthesizable at all.

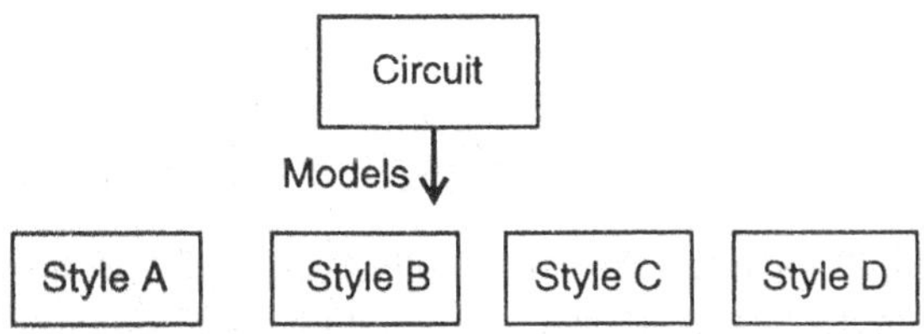

Figure 2-3 Same behavior, different styles.

This limitation creates a severe handicap because now the designer not only has to understand the VHDL language, but also has to understand the synthesis-specific modeling style before a model can be written. The ideal design process shown in Figure 2-4 can no longer be followed for VHDL synthesis.

The problem with this design process is that if the behavioral model is written without knowing the synthesis modeling style, only during the synthesis phase will the designer learn about the synthesis-specific modeling restriction and style for synthesis. A model rewrite may be necessary at this point. Also a lot of time may have been wasted in the "Write model" -> "Compile VHDL" -> "Simulate" -> "Edit model" loop. Instead, the design process shown in Figure 2-5 has to be followed for VHDL synthesis. A synthesis methodology checker is needed to check if the model being written is compatible for synthesis or not, and also this must be done within the first simulation

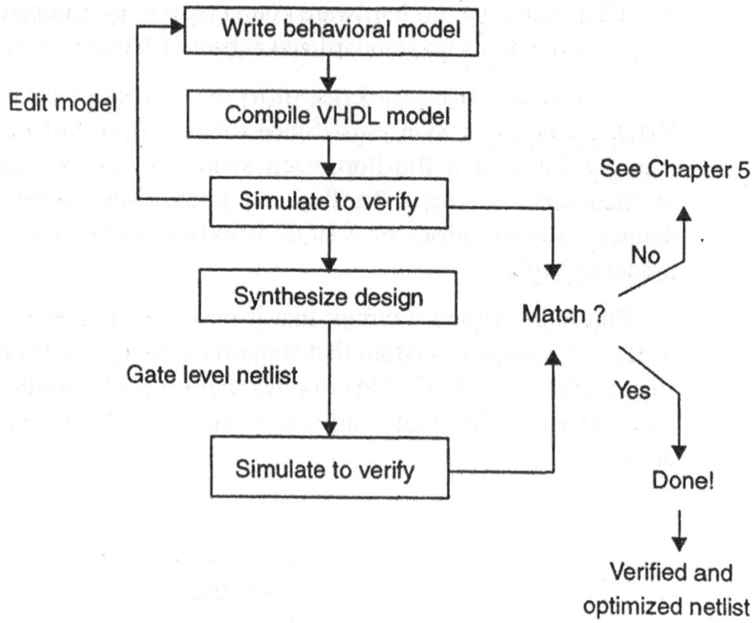

Figure 2-4 Typical design process.

loop. In this way, after the simulation results have been verified, a verified synthesizable model exists, which can then be synthesized.

2.3 Value Holders for Hardware Modeling

VHDL provides two classes of data objects, signal and variable, that can be used to model the basic value holders in hardware. The basic value holders in hardware are:

- wire
- flip-flop (an edge-triggered device)
- latch (a level-sensitive device)

In VHDL, a signal, or a variable declared in a process, retains its value through the entire simulation run, thus inferring memory. However, this is too general for synthesis. Here is an example of a variable that is used as a temporary and therefore need not be a candidate for a memory element.

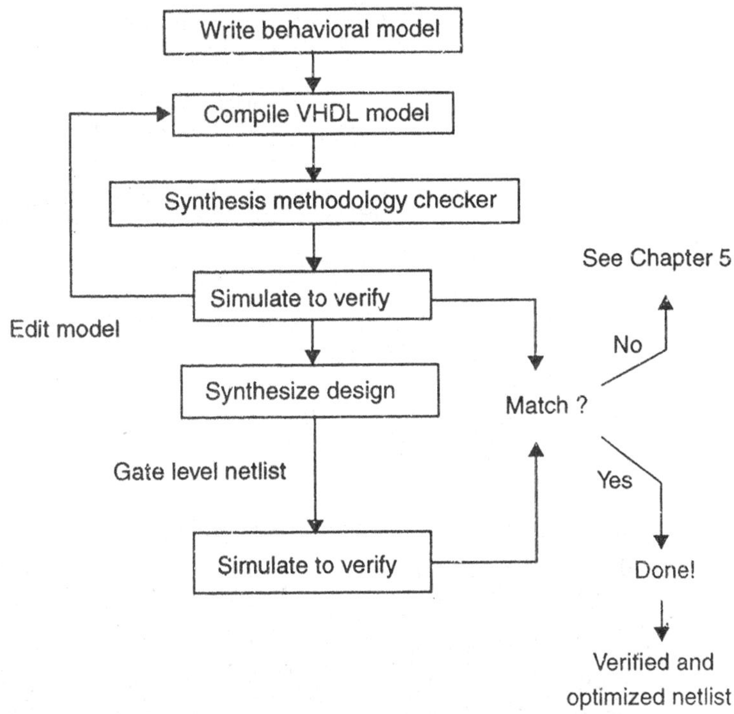

Figure 2-5 New design process.

```
signal CAR, BAR, FAR, SAR: BIT;
. . .
NO_MEMORY: process (BAR, CAR, FAR)
  variable TAR: BIT;
begin
  TAR := BAR and CAR;
  SAR <= TAR or FAR;
end process;
```

Variable *TAR* is assigned in the first statement and then used in the right-hand-side expression of the second statement. VHDL semantics indicate that variable *TAR* retains its value through the entire simulation run. However, it is not necessary to store the value of *TAR* as a memory element in hardware, since it is assigned and used immediately. Figure 2-6 shows the logic generated.

Let us look at another example. In this case, the variable *TAR* is used before its assignment.

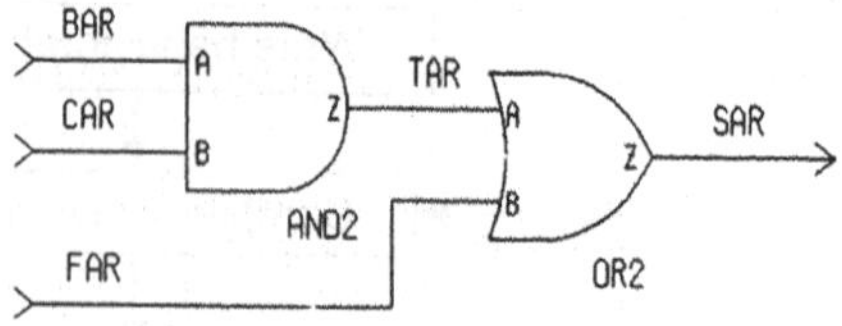

Figure 2-6 Variable *TAR* is a wire.

```
signal CAR, BAR, FAR, SAR: BIT;
...
IS_IT_A_LATCH: process (BAR, CAR, FAR)
  variable TAR: BIT;
begin
  SAR <= TAR or FAR;
  TAR := BAR and CAR;
end process;
```

The semantics of this process is very clear in VHDL. Whenever an event occurs on signal *BAR*, *CAR*, or *FAR*, execute the process. Since variable *TAR* is used before its assignment, *TAR* has to hold its value during repeated executions of the process, thus inferring memory. However, it is not clear how to build a latch for variable *TAR* because *TAR* is not assigned a value under the control of any condition. A synthesis system may issue an error or a warning message about a variable being used before its definition and produce the circuit shown in Figure 2-6. However, simulation results between pre- and post-synthesis may not match. For example, if signal *BAR* changes in the behavioral model, *SAR* is assigned a value based on the old value of *TAR* (that is, *BAR* has no effect on *SAR*), whereas in the synthesized netlist, *SAR* depends on the current value of *TAR* which is computed by taking the and of *BAR* and *CAR*.

What if *TAR* were a signal?

```
signal CAR, BAR, FAR, TAR, SAR: BIT;
...
NO_LATCH: process (BAR, CAR, FAR)
begin
  SAR <= TAR or FAR;
  TAR <= BAR and CAR;
end process;
```

This is identical to the previous case, that is, even though the value of signal *TAR* needs to be saved, it is not clear how to build a latch for *TAR*. A synthesis system may not create a latch in this case but may generate the circuit shown in Figure 2-7, which is the same as Figure 2-6. Signal *TAR* is synthesized to a wire again. However, for simulation results to match between pre- and post-synthesis, the signal *TAR* must also be in the sensitivity list of the process. If signal *TAR* is not in the sensitivity list, a synthesis system may issue a warning message about a potential simulation mismatch. More on this is discussed in Chapter 5.

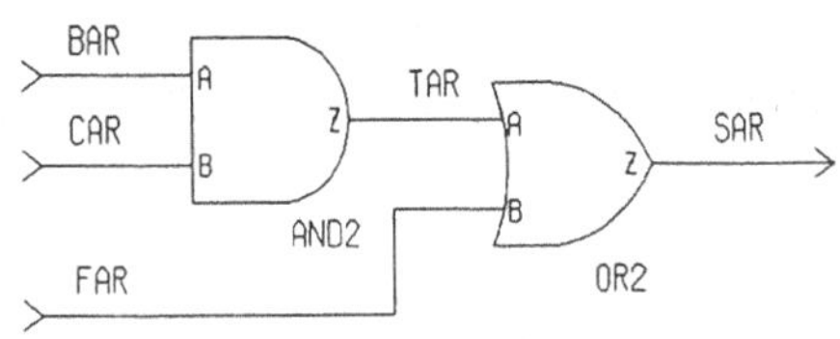

Figure 2-7 No latch for signal *TAR*.

Here is an example where a latch is inferred.

```
signal SAT, SOUT, ANT: BIT;
. . .
LATCH: process (SAT, ANT)
  variable FOX: BIT;
begin
  if SAT = '0' then
    FOX := ANT;
  end if;

  SOUT <= not FOX;
end process;
```

The variable *FOX* is not assigned in the else-branch of the `if` statement. Consequently, a latch is inferred for *FOX* since it needs to retain its value when the condition *SAT*='0' is false. The circuit synthesized in shown in Figure 2-8.

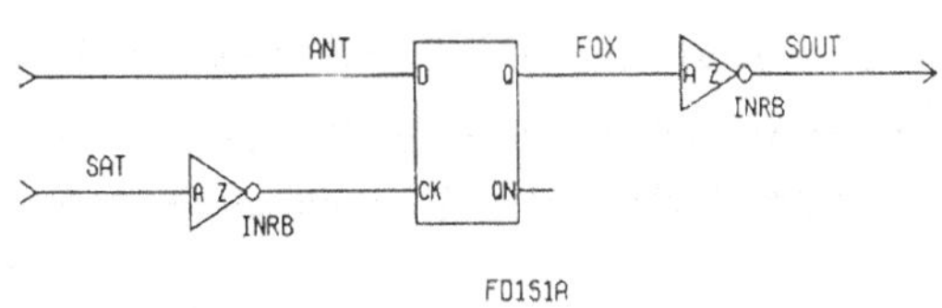

Figure 2-8 Variable *FOX* is a latch.

How is a flip-flop inferred? It depends on the modeling style being followed and the context under which a variable or a signal is assigned. This and other examples for flip-flop and latch inferencing are discussed in the next chapter. A memory can be modeled as an array of flip-flops or latches.

2.4 Logic Value System

The common values used in modeling hardware are:

- logic-0
- logic-1
- high-impedance
- don't-care
- unknown

These values are not defined explicitly in VHDL. The literal '0' in VHDL may or may not infer a logic-0 value. The literal 'Z' may or may not infer a high-impedance (or tri-state) value. Associating an interpretation for literals in VHDL is left to the designer. Also different mappings may exist from a literal to a hardware value. For synthesis purposes, this mapping needs to be explicitly provided in a form that a synthesis system can understand. The mapping of VHDL literals to the synthesis logic values is provided by using a special attribute called *ENUM_ENCODING*.

2.5 Computing Bit-widths

In VHDL, an object declaration specifies the type of the object. The size of an object, that is, the corresponding number of bits in hardware, is determined from its type. Given a signal declaration,

signal *DAK*: *INTEGER* **range** 10 **to** 31;

what should the size of *DAK* be, that is, how many bits does signal *DAK* represent in hardware? The following sections describe how this is determined.

2.5.1 Integer Types

The number of bits required for an integer type object is the minimum number of bits needed to hold the largest integer value. The bit representation for an integer can represent either an unsigned number or a signed number. If the integer type object can take a negative integer value, then the object is said to contain signed numbers. A signed number is represented using 2's complement form. If the object has only non-negative values, then the object is said to hold unsigned numbers. Here are some examples.

```
signal AX: INTEGER range 0 to 15;

type MYINT is range –128 to +15;
variable BOX: MYINT;

subtype M1 is POSITIVE range 25 downto 5;
variable CAT: M1;
```

Signal *AX* is an unsigned integer of 4 bits. *AX* contains unsigned numbers because it can hold only non-negative values. It is of size 4 bits since this is the minimum number of bits needed to encode the largest integer value, which is 15. *BOX* is a signed integer of 8 bits. Eight bits are needed, at the minimum, to represent the largest integer value, which is –128 in 2's complement form. Variable *CAT* is an unsigned number of size 5 bits.

In hardware, signal *AX* is a vector with range 3 down to 0, variable *BOX* is a vector with range 7 down to 0, and variable *CAT* is a vector with range 4 down to 0. The convention of using a descending range with the rightmost index of 0 is typical of a synthesis system. The leftmost bit is the most significant bit. For example, *AX*(3) and *CAT*(4) are the most significant bits for signal *AX* and variable *CAT* respectively.

In the above examples, the size of objects could be easily determined. What about the following variable?

```
variable ARB: INTEGER;
```

What should the size (number of bits) for *ARB* be? From the minimal range constraint of type *INTEGER* specified in the IEEE Std 1076-1993, at least 32 bits are necessary to implement it. This is an overdesign for synthesis. A synthesis system, in such a case, may automatically determine the maximum size of variable *ARB* by performing a data-flow analysis of the model. For example, given the signal assignment statement,

```
ARB <= BAR + RUB;
```

if *BAR* and *RUB* are of size 5 bits, *ARB* will be computed to be of size 6 bits.

2.5.2 Type *BIT_VECTOR*

The predefined type *BIT_VECTOR* defines an array of bit values, where a bit is either a '0' or a '1'. The bit value '0' is interpreted as representing logic-0 in hardware and bit value '1' is interpreted as logic-1. Each bit in a bit-vector is represented as one bit in hardware. The size of an object of this type is, thus, directly determined from the size of the array. Here are some examples.

```
signal RED: BIT_VECTOR (7 downto 0);
variable DHA: BIT_VECTOR (0 to 3);

subtype REST is BIT_VECTOR (26 downto 15);
variable LAP: REST;
constant CONE: BIT_VECTOR := "001";
```

Signal *RED* is an object of size 8, whose index ranges from 7 down to 0. Variable *DHA* is of size 4, with its index ranging from 0 to 3. Variable *LAP* is of size 12, with its index ranging from 26 through 15. The size of constant *CONE* is determined from the size of the constant value, which is 3, and its index ranges from 0 to 2.

VHDL does not provide any information on which bit of a bit-vector is to be treated as the most significant bit. But such information is necessary for performing arithmetic operations. In a synthesis system, values of type *BIT_VECTOR* often represent unsigned numbers and the leftmost bit is treated as the most significant bit. In the previous examples, *RED*(7), *DHA*(0), *LAP*(26) and *CONE*(0) are the most significant bits.

A value of type *BIT_VECTOR* can also be made to represent a signed number. This can be accomplished by using a package in which the operands of an arithmetic or a relational operator are treated as signed numbers. For example, here is a declaration for the "+" operator overloaded function.

```
function "+" (L, R: BIT_VECTOR) return BIT_VECTOR;
```

By writing the function body in which the operands are treated as signed numbers, an object of type *BIT_VECTOR* can then be interpreted as a signed number within the function.

2.5.3 Enumeration Types

An enumeration type specifies a user-defined set of values. These values can either be symbolic values, that is, identifiers, or character literals. Here is an example.

```
type SUMMER is (MAY, JUNE, JULY, AUG, SEPT);
signal DAC: SUMMER;
. . .
DAC <= JULY;
```

What is the size of signal *DAC*? The most common way to compute the size of an enumeration type is to compute the number of bits needed to encode the maximum position number of a literal in the enumeration type. Remember that in VHDL, every enumeration literal has a position number associated with it. The first enumeration literal in an enumeration type has position number 0, the next literal to its right has the position number 1, and so on. So in the case of signal *DAC*, the number of bits needed is 3. This is because the largest position number in the enumeration type *SUMMER* is that of the literal *SEPT*, which is 4. The value of an enumeration literal is decided by its corresponding position number. This implies that the enumeration literal *MAY* is a 3-bit value "000", *JUNE* represents the value "001", and so on. In the above example, *DAC* is being assigned the value "010".

Using the above-specified encoding technique, the predefined type *BOOLEAN* has a size of one bit, with the literal *FALSE* representing logic-0, and the literal *TRUE* representing logic-1.

This encoding of an enumeration type is consistent with the simulation semantics for this type. However, quite often, it may be desirable to specify a different encoding for the enumeration literals. The two common cases where this may be useful are in:

- state encoding of a finite state machine
- encoding of an unknown, a don't-care, or a high-impedance value.

State Encoding

Here is a VHDL code fragment.

```
type FSM_STATE is
              (RESET, APPLY, WAITS, CLEAR, SEND, COMPLETE);
signal CURR_ST, NEXT_ST: FSM_STATE;
. . .
```

```
case CURR_ST is
  when RESET =>
    NEXT_ST <= CLEAR;
...
```

This code describes part of the behavior of a finite state machine. Using the encoding scheme specified earlier, signals *CURR_ST* and *NEXT_ST* would be of size 3 bits and the enumeration literals would be encoded as *RESET* with "000", *APPLY* with "001", *WAITS* with "010", and so on.

However in finite state machine synthesis, it is well known [Reference 16. in "Bibliography"] that different encoding schemes produce different hardware representations of a finite state machine behavior. In such a case, the designer may be interested in specifying a different encoding for the enumeration literals.

In VHDL, there is no explicit mechanism for specifying such an encoding. Such an encoding may be specified using an attribute of the enumeration type. Here is an example.

```
attribute ENUM_ENCODING: STRING;
attribute ENUM_ENCODING of FSM_STATE: type
                    is "000001 000010 000100 001000 010000 100000";
```

An attribute called *ENUM_ENCODING* is first declared using an attribute declaration. Then using an attribute specification, a string containing the encoded values for each enumeration literal is specified in their respective order; the first encoded value "000001" corresponds to the first enumeration literal *RESET*, the second encoded value "000010" corresponds to the second enumeration literal *APPLY*, and so on. In this encoding mechanism, the size of the type is determined by the number of bits specified in the encoding for each of its literals. In this example, the number of bits for the type *FSM_STATE* is thus 6 bits. A synthesis system may use this encoding to synthesize the finite state machine, thereby producing a possibly more efficient implementation.

Using the above encoding in the signal assignment statement in the finite state machine example, the value "001000" is assigned to signal *NEXT_ST*. Also *NEXT_ST* is of size 6 bits. If the explicit encoding is not present, signal *NEXT_ST* is then of size 3 bits, and is assigned a value of "011".

The explicit encoding mechanism has to be used with caution since it may create differences in pre- and post- synthesis simulation results. This is because the mechanism used to specify the encoding is not a standard mechanism that a VHDL simulator understands. The encoding is specified purely for synthesis purposes only. See Chapter 5 concerning differences that may arise due to this user-defined encoding.

2.5.4 Encoding Metalogical Values

In modeling hardware, it is customary to define representations for the unknown, don't-care and high-impedance values. An unknown value (quite often, the value U) is usually used to specify unknown input values, which is useful during initial setup of a circuit. A don't-care value (quite often the value X or D) is used to specify a don't-care value, that is, a value that can either be a logic-0 or a logic-1. A high-impedance value (often the value Z) is used to set a signal to a high-impedance value, for example, in a bus so that another signal may also drive the bus.

However, such representations are not predefined in the VHDL language, and are open to different interpretations. The unknown, don't-care and high-impedance values are called *metalogical values*. In VHDL, there are no explicit reserved words or declarations that can be used to specify the metalogical values.

For a synthesis system, it is desirable to provide a mechanism that explicitly specifies the mapping of VHDL literals to correspond to the metalogical values. Such a mapping may be provided using the *ENUM_ENCODING* attribute. There are five values that a VHDL literal can be mapped to in hardware:

- 0: logic-0
- 1: logic-1
- U: unknown
- D: don't-care
- Z: high-impedance

Here is an example of an enumeration type declaration.

```
type MIDAS_VALUES is (MIDAS_U, MIDAS_0,
                      MIDAS_1, MIDAS_Z);
```

A designer may interpret the literal *MIDAS_U* to represent an unknown value, *MIDAS_0* as logic-0, *MIDAS_1* as logic-1, and *MIDAS_Z* as a high-impedance value. For synthesis, this information needs to be communicated through the VHDL model. The *ENUM_ENCODING* attribute is used to pass this information. For example, the following attribute specification can be used with the type *MIDAS_VALUES*.

```
attribute ENUM_ENCODING of MIDAS_VALUES: type
        is "U 0 1 Z";
```

This special attribute specification directs the enumeration literal *MIDAS_U* to correspond to a U value (unknown) for synthesis, the enumeration literal *MIDAS_0* to correspond to a 0 value (logic-0) for synthesis, and so on. More important is the fact that a variable or a signal of the type *MIDAS_VALUES* needs to be represented using only one bit in hardware. Here is an example.

```
variable ROY: MIDAS_VALUES;
. . .
ROY := MIDAS_0;          -- Assignment-1.

if RESET = '0' then
   ROY := MIDAS_Z;       -- Assignment-2.
end if;
```

The variable *ROY* is of size one bit. Assignment-1 is interpreted as an assignment of logic-0 value to variable *ROY* (since the literal *MIDAS_0* is encoded as a 0). Assignment-2 is interpreted as an assignment of a high-impedance value to *ROY* (since the literal *MIDAS_Z* is encoded as a Z).

If the *ENUM_ENCODING* attribute specification is not present, variable *ROY* is then of size two bits, since two bits are needed to represent the four literals of the type *MIDAS_VALUES*. Also assignment-1 is then interpreted as the assignment of value "01" to *ROY* and assignment-2 is interpreted as the assignment of value "11" to *ROY*, which may or may not be what the designer intends to do.

Note that the literals 'U', 'X', and 'Z' cannot be used directly to signify the metalogical values since these literals can be used in more than one type declaration to mean different things, as the following example shows.

```
type LOGIC5 is ('U', 'X', '0', '1', 'Z');
type CARAT is ('B', 'H', 'A', 'S', 'K', 'E', 'R', 'U', 'X', 'Z', 'D');

signal SOG: LOGIC5;
signal MY_NAME: CARAT;

SOG <= 'X';
MY_NAME <= 'U';
```

In this example, how is it determined which are the metalogical values and which are not? The *ENUM_ENCODING* attribute is again used to specify this. For example,

```
attribute ENUM_ENCODING of LOGIC5: type is "U D 0 1 Z";
```

implies that signal *SOG* is of size one bit and that the signal assignment to *SOG* assigns a value of don't-care. Signal *MY_NAME* needs four bits for its representation and the signal assignment statement infers the assignment of the value "0111" to signal *MY_NAME*.

Metalogicals in Type *STD_ULOGIC*

The type *STD_ULOGIC* is defined in the IEEE standard package *STD_LOGIC_1164* as follows.

```
type STD_ULOGIC is ('U',   -- Uninitialized
                    'X',   -- Forcing unknown
                    '0',   -- Forcing 0
                    '1',   -- Forcing 1
                    'Z',   -- High impedance
                    'W',   -- Weak unknown
                    'L',   -- Weak 0
                    'H',   -- Weak 1
                    '-'    -- Don't care
                   );
```

Given the interpretations of the literals of the enumeration type *STD_ULOGIC* as specified in the above comments, how can this information be conveyed to a synthesis system?

One option is to build it into the synthesis system. For example, if a literal '-' appears in a VHDL model, a check is made to see if this literal belongs to the type *STD_ULOGIC* that comes from the package *STD_LOGIC_1164* which resides in design library *IEEE*, then this literal is to be interpreted as a don't-care value for synthesis. This check is necessary since the literal '-' can be used in user-defined types as well.

An alternate way to specify the interpretations is by using the attribute *ENUM_ENCODING*.

```
attribute ENUM_ENCODING of STD_ULOGIC: type
   -- 'U' 'X' '0' '1' 'Z' 'W' 'L' 'H' '-'
   is "U  D   0   1   Z   D   0   1   D";
```

Using this attribute specification, the synthesis system interprets the literals in type *STD_ULOGIC* as follows. The literal 'U' implies an unknown value, the literals 'X', 'W', '-' imply a don't-care value, literal 'Z' implies a high-impedance value, literals '0' and 'L' imply the logic-0 value, and literals '1' and 'H' imply the logic-1 value for synthesis.

2.5.5 Array Types

A typical synthesis system supports array types of one dimension, and an array of an array type. The basic element of an array must be of size one bit. Arrays represent an ordered collection of wires or flip-flops. Here is an example of an array of an array.

```
type RF_TYPE is array (NATURAL range <>)
    of BIT_VECTOR(0 to 7);
signal REG_FILE_A: RF_TYPE (5 downto 0);
```

Signal *REG_FILE_A* is an array of an array with the first dimension's index ranging from 5 down to 0, and the second ranging from 0 to 7. Each array element is of type *BIT* which is of size one bit.

Let us look at another example.

```
type LOGIC5 is ('U', 'X', '0', '1', 'Z');
type REG_TYPE is array (0 to 25) of LOGIC5;
variable REG_X: REG_TYPE;
```

The variable *REG_X* represents an array of an array, 26 elements in the first dimension, with each element representing 3 bits. Three bits are needed to represent a value in type *LOGIC5*. If the literals 'U', 'X', and 'Z' in type *LOGIC5* were not intended to be actual values for synthesis but represented metalogical values, then it is necessary to specify an enumeration type encoding that identifies the metalogical values. Such an encoding is specified using the following attribute specification.

```
attribute ENUM_ENCODING of LOGIC5: type is "U D 0 1 Z";
```

With this attribute specification present, variable *REG_X* becomes an array of only one dimension with its index ranging from 0 to 25. This is because the basic element type of the array is now only one bit wide (need to represent only '0' and '1' in type *LOGIC5*, the rest are metalogical values).

2.5.6 Signed and Unsigned Types

VHDL does not provide an explicit way to model signed and unsigned numbers. A limited capability is provided in VHDL in terms of integer types. An integer type can represent a signed number depending on whether the range contains a negative number. The disadvantage of using this type is that it is not possible to directly access each element of an object of an integer type.

An alternate approach is to define two new array types, *SIGNED* and *UNSIGNED*, that are similar to type *BIT_VECTOR*. These types are interpreted by a synthesis system as signed and unsigned numbers respectively. Here are the definitions for these types.

```
type SIGNED is array (NATURAL range <>) of BIT;
type UNSIGNED is array (NATURAL range <>) of BIT;
```

Notice that both types have the same definition as type *BIT_VECTOR*. The type *SIGNED* is interpreted as a signed number. Values are stored in 2's complement form with the leftmost bit as the most significant bit. The type *UNSIGNED* is interpreted as an unsigned number. Notice that the conventions being followed for the above two types are the same as those being followed for the types discussed earlier, for example, the integer types and type *BIT_VECTOR*. The following table shows the difference in interpretation between a 4-bit *SIGNED* and *UNSIGNED* type.

Literal	UNSIGNED	SIGNED	Literal	UNSIGNED	SIGNED
"0000"	0	0	"1000"	8	-8
"0001"	1	1	"1001"	9	-7
"0010"	2	2	"1010"	10	-6
"0011"	3	3	"1011"	11	-5
"0100"	4	4	"1100"	12	-4
"0101"	5	5	"1101"	13	-3
"0110"	6	6	"1110"	14	-2
"0111"	7	7	"1111"	15	-1

Having defined the two basic types, it becomes necessary to provide operator overloading functions on these two types. Conversion functions that convert between types *SIGNED*, *UNSIGNED*, *BIT_VECTOR* and integer types become necessary and useful. Shown below is a sample list of overloaded functions and conversion functions using these types.

```
function "+" (L, R: SIGNED) return SIGNED;
function "*" (L: SIGNED; R: UNSIGNED) return SIGNED;
```

```
function "<" (L, R: SIGNED) return BOOLEAN;

function TO_SIGNED (OPD: INTEGER; SIZE: NATURAL)
  return SIGNED;
function TO_INTEGER (OPD: UNSIGNED) return INTEGER;
```

A synthesis system typically provides this capability to the user by providing a package containing these types and functions. For example, the ArchSyn system provides a package called *STD_LOGIC_ARITH*. This package contains arithmetic operations and other utility functions defined on the *SIGNED* and *UNSIGNED* types. These types are based on the element type *STD_LOGIC*. The type *STD_LOGIC* is defined in the IEEE standard package *STD_LOGIC_1164*. The declaration for the *SIGNED* and *UNSIGNED* types that appear in package *STD_LOGIC_ARITH* are as follows.

```
type SIGNED is array (NATURAL range <>) of STD_LOGIC;
type UNSIGNED is array (NATURAL range <>) of STD_LOGIC;
```

Appendix B gives a listing of the package *STD_LOGIC_ARITH*.

There are two packages that are an IEEE standard. These are described in the next section.

2.6 1076.3 Arithmetic Packages

The IEEE standard 1076.3-1997 defines two functionally equivalent packages:

i. *NUMERIC_BIT* : based on type *BIT* array types

ii. *NUMERIC_STD* : based on type *STD_LOGIC* array types

Each package defines two new types, *UNSIGNED* and *SIGNED*; these types have a numeric value semantic associated with them. Both these packages reside in library *IEEE*. Overloaded predefined operator functions on types *SIGNED* and *UNSIGNED*, including mixed integer arithmetic operator functions, are defined in the packages *NUMERIC_BIT* and *NUMERIC_STD*. The functions are classified into the following categories:

i. Arithmetic functions

ii. Comparison functions

iii. Conversion functions

iv. Shift and rotate functions

v. Resize function

vi. Edge detection functions

vii. Logical functions

The type *UNSIGNED* is a vector of bits that represents an unsigned number. The rightmost bit is the least significant bit. In package *NUMERIC_BIT*, the type *UNSIGNED* is defined as:

type *UNSIGNED* **is array** (*NATURAL* **range** <>) **of** *BIT*;

and in package *NUMERIC_STD*, the type *UNSIGNED* is defined as:

type *UNSIGNED* **is array** (*NATURAL* **range** <>) **of** *STD_LOGIC*;

A three-element vector represents values 0 to 7.

The type *SIGNED* is a vector of bits that represents a signed number. A signed number is represented in 2's complement form. The leftmost bit will necessarily be a '1' for negative numbers. The rightmost bit is the least significant bit. In package *NUMERIC_BIT*, the type is defined as:

type *SIGNED* **is array** (*NATURAL* **range** <>) **of** *BIT*;

and in package *NUMERIC_STD*, the type is defined as:

type *SIGNED* **is array** (*NATURAL* **range** <>) **of** *STD_LOGIC*;

A three-element vector represents the value range –4 to +3.

Here are some examples.

```
signal SIG: SIGNED (0 to 7);              -- Sign bit is SIG(0)
signal SGP: SIGNED (3 downto 0);          -- Sign bit is SGP(3)
signal UGI: UNSIGNED (0 to 15);
  -- UGI(0) is the most significant bit.
signal UGP: UNSIGNED (11 downto 5);
  -- UGP(11) is the most significant bit.
```

Arithmetic and comparison functions are defined for the following class of operands.

Operand type	*SIGNED*	*UNSIGNED*	*NATURAL*	*INTEGER*
SIGNED	1076.3	Not supported	Not supported	1076.3
UNSIGNED	Not supported	1076.3	1076.3	Not supported
NATURAL	Not supported	1076.3	1076	1076
INTEGER	1076.3	Not supported	1076	1076

Most of the examples in this book are based on the package *NUMERIC_STD*. Modifying the examples to use the package *NUMERIC_BIT* should be straightforward as these two packages are equivalent in terms of functionality.

2.7 Resolution Functions

A resolution function determines the effective value of a signal from the value of one or more of its drivers. In real hardware, there may or may not be logic associated with such a resolution function, since the effective value may be determined by the technology of the gates driving the signal. For synthesis purposes, one option would be to completely ignore the resolution function. However, a synthesis system may provide an option that can be preset to indicate the type of resolution function to be used: wired-and, wired-or or tri-state. For example, if the option is set to wired-and, all the drivers for a signal are connected to an `and` gate and the output of this gate becomes the effective value for the signal.

Here is an example.

```
signal SAM: WIRED_OR BIT;
  -- WIRED_OR is the name of a resolution function.
. . .
-- Following are two concurrent signal assignment statements:
SAM <= A and B;
SAM <= C or D;
```

Signal *SAM* has two drivers, one from each of the concurrent signal assignment statements. Therefore the signal *SAM* must have a resolution function associated with it so that an effective value for *SAM* can be computed. Figure 2-9 shows the logic that is represented by the above example.

However, resolution functions are not really synthesized since they represent technology-specific modeling. If such a model is synthesized with the resolution function option set to wired-or, the logic shown in Figure 2-10 is generated. Note that an explicit `or` gate is generated to mimic the logic of the *WIRED_OR* function. Therefore, as far as synthesis is concerned, resolution functions have no impact or effect, that is, no logic is synthesized from the specified resolution function; additional `and` gates or `or` gates may be generated as appropriate based on the option specified.

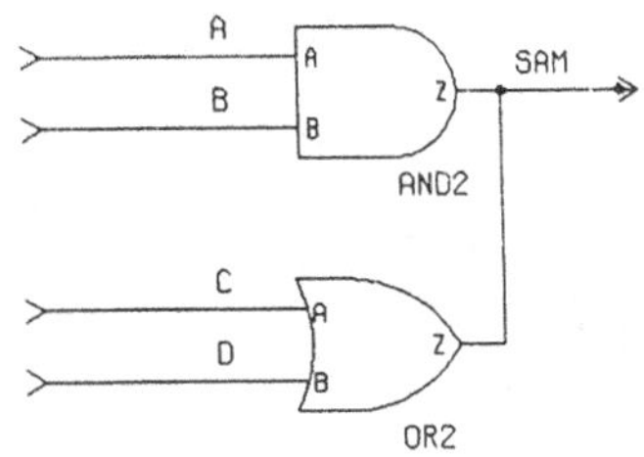

Figure 2-9 The drivers are shorted together.

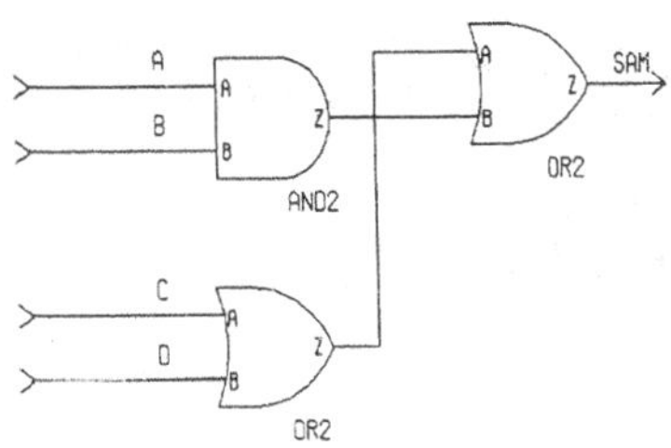

Figure 2-10 A logic gate does the resolution.

Types Used in this Book

The types used in all the examples in the rest of the book are based on the VHDL standard predefined types and the *IEEE* standard packages *STD_LOGIC_1164*, *NUMERIC_BIT* and *NUMERIC_STD*. Listing of the *NUMERIC_BIT* and *NUMERIC_STD* packages are provided in Appendix D.

❑

Chapter 3

Mapping Statements to Gates

The previous chapter described the mapping from VHDL types and literals to hardware and the mapping from VHDL objects to hardware. This chapter describes the mapping of statements in VHDL to logic gates in hardware. It also explains how operators, expressions and assignments are mapped to hardware.

Sequential or combinational logic can be synthesized from a VHDL description. There are two main styles for describing combinational logic:

a. Using concurrent signal assignment statements: This is the most natural style, since it explicitly shows the parallelism in the hardware. It also implicitly shows the structure.

b. Using sequential statements in a process: This describes the sequential nature of a combinational logic model; this is because in simulation all statements in a process statement execute sequentially.

Synchronous logic elements, that is, flip-flops and latches, can be inferred by describing statements within a process in a certain style. It is best not to synthesize a memory as a two-dimensional array of flip-flops because this is an inefficient way to design a memory. The best way to create a memory is to instantiate a predefined memory block using a component instantiation statement.

3.1 Assignment Statement

There are primarily two forms of an assignment statement:

- Signal assignment statement
- Variable assignment statement

Either of these represent, in hardware, logic that is derived from the expression on the right-hand-side of the assignment statement driving the signal or variable that appears on the left-hand-side of the assignment. Here are two examples.

```
signal STAT_OUT: STD_LOGIC;
STAT_OUT <= not STAT_IN;    -- Signal assignment statement.

variable PRESET, COUNT: UNSIGNED (0 to 3);
COUNT := PRESET + 1;        -- Variable assignment statement.
```

The first statement is a signal assignment statement that describes an inverter that has its input connected to a signal *STAT_IN* and whose output is *STAT_OUT*. See Figure 3-1. Delays, if any, specified in a signal assignment statement are usually ignored during synthesis.

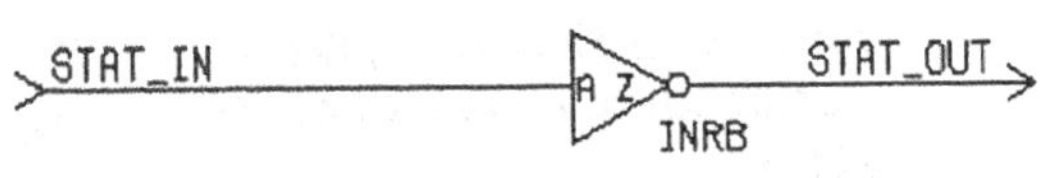

Figure 3-1 Combinational circuit from signal assignment statement.

The second statement is a variable assignment statement that describes an adder that takes *PRESET* and the integer 1 as inputs and places the result in the variable *COUNT*. Since the operator "+" is not predefined in VHDL to operate on the type *UNSIGNED* and on an integer type, it is assumed that such an overloaded "+" function exists. The synthesized circuit for the variable assignment statement is also shown in Figure 3-2.

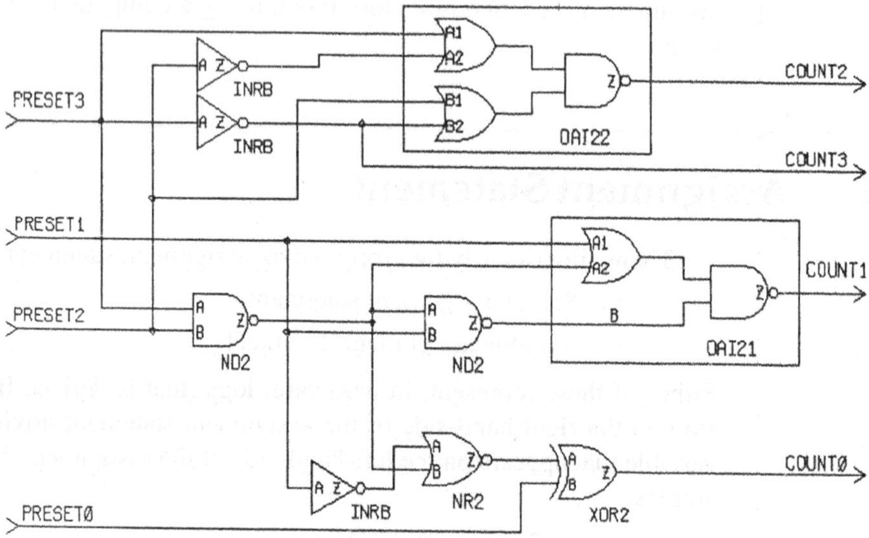

Figure 3-2 Combinational circuit from variable assignment statement.

The question of whether the target of the assignment is a wire, a flip-flop, or a latch, is decided by the context under which the assignment statement appears. For example, if the above signal assignment statement appeared, say, under the control of a clock as shown in the following example:

```
signal CLK, STAT_OUT: STD_LOGIC;
. . .
process (CLK)
begin
  if RISING_EDGE(CLK) then
    STAT_OUT <= not STAT_IN;   -- Signal assignment statement.
  end if;
end process;
```

then the target would be synthesized to be a flip-flop. This is shown in Figure 3-3.

The more subtle differences between a variable assignment statement and a signal assignment statement are described later in the section on "Process statement".

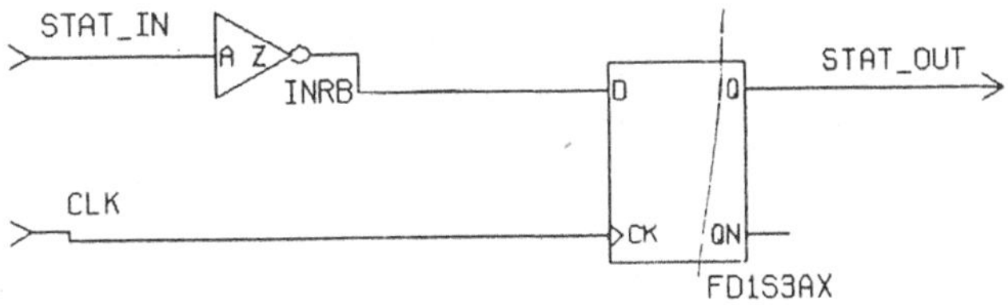

Figure 3-3 Target of an assignment is a flip-flop.

3.2 Logical Operators

Here is a model of a full-adder using concurrent signal assignment statements.

```
library IEEE;
use IEEE.STD_LOGIC_1164.all;
entity FULL_ADDER is
  port (A, B, CIN: in STD_LOGIC;
        SUM, COUT: out STD_LOGIC);
end;

architecture DATAFLOW of FULL_ADDER is
begin
  SUM <= (A xor B) xor CIN;
  COUT <= (A and B) or (B and CIN) or (A and CIN);
end;
```

The synthesized circuit is shown in Figure 3-4. The logical operators get directly mapped into primitive logic gates in hardware. Here is another example.

```
signal BI, STDY, TAP: BIT_VECTOR (0 to 3);
. . .
TAP <= BI xor STDY;
```

In this case, four exclusive-or gates are synthesized since each operand in the right-hand-side is of size 4. Figure 3-5 shows the synthesized circuit.

In the above examples, we see that there is a one-to-one correlation between a concurrent signal assignment statement and its synthesized logic. This is because a concurrent signal assignment implicitly shows the structure.

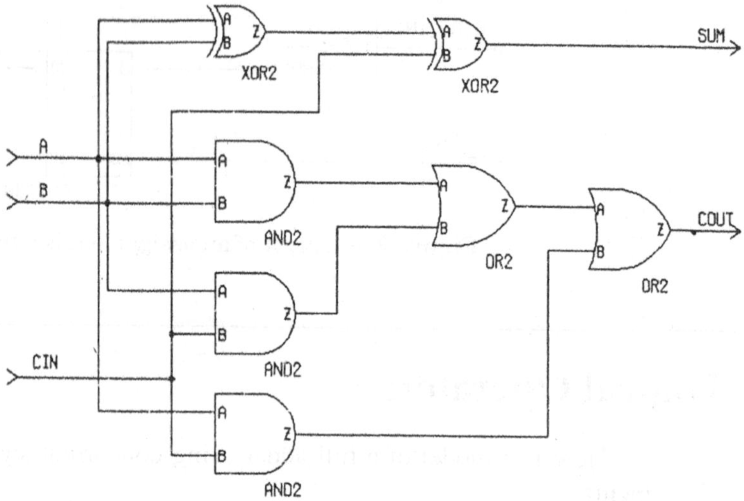

Figure 3-4 Logical operators map to primitive logic gates.

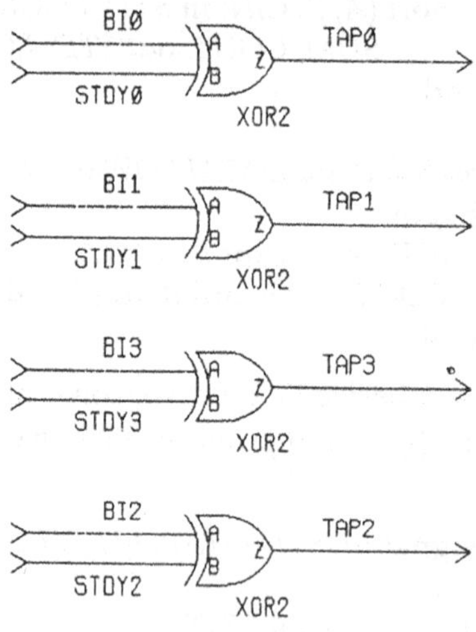

Figure 3-5 A bank of logic gates.

3.3 Arithmetic Operators

When modeling arithmetic operators on vector operands, it is necessary to identify the number system being used to represent the operands. This may be achieved by providing a special package that defines the signed and unsigned arithmetic types, and the overloaded operator functions that operate on these types. A convention also needs to be established for representing the most significant bit.

The IEEE Std 1076.3-1997 contains two packages, *NUMERIC_STD* (based on type *STD_LOGIC*) and *NUMERIC_BIT* (based on type *BIT*). Each package defines two types, *UNSIGNED* and *SIGNED*, and their corresponding overloaded operator functions. The rightmost bit is interpreted as the least significant bit. Vectors of type *SIGNED* represent values in the 2's complement form.

3.3.1 Unsigned Arithmetic

Let us look at an example that uses an arithmetic operator on unsigned numbers.

```
library IEEE;
use IEEE.NUMERIC_STD.all;
entity UNSIGNED_ADDER is
  port (ARB, BET: in UNSIGNED (0 to 3);
        LOT: out UNSIGNED (0 to 3));
end UNSIGNED_ADDER;

architecture SIMPLE of UNSIGNED_ADDER is
begin
  LOT <= ARB + BET;
end SIMPLE;
```

In this example, we are trying to model a 4-bit adder. The number system for the operands is unsigned. This is determined by the type and the package used. The type *UNSIGNED* represents unsigned numbers with the leftmost bit as the most significant bit. The synthesized netlist for the entity *UNSIGNED_ADDER* is shown in Figure 3-6.

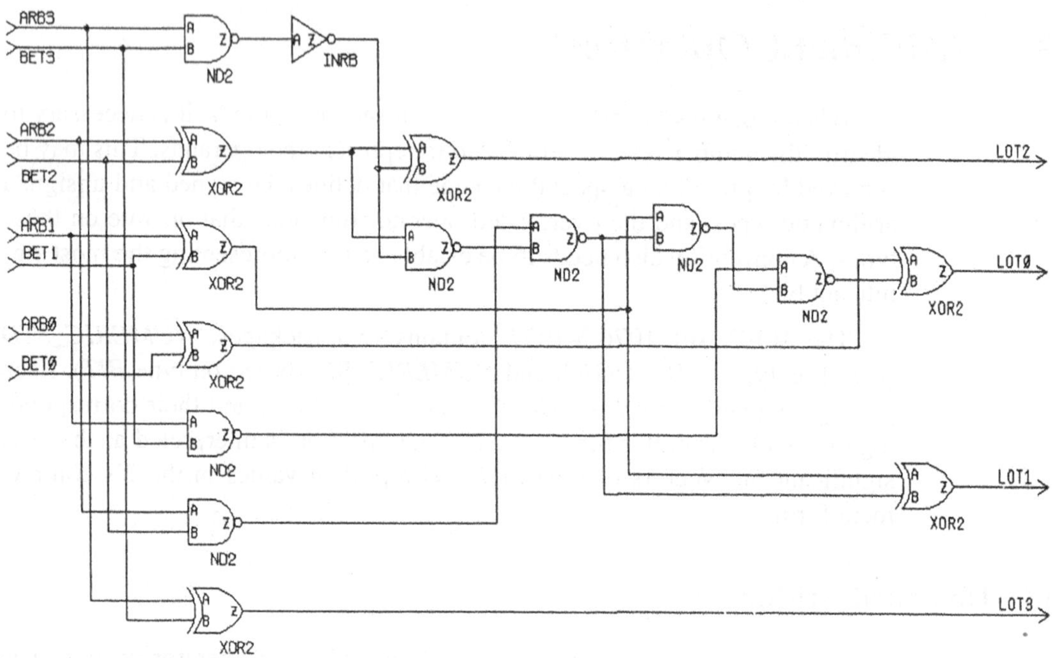

Figure 3-6 A 4-bit adder.

3.3.2 Signed Arithmetic

Here is the same example as in the previous section, except that in this case, the operands are signed numbers. The type *SIGNED* defined in the package *NUMERIC_STD* represents signed numbers in the 2's complement form.

```
library IEEE;
use IEEE.NUMERIC_STD.all;
entity SIGNED_ADDER is
   port (ARB, BET: in SIGNED (0 to 3);
         LOT: out SIGNED (0 to 3));
end SIGNED_ADDER;

architecture SIMPLE of SIGNED_ADDER is
begin
   LOT <= ARB + BET;
end SIMPLE;
```

The synthesized netlist is the same as that for the entity *UNSIGNED_ADDER* since a "+" function behaves the same for unsigned numbers as well as for signed numbers that are in the 2's complement form. The difference is that the entity *UNSIGNED_ADDER* is capable of adding numbers in the range 0 through 15, while the entity *SIGNED_ADDER* has the capability of adding numbers in the range –8 to 7.

The difference between an unsigned adder and a signed adder shows up when the size of operands are not identical. Consider the following entity.

```
library IEEE;
use IEEE.STD_LOGIC_1164.all, IEEE.NUMERIC_STD.all;
entity DIFF_ADD is
  port (AEN: in SIGNED (2 downto 0);
        BMA: in UNSIGNED (2 downto 0);
        AOT: out SIGNED (2 downto 0);
        BOT: out UNSIGNED (2 downto 0));
end DIFF_ADD;

architecture TWO_ADDERS of DIFF_ADD is
begin
  AOT <= AEN + "11";
  BOT <= BMA + "11";
end TWO_ADDERS;
```

There are two adders synthesized in this example. In the first assignment statement, the right operand "11" is sign-extended (since *AEN* is of type *SIGNED*) to 3 bits (the size of *AEN*) before the addition is performed; this is as per the semantics of the "+" operator as defined in the *NUMERIC_STD* package. In the second assignment statement, the right operand "11" is zero-extended (since *BMA* is of type *UNSIGNED*) to 3 bits (the size of *BMA*) before the addition is performed. The two concurrent signal assignment statements are equivalent to:

```
AOT <= AEN + SIGNED'("111");
BOT <= BMA + UNSIGNED'("011");
```

Thus different logic is obtained for signed addition as compared to the unsigned addition as shown in Figure 3-7.

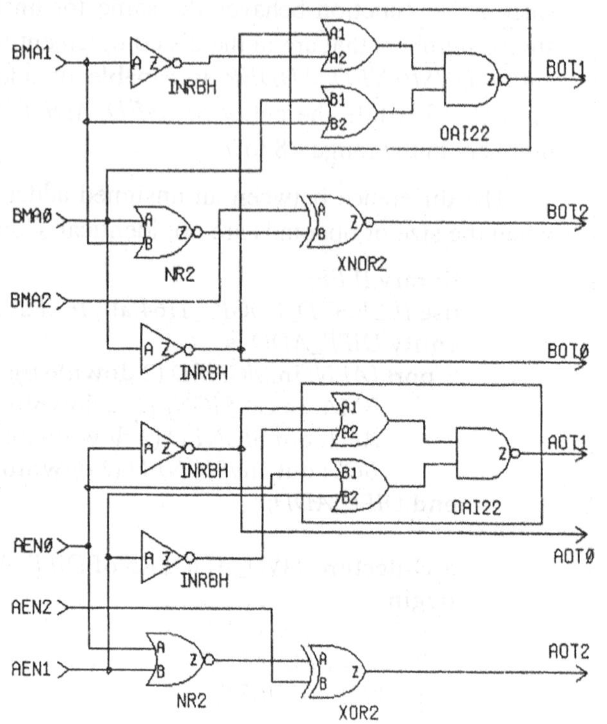

Figure 3-7 Different logic for signed and unsigned addition.

3.3.3 Computing Result Size

How is the length of a result of an arithmetic operator operating on vector operands computed? Assume *L* and *R* are the two input operands.

- +, – : Result size is the larger of *L'LENGTH* and *R'LENGTH*. For signed numbers, input operands are sign-extended to the larger of *L'LENGTH* and *R'LENGTH* before performing the appropriate operation. For unsigned numbers, operands are zero-extended.
- * : Result size is *L'LENGTH* + *R'LENGTH*.
- / : Result size is *L'LENGTH*.
- **mod**, **rem**: Result size is *R'LENGTH*.
- – (unary), **abs**: Result size is same as input operand.

What if one of the operands is an integer operand? In such a case, the integer operand is converted to its vector form of size equal to that of the other operand. Here are some examples.

```
variable USA: UNSIGNED (0 to 3);
variable SID: SIGNED (0 to 4);
. . .
USA + 2      is equivalent to      USA + "0010"
4 * SID      is equivalent to      "00100" * SID
```

3.3.4 Modeling a Carry

Note that the "+" and "–" operators return a size equal to the largest of its operands. In some cases, a "+" or a "–" operator can return a carry or a borrow respectively. The question is how can then a carry or a borrow be modeled? The trick is to provide an argument to the operator one bigger than the size of the operand. This can be achieved by using the concatenation operator. Here is such an example.

```
signal CDO_BUS: UNSIGNED (5 downto 0);
signal ONE_UP: UNSIGNED (6 downto 0);
. . .
ONE_UP <= ('0' & CDO_BUS) + 1;
```

The size of the largest operand for the "+" operator is 7, the result of the operation is 7 bits and *ONE_UP*(6) has the carry bit.

3.4 Relational Operators

Relational operators can be modeled similar to arithmetic operators. In this case, the logic produced from synthesis is different depending on whether unsigned or signed numbers are being compared. Again since the VHDL standard does not define relational operations on unsigned or signed vector operands, an arithmetic package needs to be used. Here is an example of a relational operator that is used with unsigned numbers. Figure 3-8 shows the synthesized netlist.

```
library IEEE;
use IEEE.NUMERIC_STD.all;
entity GT is
   port (A, B: in UNSIGNED (7 downto 0);
```

```
        Z: out BOOLEAN);
end GT;

architecture DF of GT is
begin
   Z <= A(3 downto 0) > B(7 downto 4);
end DF;
```

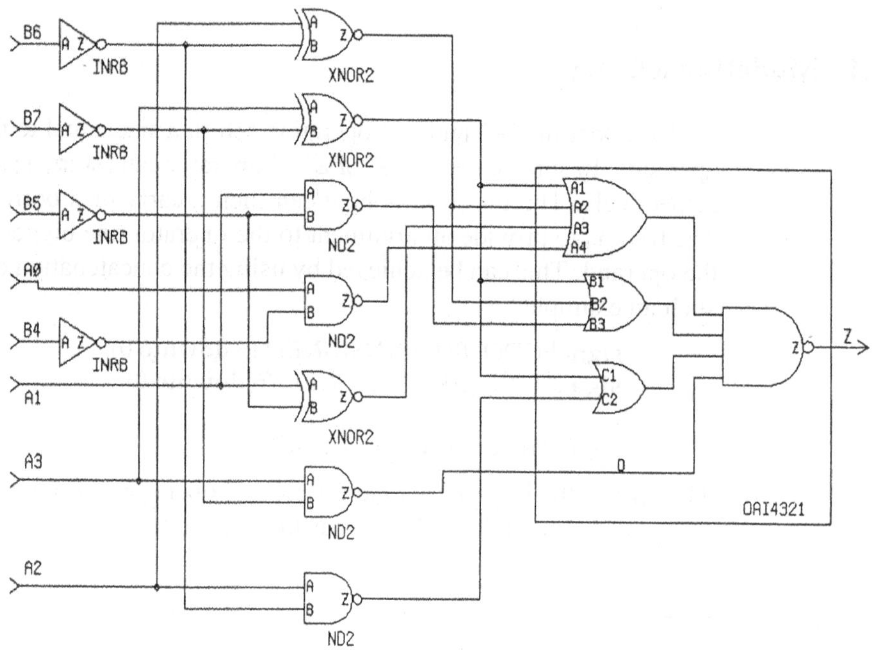

Figure 3-8 Unsigned ">" relational operator.

Here is an example that uses signed numbers. Note that in this case, we have to use the type *SIGNED* because values of type *SIGNED* represent signed numbers. Figure 3-9 shows the synthesized netlist.

```
library IEEE;
use IEEE.NUMERIC_STD.all;
entity NE is
   port (A, B: in SIGNED (0 to 7);
        Z: out BOOLEAN);
end NE;
```

```
architecture DF of NE is
begin
  Z <= A /= B;        -- Z gets assigned the value of A not equals B.
end DF;
```

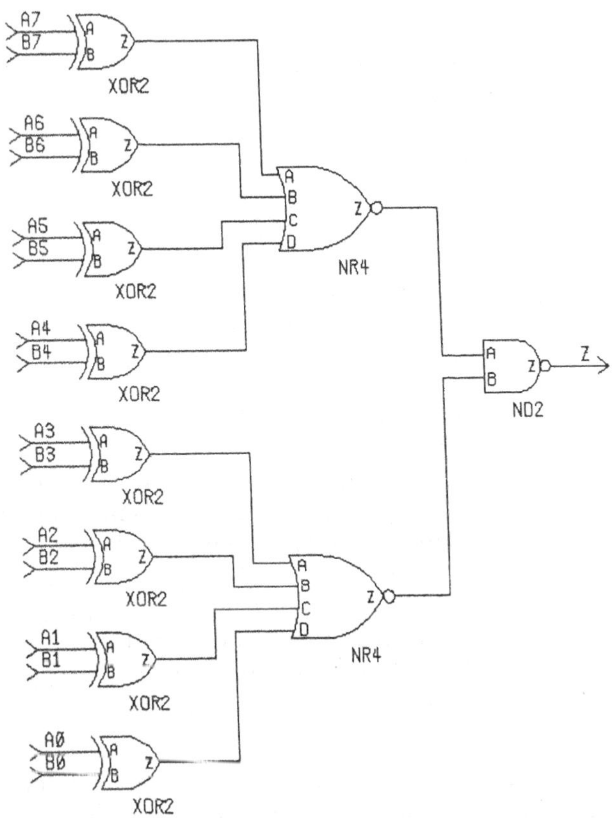

Figure 3-9 Signed "/=" relational operator.

3.5 Vectors and Slices

Operations using array vectors, slices and vector elements can be used in a model.

3.5.1 Constant Index

Here is an example that uses constant values for array indices, slice and range indices.

```
library IEEE;
use IEEE.STD_LOGIC_1164.all;
package ARRAYS is
  type BANK is array (0 to 1) of STD_LOGIC_VECTOR (3 downto 0);
end ARRAYS;

library IEEE;
use IEEE.STD_LOGIC_1164.all, WORK.ARRAYS.all;
entity VECTORS is
  port (A, B, C: in STD_LOGIC_VECTOR (3 downto 0);
        REG_FILE: inout BANK;
        ZCAT: out STD_LOGIC_VECTOR (3 downto 0));
end VECTORS;

architecture EXAMPLE of VECTORS is
begin
  ZCAT (3 downto 1) <= A(2) & C(3 downto 2);  -- This statement
    -- shows reading of an element of a vector, reading of a slice of a
    -- vector, and assigning to a slice of a vector.
  ZCAT(0) <= REG_FILE(1)(3);        -- This statement shows the
    -- reading of an element of an array of an array and assigning it
    -- to an element of another array.
  REG_FILE(0) <= A and B or C;      -- This statement shows
    -- assignment to one dimension of an array of an array.
end EXAMPLE;
```

Note that *REG_FILE* is an inout port since the port is both read and written to. Figure 3-10 shows the synthesized netlist. The concatenation operator "&" is used to generate a bigger array. The example shows an element of an array of an array being read and assigned to an element of a one-dimensional array. Also an assignment is made to a vector of an array of an array.

3.5.2 Non-constant Index

It is possible to use a non-constant as an index in an ar.ay element selection as shown in the following model.

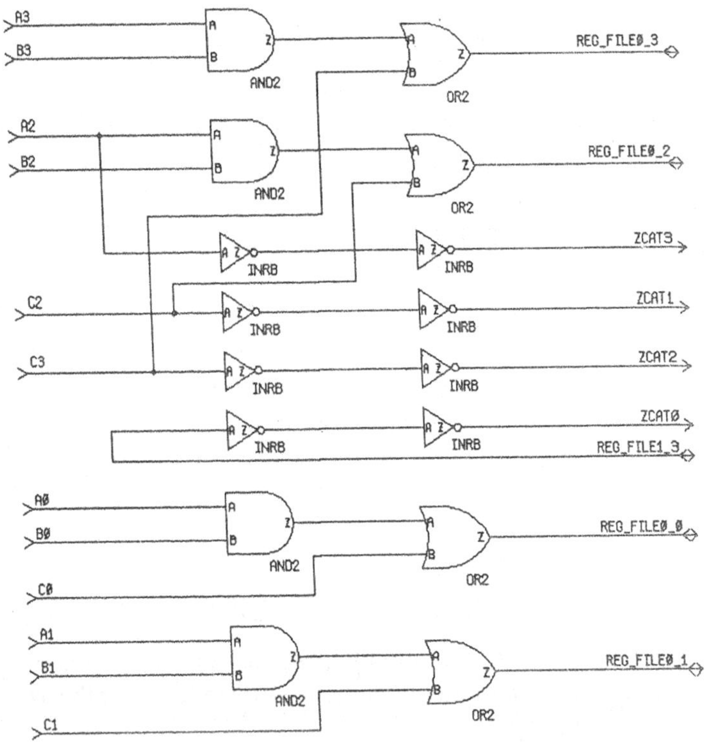

Figure 3-10 Vectors and slices.

```
library IEEE;
use IEEE.STD_LOGIC_1164.all;
entity NON_COMPUTE_RIGHT is
  port (DATA: in STD_LOGIC_VECTOR (0 to 3);
        INDEX: in NATURAL range 0 to 3;
        DOUT: out STD_LOGIC);
end;

architecture EXAMPLE of NON_COMPUTE_RIGHT is
begin
  DOUT <= DATA (INDEX);
end;
```

In this case, a multiplexer is generated as shown in the synthesized netlist of Figure 3-11.

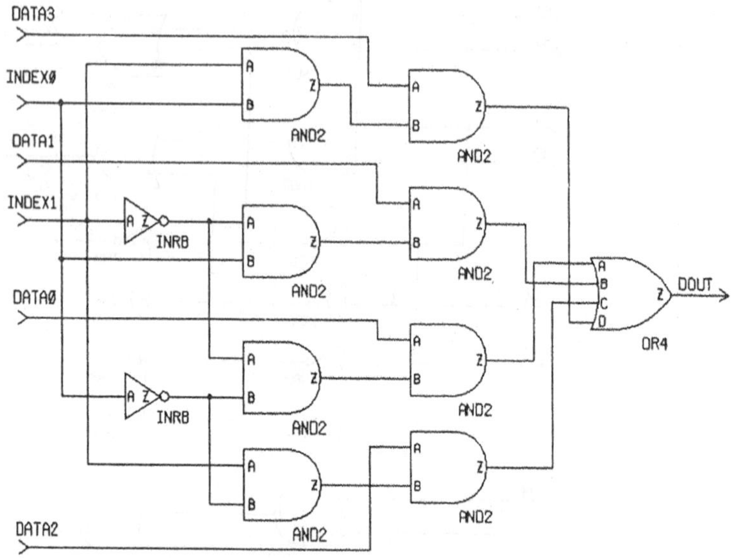

Figure 3-11 Non-constant index generates a multiplexer.

Here is another example of a non-constant index; this time it is used on the left-hand-side of an assignment. A decoder is synthesized for this behavior, as shown in Figure 3-12.

```
entity NON_COMPUTE_LEFT is
  port (MEM: out BIT_VECTOR (7 downto 0);
      STORE: in BIT;
      ADDR: in NATURAL range 0 to 7);
end NON_COMPUTE_LEFT;

architecture EXAMPLE of NON_COMPUTE_LEFT is
begin
  MEM(ADDR) <= STORE;
end EXAMPLE;
```

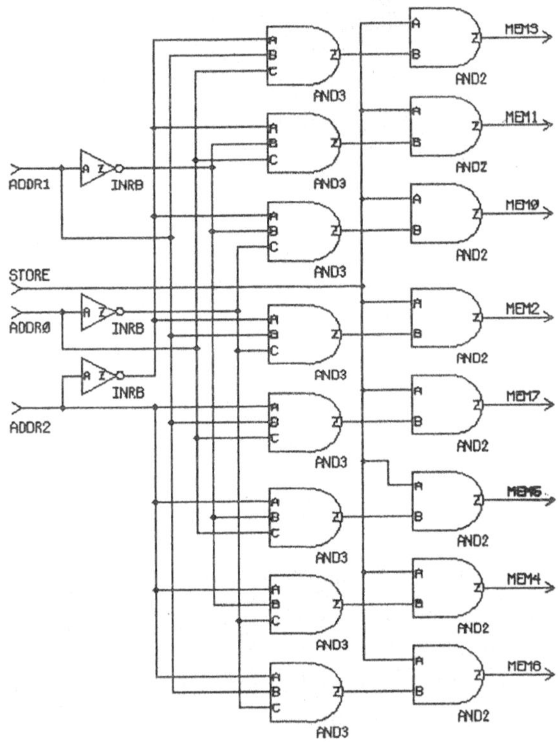

Figure 3-12 A decoder generated from a non-constant index.

3.6 Process Statement

A process statement is used to model the sequential behavior of a circuit. Here is an example of a process statement that contains variable assignment statements. Figure 3-13 shows the synthesized netlist.

```
entity PAR is
  port (A, B, C, D: in BIT;
      Z: out BIT);
end PAR;

architecture SEQ of PAR is
begin
  process (A, B, C, D)
```

```
    variable TEMP1, TEMP2: BIT;
  begin
    TEMP1 := A xor B;
    TEMP2 := C xor D;
    Z <= TEMP1 xor TEMP2;
  end process;
end SEQ;
```

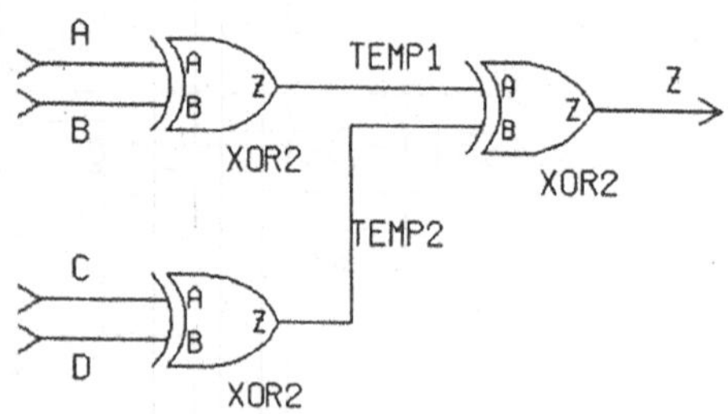

Figure 3-13 Variable assignment statements.

Signals in a sensitivity list are usually ignored during synthesis or warnings may be issued about missing signals in the sensitivity list. Consequently, the synthesized netlist may not match the simulation semantics if all signals whose values are read in a process do not appear in the sensitivity list of the process. More on this is discussed in Chapter 5.

A variable holds a temporary value and does not necessarily infer an unique wire in hardware as the following example shows.

```
VAR_EX: process (A, B, C)
  variable T1, T2: BIT;
begin
  T1 := A and B;
  T2 := T1 xor C;
  T1 := T2 nand A;
  Z <= T1 nor T2;
end process VAR_EX;
```

In the synthesized netlist, shown in Figure 3-14, the output of the *AND2* gate is the variable *T1*; so is the output of the *ND2* gate. In the above process, each assignment to a variable infers a unique wire.

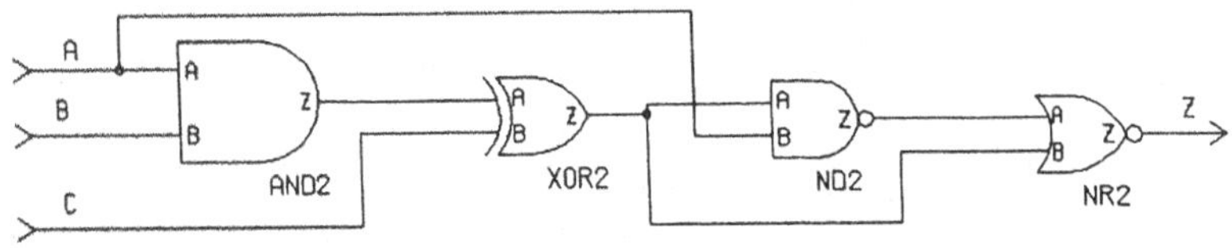

Figure 3-14 One variable can represent many wires.

3.7 If Statement

An `if` statement represents logic that is conditionally controlled. Here is an example.

```
if A > B then
  Z := A;
else
  Z := B;
end if;
```

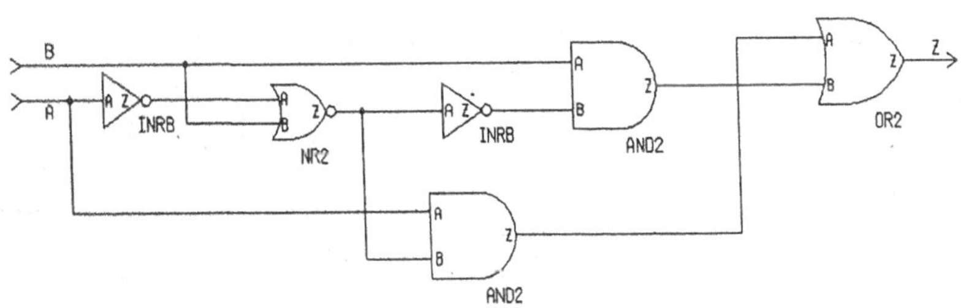

Figure 3-15 Logic derived from an `if` statement.

The logic corresponding to this `if` statement is shown in Figure 3-15. Here is another example of an `if` statement.

```
library IEEE;
use IEEE.STD_LOGIC_1164.all;
entity SIMPLE_ALU is
  port (CTRL: in BOOLEAN;
        A, B: in STD_LOGIC_VECTOR(0 to 3);
        Z: out STD_LOGIC_VECTOR(0 to 3));
end SIMPLE_ALU;
```

```
architecture EXAMPLE of SIMPLE_ALU is
begin
  process (CTRL, A, B)
  begin
    if CTRL then
      Z <= A and B;
    else
      Z <= A or B;
    end if;
  end process;
end EXAMPLE;
```

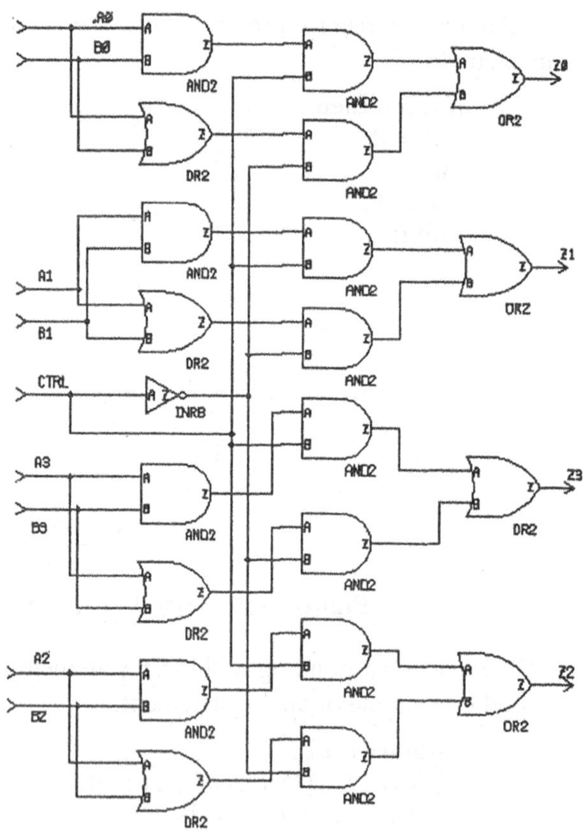

Figure 3-16 Conditional selection of operations.

The synthesized logic is shown in Figure 3-16.

The `if` statement provides a natural way of modeling a priority encoder.

```
entity PRIORITY is
  port (SEL: in BIT_VECTOR(0 to 3); Z: out BIT_VECTOR(0 to 2));
end;

architecture IF_STMT of PRIORITY is
begin
  process (SEL)
  begin
    if SEL(0) = '1' then
      Z <= "000";
    elsif SEL(1) = '1' then
      Z <= "001";
    elsif SEL(2) = '1' then
      Z <= "010";
    elsif SEL(3) = '1' then
      Z <= "011";
    else
      Z <= "111";
    end if;
  end process;
end;
```

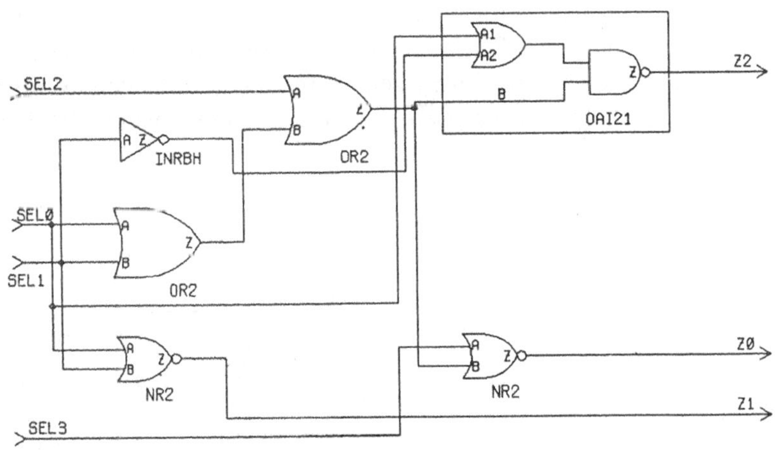

Figure 3-17 A priority encoder.

The synthesized netlist for the priority encoder is shown in Figure 3-17.

3.7.1 Inferring Latches from `if` Statements

Consider the process statement in the following entity.

```
library IEEE;
use IEEE.STD_LOGIC_1164.all;
use IEEE.NUMERIC_STD.all;
entity INCR is
  port (PHY: in BIT;
        Z: out UNSIGNED (0 to 1));
end;

architecture TEST of INCR is
begin
  INCR_L: process (PHY)
    variable ONES: UNSIGNED (0 to 1);
  begin
    if PHY = '1' then
      ONES := ONES + 1;
    end if;

    Z <= ONES;
  end process INCR_L;
end TEST;
```

The semantics for a process statement specifies that every time an event happens on signal *PHY* (denoted in the sensitivity list), the `if` statement executes and the variable *ONES* gets incremented. Between events on signal *PHY*, the value of *ONES* has to be saved; this is done using a latch, as shown in Figure 3-18.

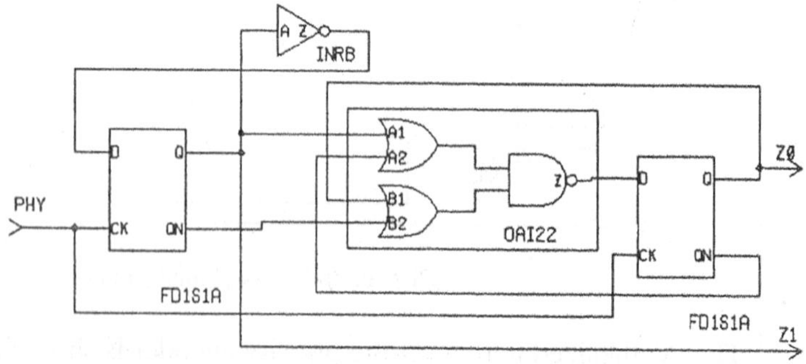

Figure 3-18 A variable is synthesized as a latch.

A general rule for latch inferencing is that if a variable declared in a process, or a signal, is not assigned in all branches of an `if` statement, then a latch is inferred. A variable declared in a subprogram never infers a latch since such a variable never retains its value through subsequent subprogram calls.

Let us now look at an example of a signal that is not assigned in all branches of an `if` statement.

```
package EXAM is
  type GRADE_TYPE is (FAIL, PASS, EXCELLENT);
end;

use WORK.EXAM.all;
entity COMPUTE is
  port (MARKS: in NATURAL range 0 to 10;
       GRADE: out GRADE_TYPE);
end;

architecture BIN of COMPUTE is
begin
  process (MARKS)
  begin
    if MARKS < 5 then
      GRADE <= FAIL;
    elsif MARKS >= 5 and MARKS < 7 then
      GRADE <= PASS;
    end if;
  end process;
end;
```

In this example, what should be the value of signal *GRADE* if *MARKS* has the value 8? From the simulation semantics viewpoint, signal *GRADE* retains its last value, since no value is assigned to the signal explicitly when *MARKS* has the value 8. Therefore a latch is inferred for the signal *GRADE* in keeping with the simulation semantics of a signal. The synthesized logic is shown in Figure 3-19.

If a signal or a variable is not assigned in all branches of an `if` statement and the intention is not to infer a latch, then the signal or variable must be assigned a value explicitly in all the branches of the `if` statement. If the previous example is modified by specifying the assignment to the signal in all branches, we get the following program.

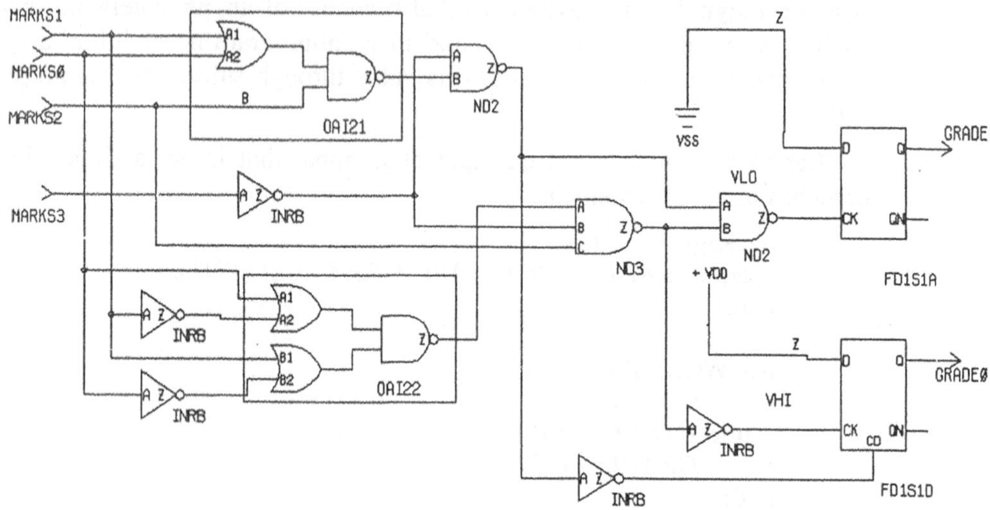

Figure 3-19 A signal is also inferred as a latch.

```
package EXAM is
   type GRADE_TYPE is (FAIL, PASS, EXCELLENT);
end;

use WORK.EXAM.all;
entity COMPUTE_MOD is
   port (MARKS: in NATURAL range 0 to 10;
         GRADE: out GRADE_TYPE);
end;

architecture BIN of COMPUTE_MOD is
begin
   process (MARKS)
   begin
      if MARKS < 5 then
         GRADE <= FAIL;
      elsif MARKS >= 5 and MARKS < 7 then
         GRADE <= PASS;
      else
         GRADE <= EXCELLENT;
      end if;
   end process;
end;
```

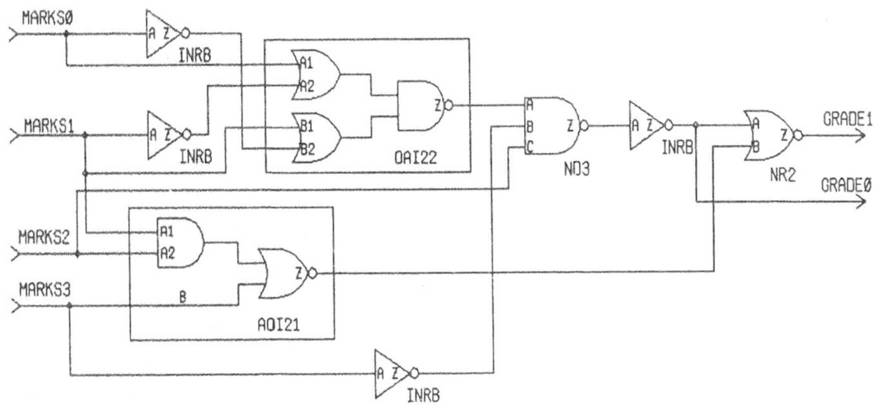

Figure 3-20 Signal *GRADE* is not a latch.

In this case, signal *GRADE* is not a latch. Figure 3-20 shows the synthesized netlist.

Exception for Variables

There is an exception to the earlier stated rule for inferring a latch. A variable that is not assigned in all branches of an `if` statement may or may not infer a latch, *depending on whether the value of the variable needs to be saved or not between multiple invocations of the process.*

Consider the variables *CRX1* and *CRX2* in the following two processes.

```
signal BBC, STATE, NEW_CLK: STD_LOGIC;
. . .
P1: process (BBC, NEW_CLK)
  variable CRX1: STD_LOGIC;
begin
  if NEW_CLK = '1' then
    STATE <= CRX1;
    CRX1 := BBC;
  end if;
end process;

P2: process (BBC, NEW_CLK)
  variable CRX2: STD_LOGIC;
begin
```

```
    if NEW_CLK = '1' then
      CRX2 := BBC;
      STATE <= CRX2;
    end if;
  end process;
```

In process *P1*, the variable *CRX1* is assigned a value only in the then-part of the `if` statement. Additionally, the value of *CRX1* is read before it is assigned. The value of *CRX1* therefore needs to be saved between multiple iterations of the process. Thus *CRX1* becomes a latch.

What about *CRX2*? In this case, the same statements are present except that the order of the assignment statements have been switched around. The variable *CRX2* is first assigned a value and then its value is read. There is no need to save the value of *CRX2*. Thus in this case *CRX2* is not synthesized to a latch.

If process *P2* were changed to the following process *P3*, the value of *CRX3* needs to be saved because if *NEW_CLK* is '0', then the saved value of *CRX3* is assigned to *STATE*.

```
P3: process (BBC, NEW_CLK)
  variable CRX3: STD_LOGIC;
begin
  if NEW_CLK = '1' then
    CRX3 := BBC;
  end if;

  STATE <= CRX3;
end process;
```

What happens if a variable is assigned in all branches of an `if` statement but its value needs to be saved? Does it become a latch? See Chapter 5 that shows examples of these conditions where no latches are inferred; consequently simulation mismatches could potentially occur.

3.8 Case Statement

Here is an example of a `case` statement.

```
package PACK_A is
  type OP_TYPE is (ADD, SUB, MUL, DIV);
end;
```

```
use WORK.PACK_A.all;
library IEEE;
use IEEE.NUMERIC_STD.all;
entity ALU is
  port (OP: in OP_TYPE;
       A, B: in UNSIGNED (0 to 1);
       Z: out UNSIGNED (0 to 1));
end ALU;

architecture SIMPLE of ALU is
begin
  process (OP, A, B)
    variable TMP: UNSIGNED (3 downto 0);
  begin
    case OP is
      when ADD =>
        Z <= A + B;
      when SUB =>
        Z <= A - B;
      when MUL =>
        TMP := A * B;       -- Result of * operator is 4 bits in this case.
        Z <= TMP(1 downto 0);
      when DIV =>
        Z <= A / B;
    end case;
  end process;
end;
```

A `case` statement behaves like a nested `if` statement, that is, the *OP* value is checked with the first case choice, if it does not match, the second case choice is checked and so on. The equivalent `if` statement for the above `case` statement is shown next.

```
if OP = ADD then
  Z <= A + B;
elsif OP = SUB then
  Z <= A - B;
elsif OP = MUL then
  Z <= A * B;
elsif OP = DIV then
  Z <= A / B;
end if;
```

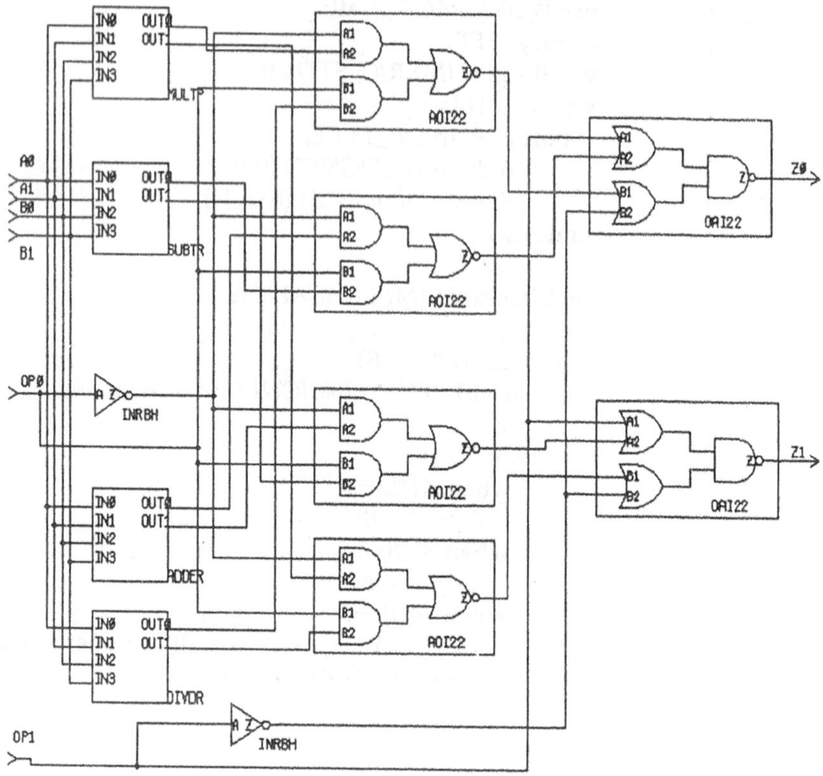

Figure 3-21 A 2-bit ALU.

The logic synthesized is shown in Figure 3-21. Note that an alternate way to generate logic is to generate a decoder for a `case` statement.

Here is another example of a `case` statement. The logic synthesized is shown in Figure 3-22.

```
package PAT is
  type WEEKDAY is (MON, TUE, WED, THU, FRI, SAT, SUN);
end PAT;

use WORK.PAT.all;
entity CASE_EX is
  port (DAY_OF_WORK: in WEEKDAY;
        SLEEP_TIME: out INTEGER range 0 to 15);
end CASE_EX;
```

```
architecture TEST of CASE_EX is
begin
  process (DAY_OF_WORK)
  begin
    case DAY_OF_WORK is
      when MON to THU =>
        SLEEP_TIME <= 6;
      when FRI =>
        SLEEP_TIME <= 8;
      when SAT =>
        SLEEP_TIME <= 9;
      when SUN =>
        SLEEP_TIME <= 7;
    end case;
  end process;
end architecture TEST;
```

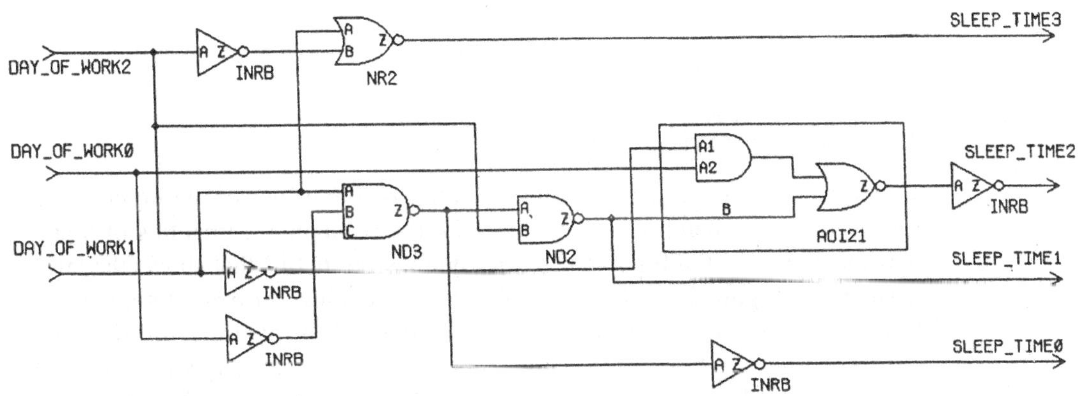

Figure 3-22 A case statement example.

3.8.1 Inferring Latches from case Statements

A latch can be inferred for a signal or a variable in a `case` statement, just like in an `if` statement. If a signal or a variable is not assigned a value in all possible branches of a `case` statement, a latch is inferred. See the following example.

```
package COLLECT is
  type STATES is (S0, S1, S2, S3);
end;

use WORK.COLLECT.all;
entity STATE_UPDATE is
  port (CURR_STATE: in STATES;
        Z: out INTEGER range 0 to 3);
end STATE_UPDATE;

architecture UPDATE of STATE_UPDATE is
begin
  process (CURR_STATE)
  begin
    case CURR_STATE is
      when S0 | S3 =>
        Z <= 0;
      when S1 =>
        Z <= 3;
      when others =>
        null;
    end case;
  end process;
end UPDATE;
```

The signal *Z* is not assigned a value for all possible values of the input signal *CURR_STATE*. Therefore in keeping with the simulation semantics of a signal, a latch is inferred for signal *Z*. The synthesized netlist that shows the latch is shown in Figure 3-23. In terms of latch inferencing, a `case` statement behaves identically to an `if` statement. If a latch is to be avoided, insert an initial value to signal *Z* before the `case` statement, as shown next. This assignment to *Z* causes it to be defined for all values of *CURR_STATE*.

```
...
process (CURR_STATE)
begin
  Z <= 0;          -- This statement added.

  case CURR_STATE is
  ...
```

The exception for inferring latches from variables described in Section 3.7 applies to a `case` statement as well.

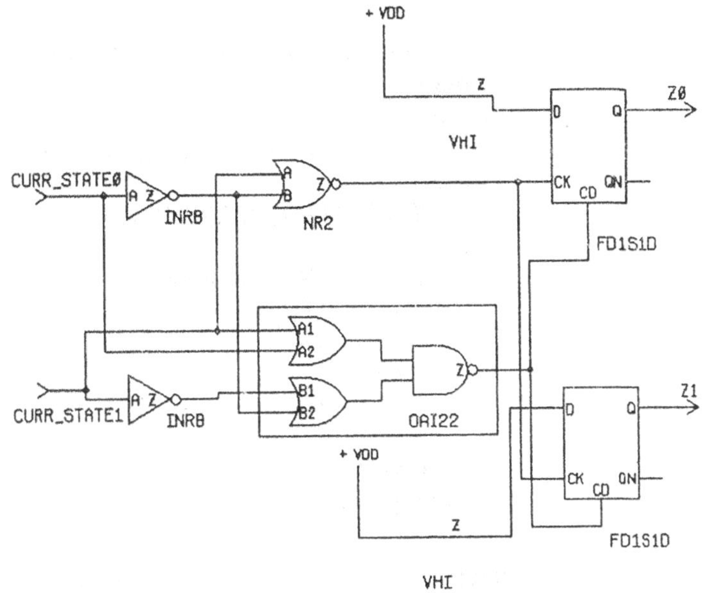

Figure 3-23 Latch inferred for a signal in a case statement.

3.9 Loop Statement

There are three kinds of loop statement in VHDL:

- while-loop
- for-loop
- loop

The for-loop statement is the one typically supported for synthesis. A for-loop is implemented by unrolling the for-loop, that is, all statements within the for-loop are replicated, once for each value of the for-loop index. This puts a restriction on the for-loop parameters, which must therefore compute to constant values during synthesis. Here is an example of a for-loop statement.

```
library IEEE;
use IEEE.STD_LOGIC_1164.all, IEEE.NUMERIC_STD.all;
entity DEMUX is
  port (A: in UNSIGNED (1 downto 0);
```

```
    Z: out UNSIGNED (3 downto 0));
end DEMUX;

architecture FOR_LOOP of DEMUX is
begin
  process (A)
    variable TEMP: INTEGER range 0 to 3;
  begin
    TEMP := TO_INTEGER (A);

    for J in Z'RANGE loop
      if TEMP = J then
        Z(J) <= '1';
      else
        Z(J) <= '0';
      end if;
    end loop;
  end process;
end;
```

The function *TO_INTEGER* converts an unsigned vector into an integer value; this function is present in the package *NUMERIC_STD*. When the for-loop is expanded, the following four `if` statements are obtained.

```
if TEMP = 3 then Z(3) <= '1'; else Z(3) <= '0'; end if;
if TEMP = 2 then Z(2) <= '1'; else Z(2) <= '0'; end if;
if TEMP = 1 then Z(1) <= '1'; else Z(1) <= '0'; end if;
if TEMP = 0 then Z(0) <= '1'; else Z(0) <= '0'; end if;
```

The synthesized logic is shown in Figure 3-24.

3.10 Null Statement

A `null` statement means to do no action. Therefore no hardware logic is generated for this statement.

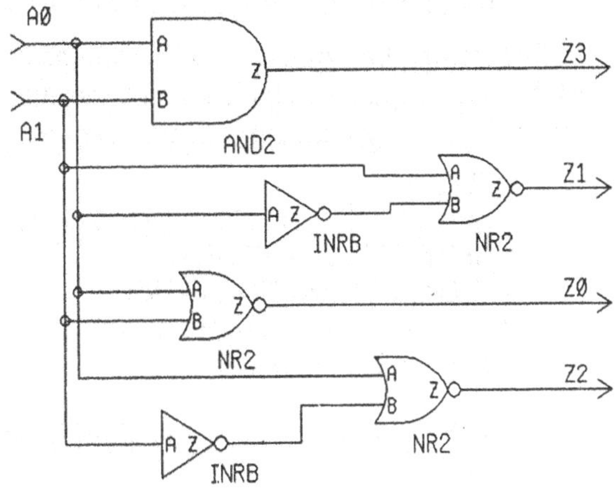

Figure 3-24 A for-loop example.

3.11 Wait Statement

There are three basic forms of the `wait` statement:

> **wait for** *time;*
> **wait until** *condition;*
> **wait on** *signal-list;*

The wait-until form is the one typically supported for synthesis. It is used to imply synchronous logic behavior. If used, the `wait` statement must be the first statement in a process, and furthermore, the condition in the `wait` statement must be one of the allowed clock expressions that indicates a falling or a rising clock edge. The `wait` statement with the various forms of clock expressions that are allowed are:

> **wait until** *clock_name = clock_value;*
> **wait until** *clock_name = clock_value* **and** *clock_name'EVENT;*
> **wait until** *clock_name = clock_value* **and not** *clock_name'STABLE;*

where the *clock_value* is either a logic-0, which indicates a falling clock edge, or a logic-1, which indicates a rising clock edge. In addition, the following two forms can be used if the clock is of type *STD_ULOGIC* or of type *STD_LOGIC*; the functions *RISING_EDGE* and *FALLING_EDGE* are defined in the package *STD_LOGIC_1164*.

```
wait until RISING_EDGE (clock_name);
wait until FALLING_EDGE (clock_name);
```

Statements that follow a `wait` statement refer to statements that execute synchronously with the clock edge. A variable or a signal assigned a value following the `wait` statement is synthesized as a flip-flop. Here is an example.

```
library IEEE;
use IEEE.STD_LOGIC_1164.all, IEEE.NUMERIC_STD.all;
entity INCREMENTOR is
  port (CLK: in STD_LOGIC;
      COUNTER: buffer UNSIGNED (1 downto 0));
end INCREMENTOR;

architecture FLOP of INCREMENTOR is
begin
  process
  begin
    wait until CLK = '1';
    COUNTER <= COUNTER + 1;
  end process;
end FLOP;
```

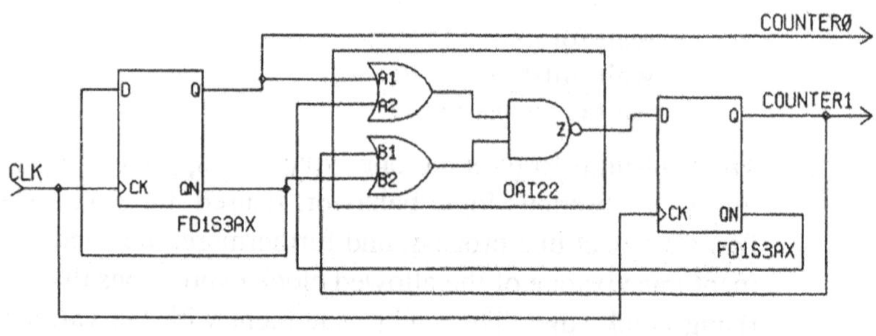

Figure 3-25 A `wait` statement implies synchronous logic.

The arithmetic package *NUMERIC_STD* needs to be included because a signal of type *UNSIGNED* is being added to an integer; the package contains the definition of the overloaded "+" operator and the definition of the type *UNSIGNED*. The logic in the process statement implies that every time signal *CLK* changes to a value '1', the counter is incremented. After synthesis, *COUNTER* is synthesized as two flip-flops with some additional combinational logic. The synthesized netlist is shown in Figure 3-25.

Here is another example of a process statement with a `wait` statement. The `if` statement following the `wait` statement is executed only on the falling edge of the clock *SYSCLK*. A register is inferred for signal *REG_A* since it is assigned synchronously under the control of the clock.

```
library IEEE;
use IEEE.STD_LOGIC_1164.all;
entity READ_RAM is
  port (SYSCLK, ENA: in STD_LOGIC;
        RAM_DATA: in STD_LOGIC_VECTOR (0 to 3);
        REG_A: out STD_LOGIC_VECTOR (0 to 3));
end READ_RAM;

architecture SAVE of READ_RAM is
begin
  process
  begin
    wait until SYSCLK = '0';

    if ENA = '0' then
      REG_A <= RAM_DATA;
    end if;
  end process;
end SAVE;
```

The synthesized netlist is shown in Figure 3-26. Notice that the output of the flip-flop for *REG_A* is fed back to the D-input of the flip-flop when *ENA* is '1', which is the way it should be; *REG_A* should retain its value when *ENA* is '1'.

Any number of sequential statements can follow the `wait` statement; the `wait` statement must be the first and the only wait statement in a process. All variables and signals assigned within such a process are implemented as flip-flops. There is, however, a slight difference in the way they are implemented to match with the semantics of a signal or a variable. Let us look at another example.

```
signal SELFIRST: STD_LOGIC;
. . .
SEQ: process
  variable RSHIFT: STD_LOGIC;
begin
  wait until CK_A = '0';
  RSHIFT := RSHIFT and STROBE;
```

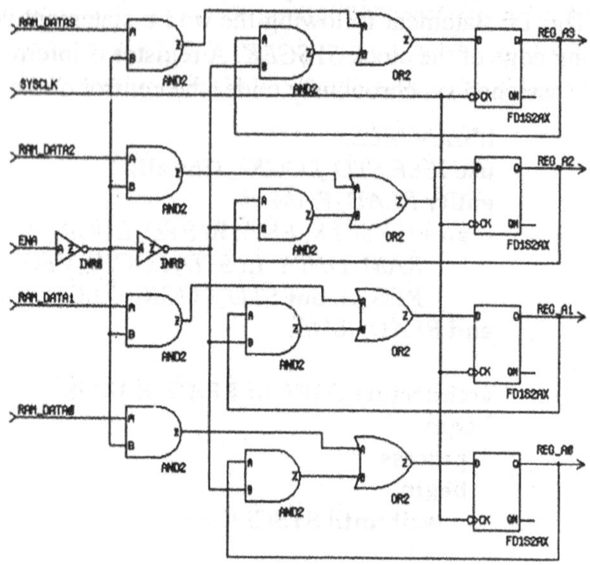

Figure 3-26 Inferring flip-flops using a `wait` statement.

SELFIRST <= *RSHIFT* **or** *XFLAG;*
CHKSTOP <= *SELFIRST* **xor** *MASK;*
end process;

In the first variable assignment statement, the variable *RSHIFT* is being used before its definition; therefore the value of this variable needs to be saved in a flip-flop. The use of *RSHIFT* in the assignment statement implies that the right-hand-side expression in the first assignment statement (the logic at the D input of the *RSHIFT* flip-flop) is used as the value of *RSHIFT* in the second assignment statement. Signals *SELFIRST* and *CHKSTOP* are also constructed as flip-flops since they are assigned under the control of a clock. The use of *SELFIRST* in the last statement implies that the output of the flip-flop, that is, the old value of *SELFIRST,* is used. This is because a signal is never assigned a value immediately but always after a certain delay. Thus, signal *SELFIRST* used in the last statement refers to the old value of *SELFIRST* and not to the value assigned in the previous statement.

Contrasting a signal assignment to a variable assignment, a variable gets assigned instantaneously in VHDL without any delays. *RSHIFT* is inferred as a flip-flop since it is used before its definition. Since *RSHIFT* is a variable, the input of the *RSHIFT* flip-flop (the current value of the variable) is used as the value of the operand in the second assignment statement. The synthesized netlist is shown in Figure 3-27.

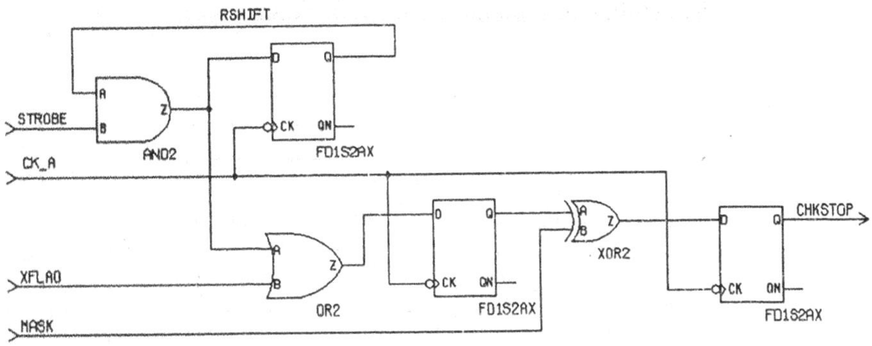

Figure 3-27 Variable vs. signal assignment following a `wait` statement.

Here is another example of a `wait` statement that is used to model an up-down counter.

```
library IEEE;
use IEEE.STD_LOGIC_1164.all, IEEE.NUMERIC_STD.all;
entity UPDOWN is
  port (CTRL: in STD_LOGIC;
      CLK_B: in STD_LOGIC;
      COUT: out STD_LOGIC_VECTOR(1 downto 0));
end UPDOWN;

architecture WAIT_EX of UPDOWN is
  signal COUNTER: UNSIGNED (1 downto 0);
begin
  process
  begin
    wait until CLK_B = '0';

    if CTRL = '1' then
      COUNTER <= COUNTER + 1;
    else
      COUNTER <= COUNTER – 1;
    end if;
  end process;
```

```
        COUT <= STD_LOGIC_VECTOR (COUNTER);
          -- The right-hand-side of the assignment is an
          -- example of a type conversion.
      end WAIT_EX;
```

The synthesized netlist is shown in Figure 3-28.

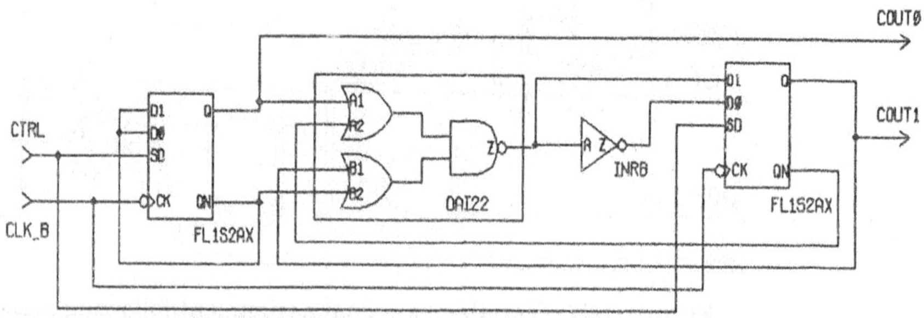

Figure 3-28 Up-down counter generated using a `wait` statement.

Exception for Variables

Not all variables that are assigned a value under the control of a `wait` statement become flip-flops. The exception is that if a variable is used temporarily, that is, if it's value does not have to be saved between multiple iterations of the process, then no flip-flop is inferred for that variable. This is very similar to the exception for inferring latches for variables described in Section 3.7.

Consider the following two processes.

```
signal BBC, STATE, NEW_CLK: STD_LOGIC;
. . .
P1: process
  variable CRX1: STD_LOGIC;
begin
  wait until NEW_CLK = '1';
  STATE <= CRX1;
  CRX1 := BBC;
end process;

P2: process
  variable CRX2: STD_LOGIC;
begin
```

```
    wait until NEW_CLK = '1';
    CRX2 := BBC;
    STATE <= CRX2;
end process;
```

In process *P1*, the value of variable *CRX1* has to be saved between multiple iterations of the process. Thus variable *CRX1* is inferred as a flip-flop. In process *P2*, *CRX2* is assigned and used in the same iteration of a process and it is not necessary to save its value between different iterations of the process. In this case, variable *CRX2* does not synthesize to a flip-flop.

What about variable *CRX3* in the following process *P3*? Careful examination reveals that the value of *CRX3* has to be saved since the previous value of *CRX3* is assigned to *STATE* when *CTL* is '0'. Thus variable *CRX3* is inferred as a flip-flop.

```
signal CTL: STD_LOGIC;
. . .
P3: process
    variable CRX3: STD_LOGIC;
begin
    wait until NEW_CLK = '1';

    if CTL = '1' then
        CRX3 := BBC;
    end if;

    STATE <= CRX3;
end process;
```

3.12 Modeling Flip-flops

In the previous section, we saw how flip-flops can be inferred from signals and variables when they are assigned values within a process that contains a `wait` statement as the first statement. A flip-flop can also be inferred by using a special `if` statement in a process. The syntax is of the form:

```
if clock-expression then
    sequential-statements
end if;
```

where a *clock-expression* is one of the following:

```
RISING_EDGE (clock_name)
FALLING_EDGE (clock_name)
clock_name = clock_value and clock_name'EVENT
clock_name = clock_value and not clock_name'STABLE
```

where *clock_value* is either a logic-0 or a logic-1. The first two forms are allowed only if the clock is of type *STD_ULOGIC* or *STD_LOGIC*; the functions are defined in the package *STD_LOGIC_1164*.

A signal assigned in such an `if` statement is inferred as a flip-flop. A flip-flop is inferred for a variable if its value is read before it is assigned a value. Here is an example.

```
library IEEE;
use IEEE.STD_LOGIC_1164.all, IEEE.NUMERIC_STD.all;
entity COUNT4 is
  port (CLK, PRESET, UPDOWN: in STD_LOGIC;
       DATAIN: in UNSIGNED (1 downto 0);
       DOUT: out UNSIGNED (1 downto 0));
end COUNT4;

architecture EXAMPLE of COUNT4 is
  signal COUNTER: UNSIGNED (1 downto 0);
begin
  process (CLK, PRESET, UPDOWN, DATAIN)
  begin
    if RISING_EDGE (CLK) then
      if PRESET = '1' then
        COUNTER <= DATAIN;
      else
        if UPDOWN = '1' then
          COUNTER <= COUNTER + 1;
        else
          COUNTER <= COUNTER - 1;
        end if;
      end if;
    end if;

    DOUT <= COUNTER;
  end process;
end EXAMPLE;
```

In this example, signal *COUNTER* is assigned a value within a special `if` statement, thus inferring flip-flops. Notice that signal *DOUT* is not a flip-flop

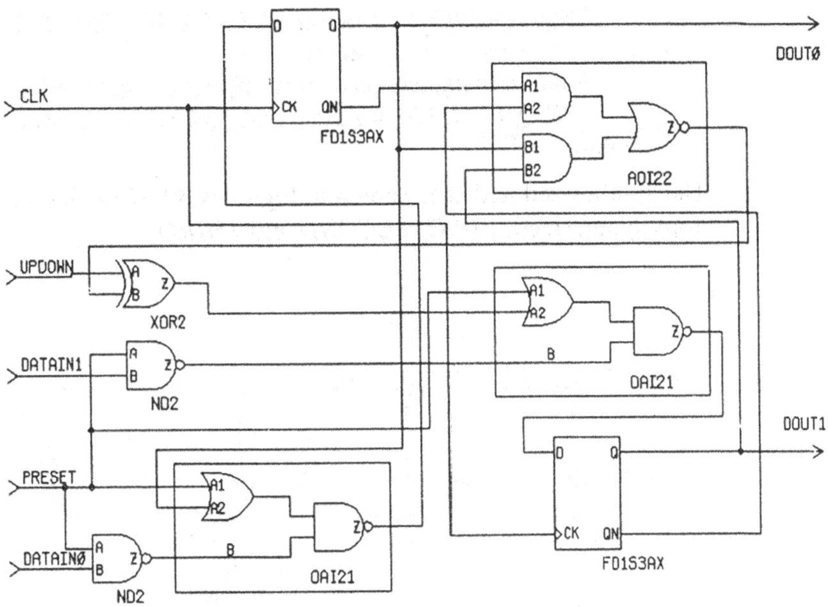

Figure 3-29 Modeling synchronous logic using an `if` statement.

since it is assigned a value outside the `if` statement. The synthesized netlist for this model is shown in Figure 3-29.

Here is an example of a pipelined sequence detector that is modeled using the `wait` statement style. The output of the detector is a '1' if a sequence "101" has been detected in the input data stream.

```
entity SEQ_DET is
  port (CLK, DATA: in BIT;
        SEQ_FOUND: out BIT);
end;

architecture PIPELINE of SEQ_DET is
  signal FIRST, SECOND, THIRD: BIT;
begin
  process
  begin
    wait until CLK = '1';       -- Save data on every rising edge.
    FIRST <= DATA;
    SECOND <= FIRST;
    THIRD <= SECOND;
  end process;
```

```
        SEQ_FOUND <= '1' when (FIRST & SECOND & THIRD = "101")
                         else '0';
        -- Alternately, the concurrent signal assignment can be written as:
        -- SEQ_FOUND <= FIRST and (not SECOND) and THIRD;
    end;
```

The synthesized netlist is shown in Figure 3-30. Note that there are three flip-flops synthesized, *FIRST*, *SECOND* and *THIRD*.

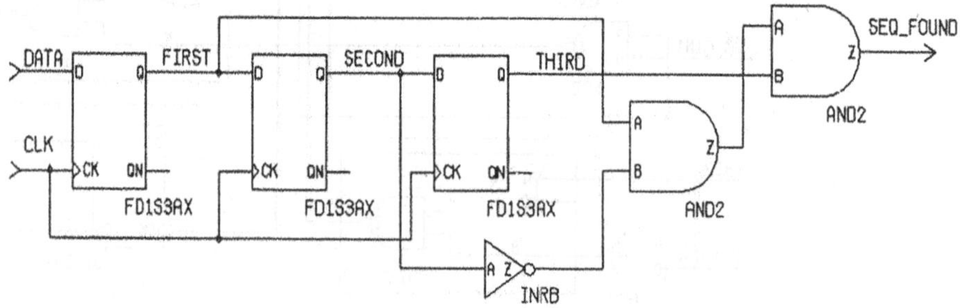

Figure 3-30 A pipelined sequence detector.

The difference between the `if` statement style and the `wait` statement style is that in the `if` statement style more than one clock can be modeled in a single process. More importantly, the description of combinational logic and sequential logic can be lumped into one process. Using the `wait` statement style, logic associated with each clock has to be described in a different process, and synchronous logic has to be separated from combinational logic, with each having its own process statement.

Using the `wait` statement style, a design might be described using more than one process, such as the one shown in the following template.

```
    process
    begin
        wait until clock-expression-1;
        synchronous-logic-description-1
    end process;

    process
    begin
        wait until clock-expression-2;
        synchronous-logic-description-2
```

```
end process;

process ( sensitivity-list )
begin
  combinational-logic-description
end process;
```

Using the `if` statement style, the same three processes can be merged into one single process, such as the one shown in the following template.

```
process ( sensitivity-list-with-clocks )
begin
  if clock-expression-1 then
    synchronous-logic-description-1
  end if;

  if clock-expression-2 then
    synchronous-logic-description-2
  end if;

  combinational-logic-description
end process;
```

The exception for inferring latches for variables described in Section 3.7 also applies to this form of inferring flip-flops.

3.12.1 Multiple Clocks

Here is an example of multiple clocks used in a single model. The synthesized netlist is shown in Figure 3-31.

```
library IEEE;
use IEEE.STD_LOGIC_1164.all;
entity MULT_CLKS is
  port (VT15CK, ADDCLK, ADN,
        RESETN, SUB_CLR, SUBN,
        DS1CK: in STD_LOGIC;
        DS1_ADD, DS1_SUB: out STD_LOGIC);
end;

architecture TEST of MULT_CLKS is
  signal ADD_STATE, SUB_STATE: STD_LOGIC;
begin
```

```
process (VT15CK, DS1CK)
begin
  if RISING_EDGE (VT15CK) then
    ADD_STATE <= ADDCLK nor (ADN or RESETN);
    SUB_STATE <= SUB_CLR xor (SUBN and RESETN);
  end if;

  if RISING_EDGE (DS1CK) then
    DS1_ADD <= ADD_STATE;
    DS1_SUB <= SUB_STATE;
  end if;
 end process;
end;
```

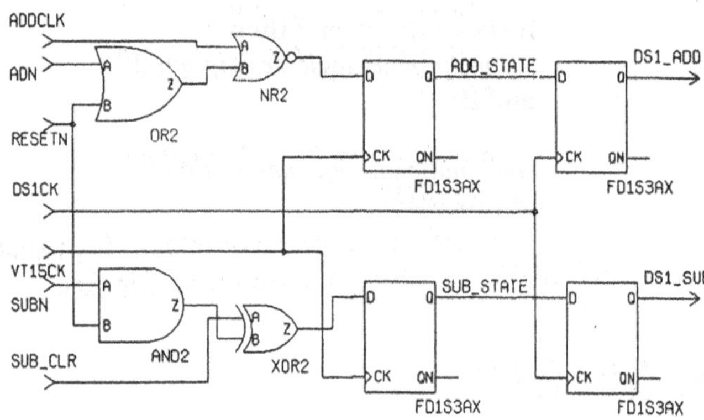

Figure 3-31 Multiple clocks within a process.

A typical restriction in this case is that a signal or a variable cannot be assigned under the control of more than one clock.

3.12.2 Multi-phase Clocks

Here is an example where two different phases of the same clock are used. Figure 3-32 shows the synthesized netlist.

```
library IEEE;
use IEEE.STD_LOGIC_1164.all;
entity MULTIPHASE_CLKS is
  port (CLK_A, A, B, C: in STD_LOGIC;
        E: out STD_LOGIC);
end;
```

```
architecture TEST of MULTIPHASE_CLKS is
  signal D: STD LOGIC;
begin
  process (CLK_A)
  begin
    if RISING_EDGE (CLK_A) then
      E <= D and C;
    end if;

    if FALLING_EDGE (CLK_A) then
      D <= A and B;
    end if;
  end process;
end;
```

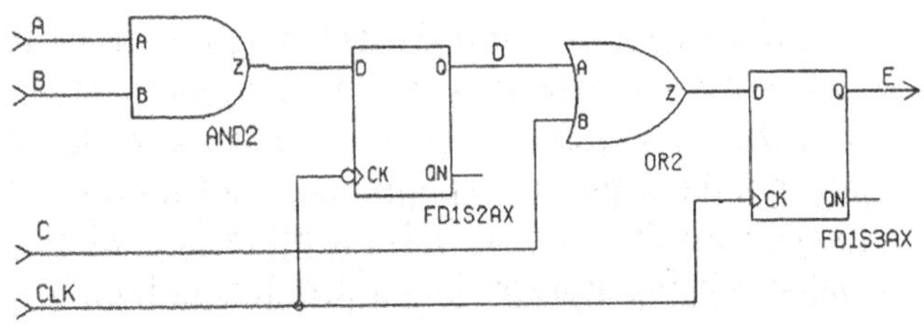

Figure 3-32 Different edges of the same clock within a process.

A typical restriction in this case is that a variable or a signal cannot be assigned under two different clock conditions or for that matter, under different clock edges.

3.12.3 With Asynchronous Preset and Clear

So far we have talked about simple D-type flip-flops. What if we wanted to infer a flip-flop with asynchronous preset and clear? To generate such a flip-flop, a special form of `if` statement has to be used. This is of the form:

```
if condition-1 then
  asynchronous-logic-1
elsif condition-2 then
  asynchronous-logic-2
elsif condition-3 then
  asynchronous-logic-3
```

```
-- Any number of elsif's
...
elsif clock-expression then
  synchronous-logic
end if;
```

The `if` statement may have one or more `elsif`'s but must not have any `else` clause. The last `elsif` clause must have a valid clock expression as its condition. A valid clock expression is of the form:

```
RISING_EDGE (clock_name)
FALLING_EDGE (clock_name)
clock_name = clock_value and clock_name'EVENT
clock_name = clock_value and not clock_name'STABLE
```

where *clock_value* is either a logic-0 or a logic-1. The logic in the last `elsif` clause describes synchronous logic. All other `elsif` branches describe asynchronous logic.

If a signal is assigned a value in any of the asynchronous sections and is also assigned in the synchronous part, that signal will get synthesized as a flip-flop with asynchronous preset and or clear. Depending on the value being assigned, the flip-flop could either be a flip-flop with asynchronous preset (if a non-zero value is assigned), or a flip-flop with asynchronous clear (if a zero value is being assigned), or a flip-flop with both.

Here is an example of an up-down counter with asynchronous preset and clear. The synthesized netlist is shown in Figure 3-33.

```
library IEEE;
use IEEE.STD_LOGIC_1164.all;
use IEEE.NUMERIC_STD.all;
entity ASYNC_COUNT2 is
  port (CLK, PRESET, UPDOWN, CLEAR: in STD_LOGIC;
      DIN: in STD_LOGIC_VECTOR (1 downto 0);
      DOUT: out STD_LOGIC_VECTOR (1 downto 0));
end;

architecture EXAMPLE of ASYNC_COUNT2 is
  signal COUNTER: UNSIGNED (1 downto 0);
begin
  process (CLK, PRESET, UPDOWN, DIN, CLEAR, COUNTER)
  begin
    if PRESET = '1' then
      COUNTER <= UNSIGNED (DIN);
```

```
    elsif CLEAR = '1' then
      COUNTER <= (others => '0');
    elsif CLK = '1' and CLK'EVENT then
      if UPDOWN = '1' then
        COUNTER <= COUNTER + 1;
      else
        COUNTER <= COUNTER - 1;
      end if;
    end if;

    DOUT <= STD_LOGIC_VECTOR(COUNTER);
  end process;
end;
```

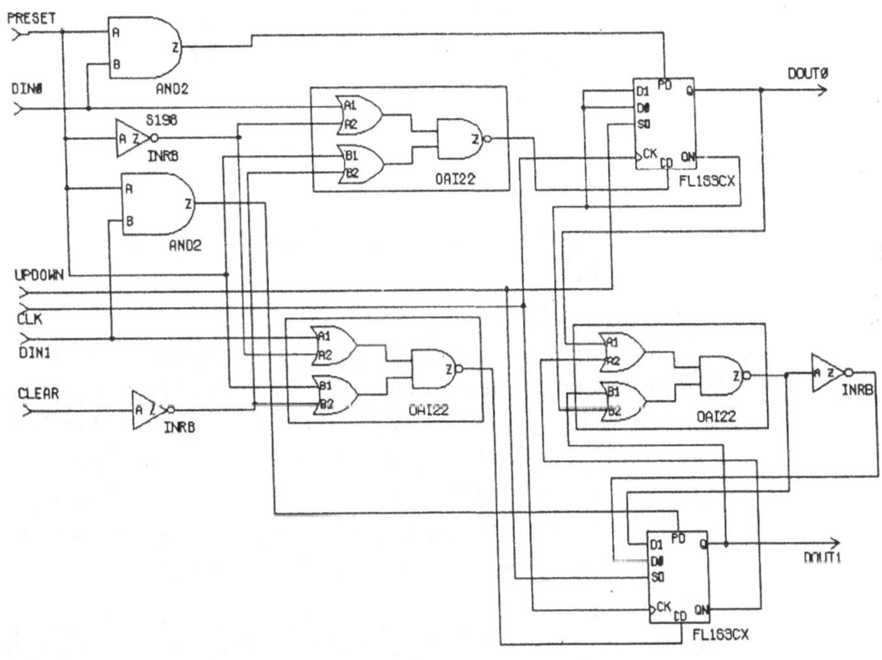

Figure 3-33 Flip-flops with asynchronous preset and clear.

A word of caution. It is very tempting to write the following code to infer a D-type flip-flip for *ODL*.

```
library IEEE;
use IEEE.STD_LOGIC_1164.all, IEEE.NUMERIC_STD.all;
entity MUX_FF is
  port (CLK, SET, BRV: in STD_LOGIC;
        DIN: in STD_LOGIC_VECTOR (1 downto 0);
        ODL: out STD_LOGIC;
        DOUT: out STD_LOGIC_VECTOR (1 downto 0));
end;

architecture EXAMPLE of MUX_FF is
  signal COUNT: UNSIGNED (1 downto 0);
begin
  process (CLK, SET, DIN, COUNT, BRV)
  begin
    if SET = '1' then
      COUNT <= UNSIGNED(DIN);
    elsif CLK = '1' and CLK'EVENT then
      ODL <= BRV;
      COUNT <= COUNT + 1;
    end if;
  end process;

  DOUT <= STD_LOGIC_VECTOR(COUNT);
end;
```

In this case, *ODL* is not synthesized to a simple D-type flip-flop but to an asynchronous preset/clear D-type flip-flop. This is because the assignment to *ODL* is dependent on the value of *SET* as well. What should the value of *ODL* be when *SET* is '1'? The answer is that the value of *ODL* must be retained; this implies that there is an implicit "*ODL* <= *ODL*;" assignment in the *SET* = '1' branch. Figure 3-34 shows the synthesized netlist. Note that as long as *SET* is '1', all clock edges are ignored; this is because the first `if` condition is always true and the clock edge condition is never checked.

If it is not intended for *ODL* to be dependent on the signal *SET*, a good alternative is to break the process into two processes as shown next.

```
-- This process is for asynchronous preset/clear flip-flops:
process (CLK, SET, DIN, COUNT)
begin
  if SET = '1' then
    COUNT <= UNSIGNED(DIN);
  elsif CLK = '1' and CLK'EVENT then
    COUNT <= COUNT + 1;
```

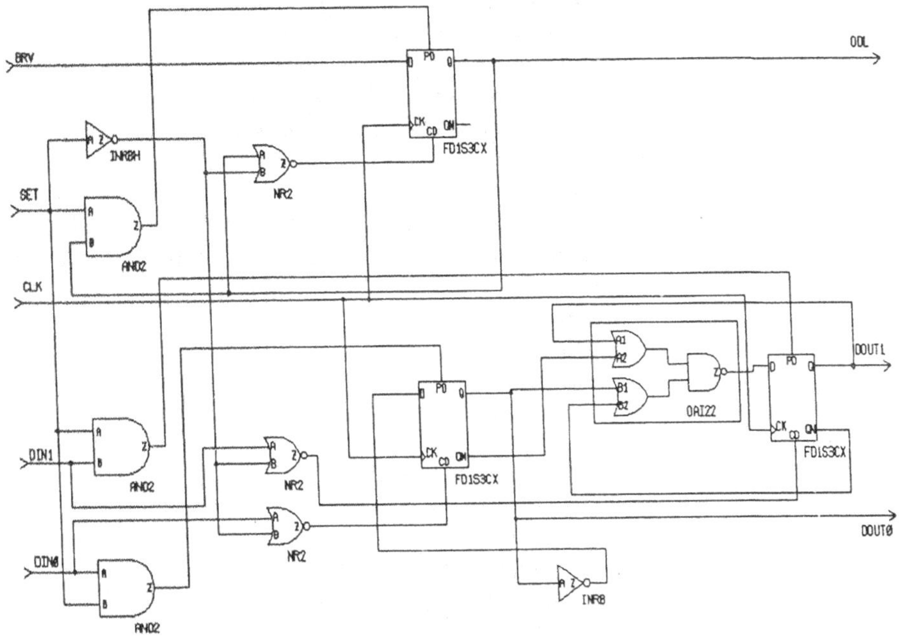

Figure 3-34 An extra asynchronous preset clear flip-flop.

```
  end if;
end process;

-- This process is for simple D-type flip-flops:
process
begin
  wait until CLK = '1';
  ODL <= BRV;
end process;
```

The first process is for inferring a asynchronous preset/clear flip-flop for *COUNT*, while the second process is for inferring a simple D-type flip-flop for *ODL*; *ODL* now has no dependency on signal *SET*.

3.12.4 With Synchronous Preset and Clear

What if we want to model a flip-flop with synchronous preset and clear? Let us first examine the following process statement.

```
library IEEE;
use IEEE.STD_LOGIC_1164.all;
use IEEE.NUMERIC_STD.all;
entity PRESET_COUNTER is
  port (CLK, PRESET, UPDOWN: in STD_LOGIC;
        DIN: in UNSIGNED (0 to 1);
        DOUT: out UNSIGNED(0 to 1));
end;

architecture IS_IT_SYNC_FF of PRESET_COUNTER is
  signal COUNTER: UNSIGNED (0 to 1);
begin
  process
  begin
    wait until CLK = '0';

    if PRESET = '1' then
      COUNTER <= DIN;
    else
      if UPDOWN = '1' then
        COUNTER <= COUNTER + 1;
      else
        COUNTER <= COUNTER - 1;
      end if;
    end if;
  end process;

  DOUT <= COUNTER;
end;
```

In this case, there are two (maybe more) ways of implementing the logic for signal *COUNTER*. First of all, there will be two flip-flops synthesized for signal *COUNTER*. The flip-flops could either be simple D-type flip-flops or they could be D-type flip-flops with synchronous preset and clear. This depends on how the signal *DIN* is used. If signal *DIN* is part of the data input of the flip-flops, simple D-type flip-flops are synthesized; such a synthesized netlist is shown in Figure 3-35. If signal *DIN* is part of the preset clear logic, synchronous preset clear flip-flops are synthesized; such a synthesized netlist is shown in Figure 3-36. A synthesis system may implement either of these depending on an option.

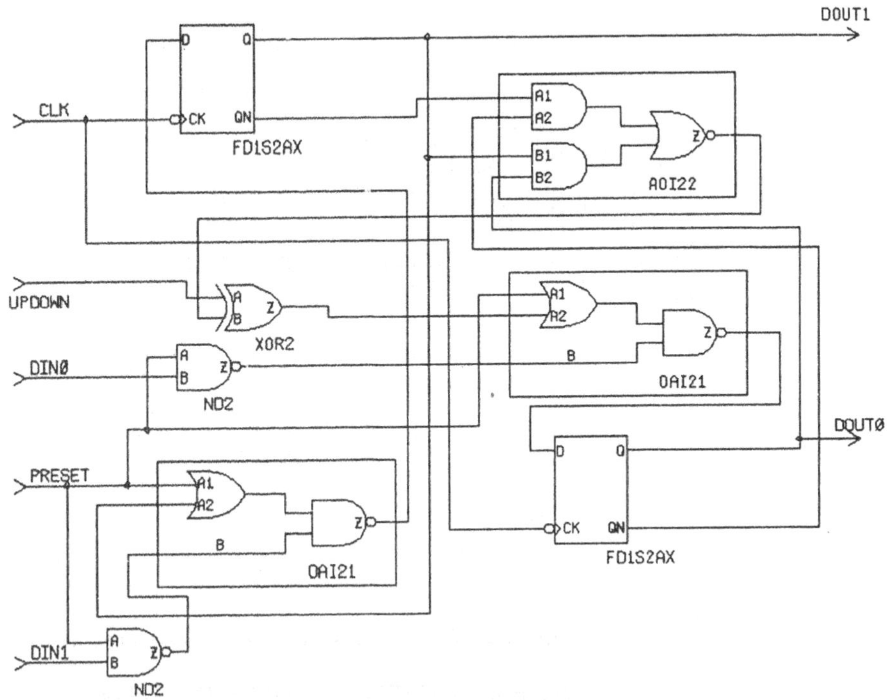

Figure 3-35 Synchronous preset and clear synthesized as combinational logic.

3.13 Modeling Latches

In sections 3.7.1 and 3.8.1, we saw how latches can be inferred when a signal or a variable is not assigned in all possible branches of an `if` or a `case` statement.

Here is another example. The synthesized netlist is shown in Figure 3-37.

```
library IEEE;
use IEEE.STD_LOGIC_1164.all;
entity LATCHED_ALU is
  port (A, B: in SIGNED(0 to 2);
        CLK: in STD_LOGIC;
        Z: out SIGNED(0 to 2));
end;
```

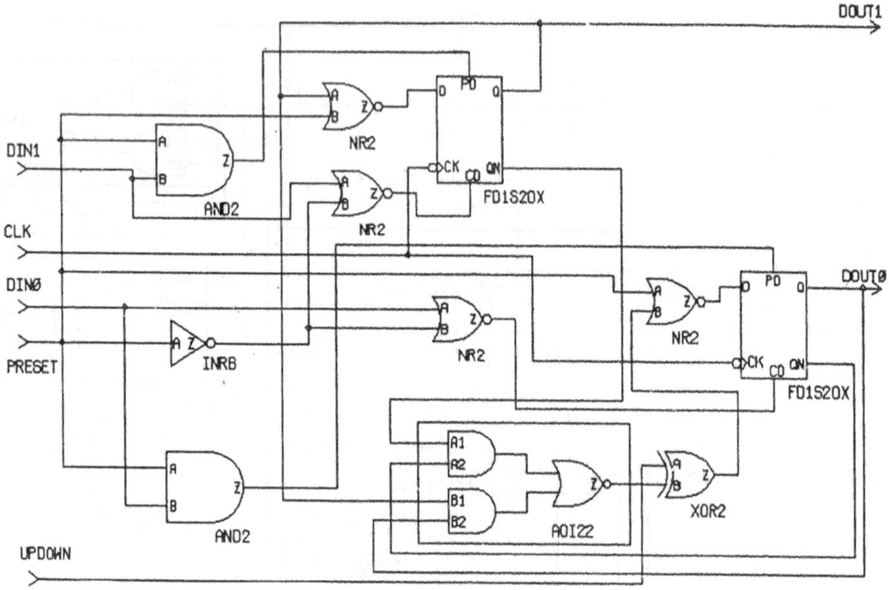

Figure 3-36 Flip-flops with synchronous preset and clear.

```
architecture EXAMPLE of LATCHED_ALU is
begin
  process (CLK, A, B)
  begin
    if CLK = '1' then
      Z <= A nor B;
    end if;
  end process;
end;
```

Since signal *Z* is not assigned a value when *CLK* is '0', a latch is synthesized for Z.

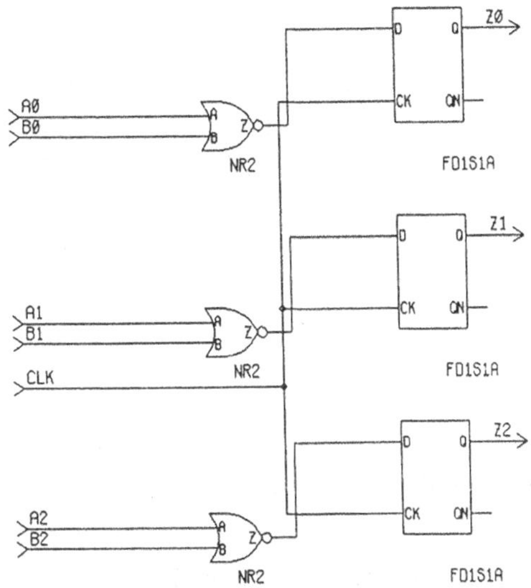

Figure 3-37 Level-sensitive latches.

3.14 Other Forms of Signal Assignment

3.14.1 Conditional Signal Assignment Statement

A conditional signal assignment statement is used to model combinational logic. It is implemented just like an `if` statement. However, no clock edges (for example, *CLK'EVENT*) are allowed as conditions. Here is an example.

```
library IEEE; use IEEE.STD_LOGIC_1164.all;
entity COND_ASSIGN is
  port ( START_XM, SHIFT_VAL, RESET: in STD_LOGIC;
         STOP_XM: out STD_LOGIC);
end;

architecture TEST of COND_ASSIGN is
begin
  STOP_XM <= START_XM xor SHIFT_VAL when RESET = '0'
               else START_XM or SHIFT_VAL;
end;
```

The synthesized netlist is shown in Figure 3-38.

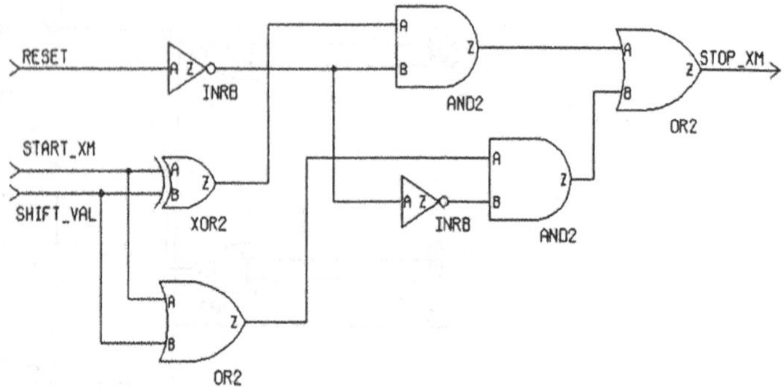

Figure 3-38 Logic generated from a conditional signal assignment statement.

3.14.2 Selected Signal Assignment Statement

A selected signal assignment statement is used to model combinational logic. It is implemented just like a `case` statement. Here is an example.

```
package P1 is
  type STATES is (RESET, WAITS, APPLY, DONE);
end;

use WORK.P1.all;
library IEEE; use IEEE.STD_LOGIC_1164.all;
entity SEL_ASSIGN is
  port (CURR_STATE: in STATES;
      RFLAG: out STD_LOGIC_VECTOR(0 to 1));
end;

architecture TEST of SEL_ASSIGN is
  signal CURR_STATE: STATES;
begin
  with CURR_STATE select
    RFLAG <= "00" when RESET | WAITS,
             "10" when APPLY,
             "11" when others;
end;
```

The synthesized netlist is shown in Figure 3-39.

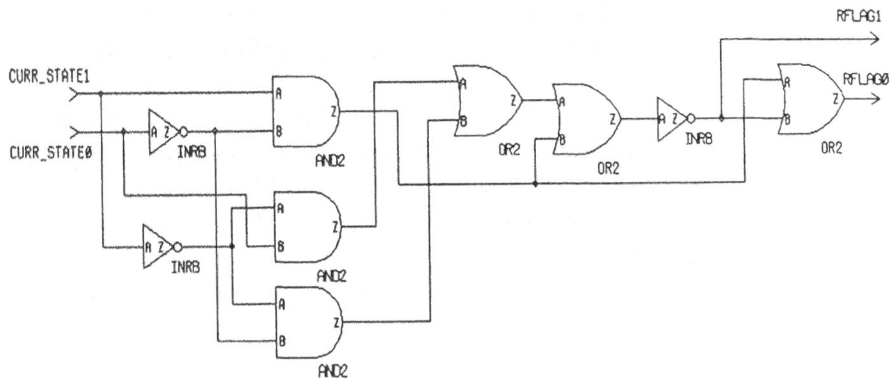

Figure 3-39 Logic generated from a selected signal assignment statement.

3.14.3 Sequential Signal Assignment Statement

Here is an example of a process statement with some sequential signal assignment statements.

```
entity SEQ_SIG is
  port (MERGE: in BOOLEAN;
        ER, XMT, FDDI: in BIT;
        CLAIM: out BIT);
end SEQ_SIG;

architecture TEST of SEQ_SIG is
  signal FCR: BIT;
begin
  process (MERGE, ER, XMT, FDDI)
  begin
    FCR <= ER or XMT;            -- Assignment 1.

    if MERGE then
      CLAIM <= FCR and FDDI;     -- Assignment 2.
    else
      CLAIM <= FDDI;
    end if;
  end process;
end;
```

There are three signal assignment statements in this example. Statements within a process statement execute sequentially. However, a signal is always assigned a value after a certain delay. Therefore the use of *FCR* in assignment 2 is the old value of *FCR* and not the value assigned in assignment 1. Most synthesis systems, however, ignore the delay in the signal assignment and the logic produced is as if the value assigned in assignment 1 is used in assignment 2. Note that simulation semantics may be different since signal *FCR* is not in the sensitivity list. To make the simulation results match between pre-synthesis and post-synthesis, the signal *FCR* must also appear in the sensitivity list so that when the value of *FCR* changes, the simulator executes the process a second time. If signal *FCR* is not in the sensitivity list, a warning message about a potential simulation mismatch may be produced. The synthesized netlist is shown in Figure 3-40.

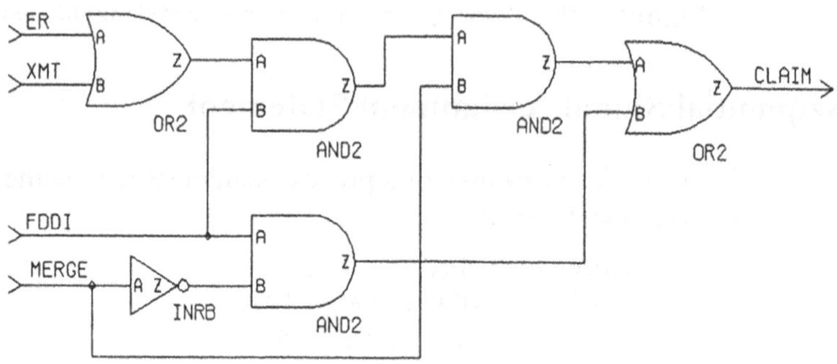

Figure 3-40 Signal assignments within a process.

Now let us look at the same case when a `wait` statement is introduced as the first statement in the process. Such an example is shown next.

```
architecture TEST of SEQ_SIG_FF is
  signal FCR: BIT;
begin
  process
  begin
    wait until CK = '1';
    FCR <= ER or XMT;                -- Assignment 1.

    if MERGE then
      CLAIM <= FCR and FDDI;         -- Assignment 2.
    else
      CLAIM <= FDDI;
    end if;
```

```
    end process;
end;
```

In this case, the sequential statements infer synchronous logic. Signals *FCR* and *CLAIM* both infer flip-flops. Usage of signal *FCR* in assignment 2 now refers to the output of the flip-flop *FCR*, that is, the old value, rather than the value assigned in assignment 1. Simulation results between behavior and synthesized netlist now match. The synthesized netlist for this example in shown in Figure 3-41.

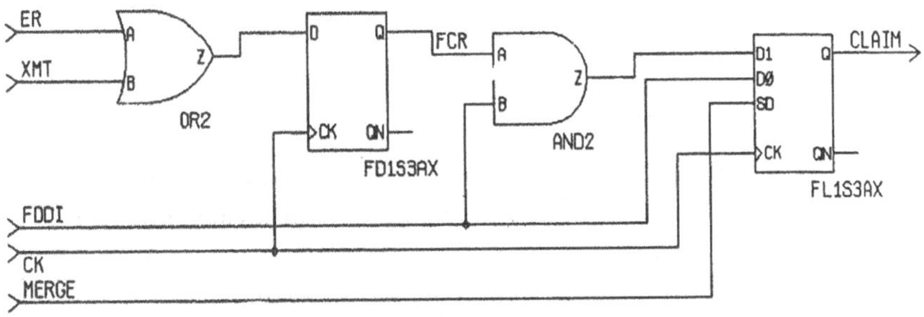

Figure 3-41 Signal assignments following a `wait` statement.

3.15 Functions

A function call represents combinational logic since a function call is always part of an expression in VHDL. A function call is synthesized by expanding the function call into in-line code. Any local variable declared within the function is treated as a pure temporary, in keeping with the simulation semantics of a variable declared within a subprogram; such a variable gets synthesized as a wire. Here is an example of a function call.

```
entity FUNC_CALL is
  port (XBC: out BOOLEAN;
        DATAIN: in BIT_VECTOR(0 to 5));
end;

architecture EXAMPLE of FUNC_CALL is
  function ODD_ONES (A: BIT_VECTOR) return BOOLEAN is
    variable RESULT: BIT;
  begin
```

```
        RESULT := '0';

        for K in A'RANGE loop
          RESULT := RESULT xor A(K);
        end loop;

        if RESULT = '0' then
          return FALSE;
        else
          return TRUE;
        end if;
      end ODD_ONES;
    begin
      XBC <= ODD_ONES (DATAIN);
    end;
```

After in-line expansion of the function call and further in-line expansion of the for-loop statement, we get the following code.

```
RESULT := '0';
RESULT := RESULT xor DATAIN(0);
RESULT := RESULT xor DATAIN(1);
RESULT := RESULT xor DATAIN(2);
RESULT := RESULT xor DATAIN(3);
RESULT := RESULT xor DATAIN(4);
RESULT := RESULT xor DATAIN(5);
XBC <= RESULT;
```

The synthesized netlist is shown in Figure 3-42. Note that a variable defined within a function can never be synthesized as a latch since the value of a variable defined in a function is never saved between subsequent function calls.

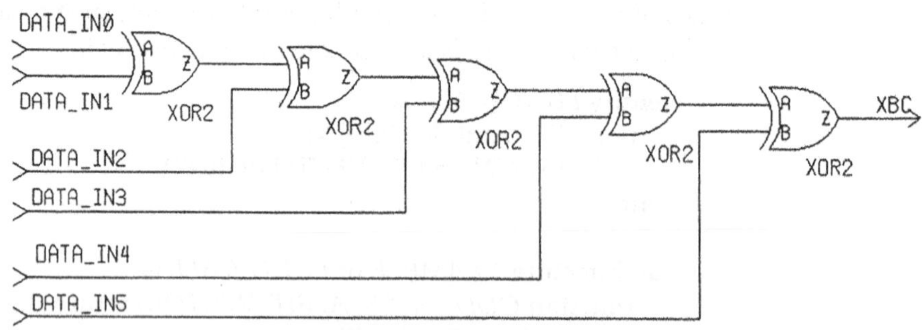

Figure 3-42 A function call example.

3.16 Procedures

A procedure call can represent either combinational logic or sequential logic depending on the context under which the procedure call occurs. By this, we mean that the output parameters of a procedure call may imply memory depending on the context in which they are assigned. For example, if a procedure call occurs in a process statement with a `wait` statement as the first statement, then any signal output parameter in a procedure call is synthesized as a flip-flop. Here is an example of a procedure call that represents pure combinational logic.

```
library IEEE;
use IEEE.STD_LOGIC_1164.all;
entity PROC_CALL is
  port (SHA, SHB: in STD_LOGIC_VECTOR(0 to 3);
        SHCARR: in STD_LOGIC;
        SHSUM: out STD_LOGIC_VECTOR(0 to 3);
        SHCARROUT: out STD_LOGIC);
end;

architecture EXAMPLE of PROC_CALL is
  procedure ADD (A, B, CIN: in STD_LOGIC;
                 COUT, SUM: out STD_LOGIC) is
  begin
    SUM := A xor B xor CIN;
    COUT := A and B and CIN;
  end;
begin
  process
    variable TCARR: STD_LOGIC_VECTOR (0 to 4);
    variable TSUM: STD_LOGIC_VECTOR (0 to 3);
  begin
    TCARR(0) := SHCARR;

    for J in SHA'RANGE loop
      ADD (SHA(J), SHB(J), TCARR(J), TSUM(J), TCARR(J+1));
    end loop;

    SHCARROUT <= TCARR(4);
    SHSUM <= TSUM;
```

```
        end process;
    end;
```

After in-line expansion of the procedure call and the for-loop statement, we get the following code.

```
TCARR(0) := SHCARR;
TSUM(0) := SHA(0) xor SHB(0) xor TCARR(0);
TCARR(1) := SHA(0) and SHB(0) and TCARR(0);
TSUM(1) := SHA(1) xor SHB(1) xor TCARR(1);
TCARR(2) := SHA(1) and SHB(1) and TCARR(1);
TSUM(2) := SHA(2) xor SHB(2) xor TCARR(2);
TCARR(3) := SHA(2) and SHB(2) and TCARR(2);
TSUM(3) := SHA(3) xor SHB(3) xor TCARR(3);
TCARR(4) := SHA(3) and SHB(3) and TCARR(3);
SHCARROUT <= TCARR(4);
SHSUM <= TSUM;
```

The synthesized logic is shown in Figure 3-43. Next is an example of a procedure call that is called under the control of a clock edge.

```
library IEEE;
use IEEE.STD_LOGIC_1164.all;
entity PROC_CALL_2 is
  port (BYTEREC: in STD_LOGIC_VECTOR (3 downto 0);
        CLK_FA: in STD_LOGIC;
        RFIF: out STD_LOGIC);
end;

architecture EXAMPLE of PROC_CALL_2 is
  procedure AND_BITS (A: in STD_LOGIC_VECTOR;
                signal Z: out STD_LOGIC) is
    variable RES: STD_LOGIC;
  begin
    RES := '1';

    for J in A'RANGE loop
      RES := RES and A(J);
    end loop;

    Z <= RES;
  end;
begin
  process
  begin
```

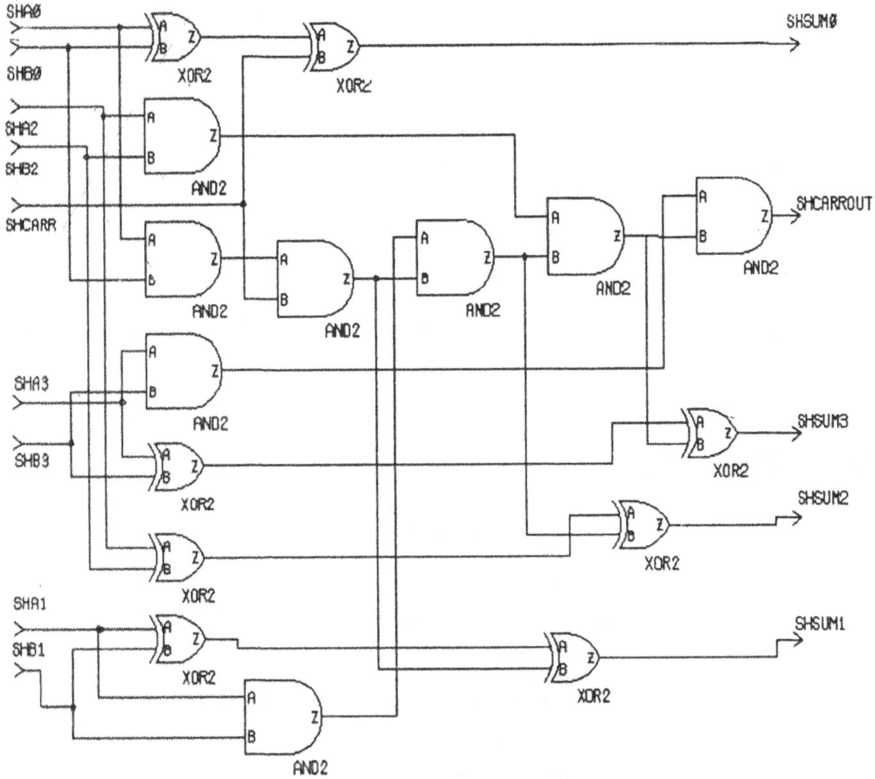

Figure 3-43 A procedure call example.

```
    wait until FALLING_EDGE(CLK_FA);
    AND_BITS (BYTEREC, RFIF);
  end process;
end;
```

In this example, signal *RFIF* is assigned a value under the control of clock *CLK_FA*; thus, signal *RFIF* gets synthesized as a flip-flop. The code after in-line expansion of the procedure call looks like this:

```
RES := '1';
RES := RES and BYTEREC(3);
RES := RES and BYTEREC(2);
RES := RES and BYTEREC(1);
RES := RES and BYTEREC(0);
RFIF <= RES;
```

The synthesized netlist is shown in Figure 3-44.

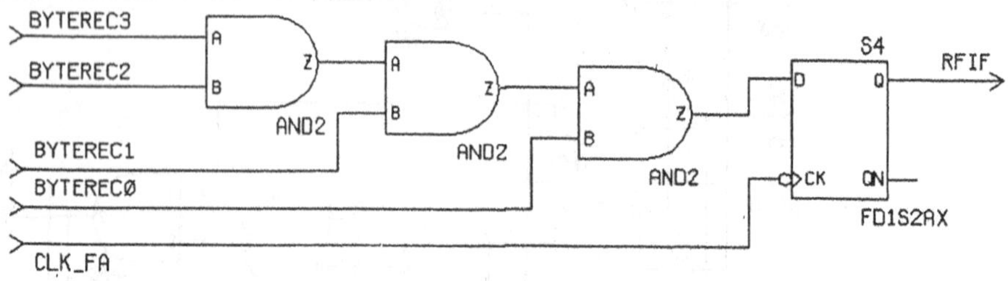

Figure 3-44 A procedure call following a `wait` statement.

3.17 Records

Here is an example that uses a record type.

```
package PACK is
  type STATES is (XMIT, RCV, INIT, DONE);
  type PACKET is
    record
      PACKET_ID: INTEGER range 0 to 3;
      PACKET_STATE: STATES;
    end record;
end;

use WORK.PACK.all;
entity INIT_PACKET is
  port (TSQ: out PACKET;
        SEND, CLK: in BIT);
end;

architecture RECORD_EXAMPLE of INIT_PACKET is
begin
  process
    variable PACK_INDEX: NATURAL;
  begin
    wait until CLK = '1';

    if SEND = '1' then
      PACK_INDEX := (PACK_INDEX + 1) mod 4;
```

```
            TSQ.PACKET_ID <= PACK_INDEX;
            TSQ.PACKET_STATE <= INIT;
        end if;
    end process;
end;
```

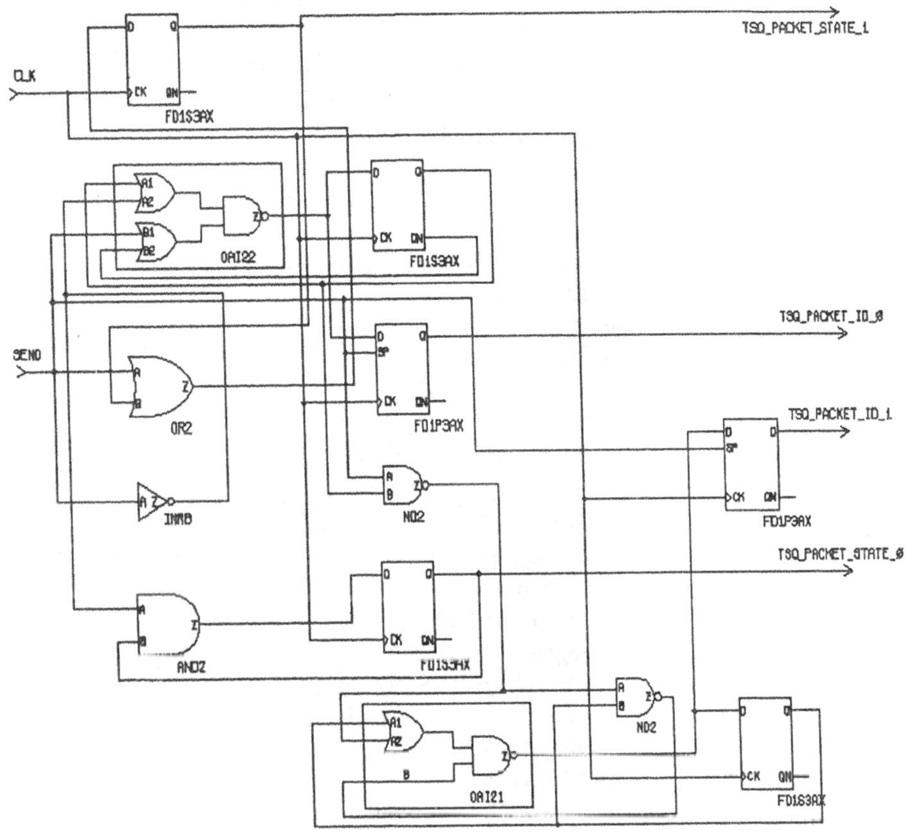

Figure 3-45 An example using a record type.

A record is split up into its individual elements for synthesis. Thus, for packet *TSQ*, two output ports *TSQ.PACKET_ID* and *TSQ.PACKET_STATE* are identified. Figure 3-45 shows the synthesized netlist for the above example.

3.18 Block Statement

A block statement can be used to specify a guard, to limit signal scope and to partition a design as blocks. Block statements that specify a guard expression are usually not supported for synthesis. A block statement does not cause any semantics or logic changes to occur, other than to limit the scope of signals declared within it. Here is an example.

```
entity BLOCK_STMT is
  port (CIN, DIN: in BIT;
        REC_OUT: out BIT);
end;

architecture NESTED of BLOCK_STMT is
  signal STAT: BIT;
begin
  B1: block
    signal STAT: BIT;
  begin
    STAT <= CIN and DIN;
      -- Refers to STAT declared in block B1.
    NESTED.STAT <= CIN or DIN;
      -- Refers to STAT declared in architecture NESTED.
    B2: block
      signal STAT: BIT;
    begin
      STAT <= B1.STAT xor NESTED.STAT;
      REC_OUT <= B2.STAT;    -- Alternately, refer simply as STAT.
    end block B2;
  end block B1;
end NESTED;
```

Figure 3-46 shows the synthesized netlist.

3.19 Using Metalogical Values

In the previous chapter, we described the three metalogical values: don't-care, unknown, and high-impedance. These are specified in an encoding scheme using the attribute *ENUM_ENCODING* with the values D, U, and Z.

Because of their restrictive interpretation, each metalogical value has certain constraints with its usage. In this section, we specify the domain under which these metalogical values can be used and their interpretations for synthesis.

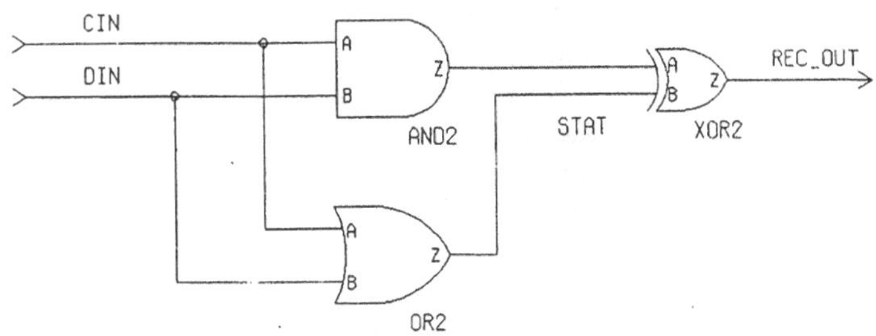

Figure 3-46 A block statement example.

The following entity is used as an example to explain the encoding of the metalogical values.

```
library IEEE;
use IEEE.STD_LOGIC_1164.all;
entity FIND_TWO is
  port (CLOCK, A: in STD_LOGIC; Y: out STD_LOGIC);
end;

architecture VERSION1 of FIND_TWO is
  attribute ENUM_ENCODING: STRING;
  type STATE is (INIT, FND1, FND2);
  attribute ENUM_ENCODING of STATE: type is "01 10 11";
  signal PRST, NXST: STATE;
begin
  process (CLOCK)
  begin
    if CLOCK'EVENT and CLOCK = '1' then
      PRST <= NXST;
    end if;
  end process;

  process (PRST, A)
  begin
    if PRST = INIT then                -- LineA
      if A = '0' then
        NXST <= INIT;                  -- LineB
```

```
        else
          NXST <= FND1;                     -- LineC
        end if;
      elsif PRST = FND1 then                -- LineF
        if A = '0' then
          NXST <= INIT;
        else
          NXST <= FND2;                     -- LineD
        end if;
      elsif PRST = FND2 then                -- LineE
        if A = '0' then
          NXST <= INIT;
        else
          NXST <= FND1;
        end if;
      end if;
    end process;

    Y <= '1' after 20 ns when PRST = FND2 else '0' after 20 ns;
  end;
```

Note that an explicit encoding has been specified for the enumeration literals, *INIT* has value "01", *FND1* has value "10", and *FND2* has value "11". In this encoding, no metalogical values have been used.

3.19.1 The Don't-care Value (D)

A don't-care value can be assigned to any signal or variable. Either a logic-0 or a logic-1 value that can lead to minimal logic is automatically selected.

A don't-care value can be compared using the "=" (equality) operator or the "/=" (inequality) operator in an `if` statement. In such a case, the "=" operator always returns false while the "/=" operator always returns true. Here are some examples.

```
-- Assume that literal '-' is encoded as the metalogical
-- don't-care value.

RESET <= '-';     -- Assign a don't-care value to signal RESET.
  -- Synthesis system will automatically select logic-0 or logic-1.

if SELECT = "----" then
```

```
    -- The if condition always evaluates to false.
  ...

  elsif BSQ /= "---" then
    -- elsif condition always evaluates to true.
  ...
```

Assume that the following encoding is used for the enumeration type *STATE* in entity *FIND_TWO*.

```
attribute ENUM_ENCODING of STATE: type is "01 10 DD";
```

On *LineD*, *NXST* gets assigned a don't-care value; a synthesis tool may appropriately choose a value for *NXST* in such a case. The condition on *LineE* evaluates to false and therefore none of the statements in that `if` branch are synthesized.

Here is an example of a 8-to-3 encoder that assigns a don't-care value to the output under a certain condition.

```
library IEEE;
use IEEE.STD_LOGIC_1164.all;
entity ENCODER8x3 is
  port (DATA: in STD_LOGIC_VECTOR(0 to 7);
      YOUT: out STD_LOGIC_VECTOR(0 to 3));
end ENCODER8x3;

architecture CONC_SIG of ENCODER8x3 is
begin
  with DATA select
    YOUT <=  "000" when "00000001",
             "001" when "00000010",
             "010" when "00000100",
             "011" when "00001000",
             "100" when "00010000",
             "101" when "00100000",
             "110" when "01000000",
             "111" when "10000000",
             "---" when others;
end CONC_SIG;
```

When *DATA* has a value other than any of those explicitly listed, a don't-care value is assigned to signal *YOUT*. This means that a synthesis tool is free to choose any value for *YOUT* (most synthesis tools will pick a value that leads to reduction of the synthesized logic). Note that this interpretation is different from what occurs during simulation; in simulation, the value "---" is assigned to signal *YOUT*, not any arbitrary value. This mismatch of interpretation between synthesis and simulation can lead to different simulation results. See Chapter 5 for more examples.

3.19.2 The Unknown Value (U)

The unknown metalogical value cannot be used in an expression on the right-hand-side of an assignment. However it can be used with the "=" (equality) and the "/=" (inequality) operator in an `if` statement.

```
-- Assume literal 'U' is encoded to represent the metalogical
-- unknown value.

if SAM /= "UUUUU" then
  -- The if condition always evaluates to true.
...

if BAR = 'U' then
  -- The if condition always evaluates to false.
...
```

Consider the following encoding for the enumeration type *STATE* in the entity *FIND_TWO*.

```
attribute ENUM_ENCODING of STATE: type is "01 UU 11";
```

In this case, *LineC* will report an error since an unknown value (enumeration literal *FND1*) is being assigned to *NXST*. Additionally, the condition on *LineF* will evaluate to false.

3.19.3 The High-impedance Value (Z)

The high-impedance value is used to generate a tri-state gate. A high-impedance value can be assigned to a signal or a variable; however, such an assignment must occur under the control of a condition, either in an `if` statement, or in a `case` statement. Here is an example.

```
library IEEE;
use IEEE.STD_LOGIC_1164.all;
entity TRI_STATE is
  port (RDY: in BOOLEAN;
       DINA, DINB: in STD_LOGIC;
       SEL1: out STD_LOGIC);
end TRI_STATE;
```

```
architecture EXAMPLE of TRI_STATE is
begin
  process (RDY, DINA, DINB)
  begin
    if RDY then
      SEL1 <= 'Z';
        -- Literal 'Z' is encoded as a high-impedance
        -- metalogical value in package STD_LOGIC_1164 using
        -- the attribute ENUM_ENCODING.
    else
      SEL1 <= DINA and DINB;
    end if;
  end process;
end EXAMPLE;
```

Figure 3-47 shows the synthesized netlist.

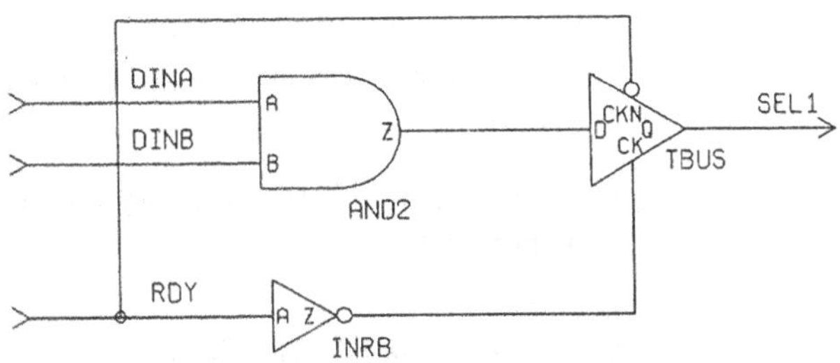

Figure 3-47 A high-impedance value produces a tri-state gate.

Furthermore, a high-impedance value can be compared using the "=" (equality) and the "/=" (inequality) operator in an `if` statement. The "=" operator always returns false while the "/=" operator always returns true. Here is an example.

```
-- Assume literal 'Z' is encoded as a high-impedance
-- metalogical value.
if DACK /= "ZZZ" then -- The if condition always evaluates to true.
...
```

Consider the use of high-impedance encoding for literal *FND2* in entity *FIND_TWO* as shown in the following attribute specification.

```
attribute ENUM_ENCODING of STATE: type is "01 10 ZZ";
```

In this case, *LineD* will cause a tri-state gate to be inferred for *NXST*. Additionally, the condition on *LineE* will evaluate to false.

3.19.4 Wild Card Matching

Wild card matching of don't-care values is provided by the function *STD_MATCH* defined in package *NUMERIC_STD*. The function *STD_MATCH* compares two values of base type *STD_ULOGIC*, and returns true iff:

i. both values are same, or
ii. one value is '0' and the other is a 'L', or
iii. one value is '1' and the other value is a 'H', or
iv. at least one of the values is a '-' (the don't-care value)

The function *STD_MATCH* can also be used for comparing two vectors. In this case, the function returns true iff:

i. both vectors are of same size, and
ii. the *STD_MATCH* function applied to each corresponding element returns true.

Here is an example of a 3-line priority encoder that shows the use of the *STD_MATCH* function.

```
library IEEE;
use IEEE.STD_LOGIC_1164.all;
use IEEE.NUMERIC_STD.all;
entity PRIORITY_WC is
  port (CTRL: in STD_LOGIC_VECTOR(0 to 3);
      POUT: out STD_LOGIC_VECTOR(0 to 3));
end;

architecture WILD_CARD of PRIORITY_WC is
begin
  process (CTRL)
  begin
    if STD_MATCH (CTRL, "1--") then
      -- Check if first bit is a '1', ignore others.
      POUT <= "100";
    elsif STD_MATCH (CTRL, "-1-") then
      -- Check if second bit is a '1', ignore others.
      POUT <= "010";
```

```
      elsif STD_MATCH (CTRL, "--1") then
        -- Check if third bit is a '1', ignore others.
        POUT <= "001";
      else
        POUT <= "000";
      end if;
    end process;
  end;
```

3.20 Component Instantiation Statement

A component instantiation statement can be written within an architecture body. Such a component is treated as a black box, that is, the component appears in the synthesized netlist as if it were a primitive component. Here is an example of a full-adder entity that contains one component instantiation statement. Notice that in the synthesized netlist, shown in Figure 3-48, the *MY_XOR* block appears as it is described in the architecture body.

```
entity FA_MIX is
  port (A, B, CIN: in BIT;
        SUM, COUT: out BIT);
end FA_MIX;

architecture MIXED of FA_MIX is
  component MY_XOR
    port (IN0, IN1: in BIT;
          OUT0: out BIT);
  end component;

  signal SFT: BIT;
begin
  X1: MY_XOR port map (IN0 => A, IN1 => B, OUT0 => SFT);

  COUT <= A and B and CIN;
  SUM <= SFT xor CIN;
end MIXED;
```

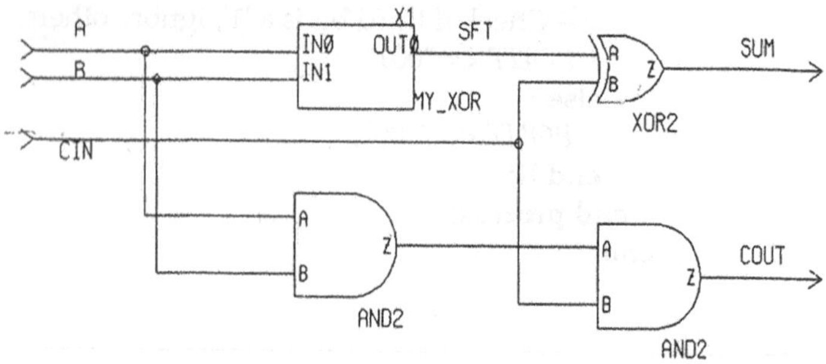

Figure 3-48 A component instance mixed with behavior.

3.21 Using Predefined Blocks

Component instantiation statements are often used when a designer is not satisfied with the quality of circuits produced by a synthesis tool. A designer may also have a library of predefined blocks such as memories. In such a case, the designer may prefer to instantiate a predefined block using a component instantiation statement instead of writing a behavioral description for the block. Thus a component instantiation statement provides flexibility in controlling the logic that is synthesized, and allows mixing of one or more predefined blocks as well.

Instantiating User-built Multipliers

As a first example, consider the case where a designer is not happy with the multiplication logic generated by a synthesis tool. This logic might have been generated from the following code.

```
library IEEE;
use IEEE.STD_LOGIC_1164.all;
use IEEE.NUMERIC_STD.all;
entity MULT_RED is
   port (A, B: in UNSIGNED(1 downto 0);
         Z: out STD_LOGIC);
end MULT_RED;
```

```
architecture EXAMPLE of MULT_RED is
  signal TEST: UNSIGNED (3 downto 0);
begin
  TEST <= A * B;              -- Multiply.
  Z <=  '1' when TEST = "1111" else
        '0';
end EXAMPLE;
```

In this example, the designer may instantiate a predefined multiplier as follows.

```
architecture OWN_INST of MULT_RED is
  component MY_MULT
    port (L, M: in UNSIGNED;
          P: out UNSIGNED);
  end component;

  signal TEST: UNSIGNED (3 downto 0);
begin
  M1: MY_MULT port map (L => A, M => B, P => TEST);
  Z <=  '1' when TEST = "1111" else
        '0';
end;
```

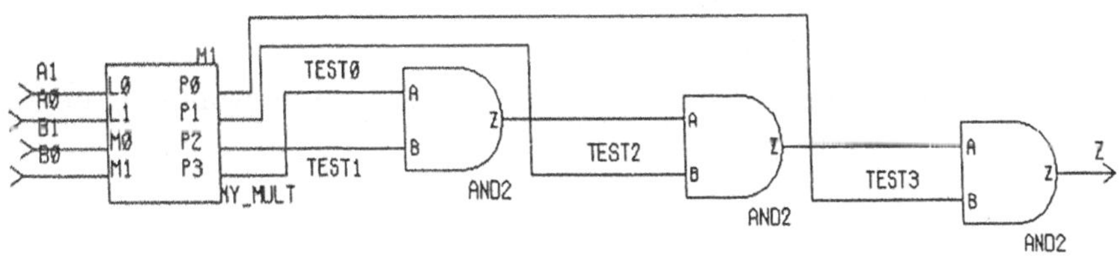

Figure 3-49 Instantiating a predefined multiplier.

The synthesized netlist for this example is shown in Figure 3-49. The designer may now use the predefined multiplier in the block *MY_MULT*.

Instantiating User-specific Flip-flops

A flip-flop is yet another case where a designer may want to control the type of flip-flop being generated. Normally a flip-flop is inferred for a signal or a variable that is assigned a value within a process that has a special `wait` statement or a special `if` statement. However, such a synthesized flip-flop may not be optimal for the designer. A designer may want to use a custom-made flip-flop instead of the flip-flop generated by the synthesis tool. This can be modeled again by instantiating the predefined flip-flop as a component. Here is an example.

```
component MY_FF
  port (IN0, IN1: in STD_LOGIC;
       OUT0: out STD_LOGIC);
end component;
. . .
F1: MY_FF port map (IN0 => REQ, IN1 => DCK, OUT0 => NREQ);
-- The component instantiation statement replaces the following
-- process statement:
  -- process
  -- begin
  --   wait until DCK = '1';
  --   NREQ <= REQ;
  -- end process;
process (NREQ, DYP, DLY)
begin
  if NREQ = '1' then
    FOP <= DYP;
  else
    FOP <= DLY;
  end if;
end process;
```

The synthesized netlist for this example is shown in Figure 3-50.

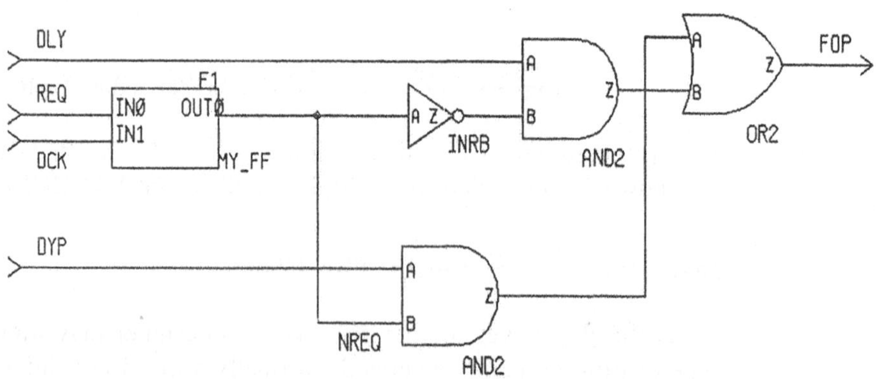

Figure 3-50 Instantiating a predefined flip-flop.

3.22 Generics

Generics provide a powerful mechanism in VHDL to model parameterized designs. Here is a simple example of an *N*-input and gate.

```
library IEEE;
use IEEE.STD_LOGIC_1164.all;
entity GENERIC_AND is
  generic (SIZE: INTEGER);
  port (A: STD_LOGIC_VECTOR (0 to SIZE-1);
        Z: out STD_LOGIC);
end GENERIC_AND;

architecture EXAMPLE of GENERIC_AND is
begin
  process (A)
    variable RES: STD_LOGIC;
  begin
    RES := '1';

    for K in A'RANGE loop
      RES := RES and A(K);
    end loop;

    Z <= RES;
  end process;
end EXAMPLE;
```

The entity *GENERIC_AND* cannot be synthesized by itself since the value of *SIZE* is not yet specified. Such an entity is synthesized when it is instantiated within other entities. An example is shown next.

```
library IEEE;
use IEEE.STD_LOGIC_1164.all;
entity GENERIC_INSTANTIATE is
  port (TSQ: in STD_LOGIC_VECTOR (0 to 5);
        RSQ: out STD_LOGIC);
end;

architecture EXAMPLE of GENERIC_INSTANTIATE is
  component GENERIC_AND
    generic (SIZE: INTEGER);
    port (A: in STD_LOGIC_VECTOR (0 to SIZE-1);
```

```
        Z: out STD_LOGIC);
    end component;

    signal SV1, SV2: STD_LOGIC;
begin
    G1: GENERIC_AND generic map (SIZE => 2)
            port map (A => TSQ(0 to 1), Z => SV1);
    G2: GENERIC_AND generic map (SIZE => 4)
            port map (A => TSQ(2 to 5), Z => SV2);
    RSQ <= SV1 xor SV2;
end;
```

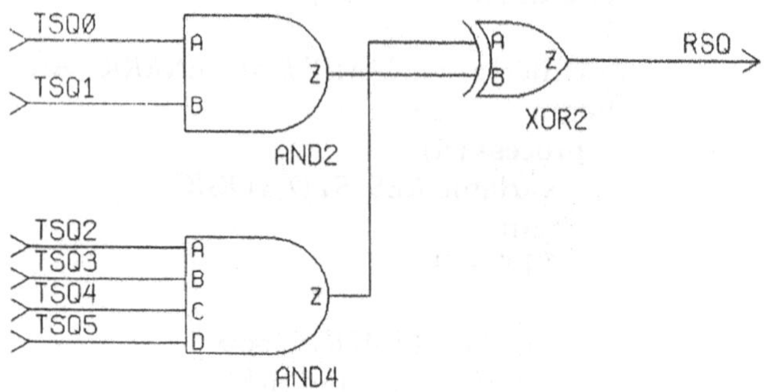

Figure 3-51 Using a 2-input and a 4-input generic and gate.

During the synthesis of entity *GENERIC_INSTANTIATE*, if a component instantiation with a generic map is found, the default entity is searched and the generic values are passed in before the generic entity is synthesized. In this example, the entity *GENERIC_AND* is synthesized twice, once for each instantiation of the generic entity. The synthesized netlist for the entity *GENERIC_INSTANTIATE* is shown in Figure 3-51.

3.23 Generate Statement

There are two forms of the generate statement: the if-generate scheme and the for-generate scheme. A generate statement causes the concurrent statements that appear within it to be conditionally selected if it is an if-generate statement, or the concurrent statements are expanded in-line if it is a for-generate statement. Here is an example of a ripple counter described using a generate statement. The number of elements in the counter is specified via a generic. The synthesized netlist is shown in Figure 3-52.

```
entity RIPPLE is
  generic (WIDTH: POSITIVE := 4);
  port (CLEAR, COUNT: in BIT;
      Q: out BIT_VECTOR (0 to WIDTH – 1));
end RIPPLE;

architecture COUNTER of RIPPLE is
  component TOGGLE_FF
    port (PC, CLK: in BIT;
        Z: out BIT);
  end component;

  signal CT: BIT_VECTOR (0 to WIDTH – 1);
begin
  G1: for J in 0 to WIDTH – 1 generate
    G2: if J = 0 generate
      T1: TOGGLE_FF port map (CLEAR, COUNT, CT(J));
    end generate G2;

    G3: if J > 0 generate
      T2: TOGGLE_FF port map (CLEAR, CT(J–1), CT(J));
    end generate G3;
  end generate G1;

  Q <= CT;
end COUNTER;
```

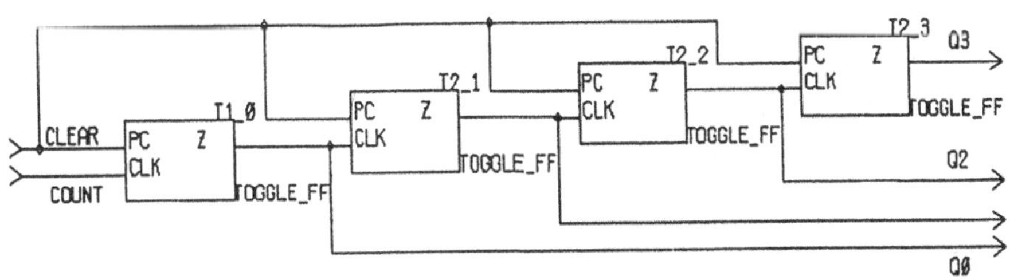

Figure 3-52 Logic generated using a generate statement.

Chapter 6 shows many more modeling examples that show the collective usage of multiple VHDL constructs.

❑

Chapter 4

Model Optimizations

This chapter describes optimizations that can be performed on a VHDL model to improve the circuit performance. In a C programming language compiler, an optimizer produces optimized machine code: code is rearranged, moved around, and so on, to reduce the C code execution time. Such optimizations may also be performed by a logic optimizer. Also in synthesis, the logic generated is very sensitive to the way a model is described. Moving a statement from one place to another or splitting up expressions may have a profound impact on the generated logic; it might increase or decrease the number of synthesized gates.

Figure 4-1 shows that different endpoints for best area and best speed are reached by a logic optimizer depending on the starting point provided by a netlist synthesized from VHDL. The various starting points are provided by rewriting the same VHDL model using different constructs. Unfortunately, no algorithms are known that determine what coding style or optimizations produce the desired balance between area and delay.

This chapter explores some of these optimizations that may be performed by a designer by rewriting appropriate code in the VHDL synthesis model.

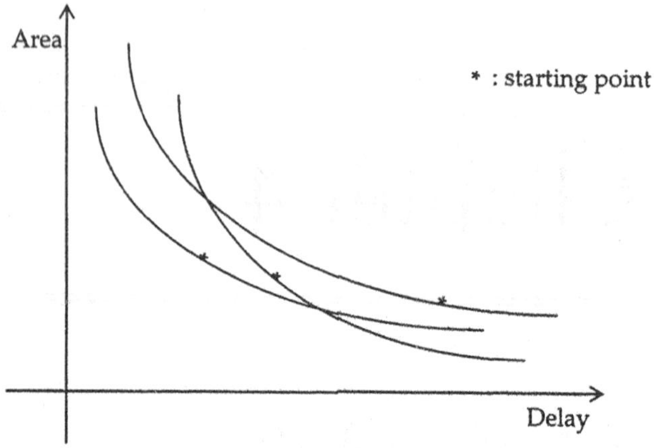

Figure 4-1 Different writing styles produce different area-delay trade-offs.

These optimizations provide a way to reduce the number of arithmetic and relational operators in the design yielding better quality designs. Synthesis run times may also be reduced.

4.1 Resource Allocation

Resource allocation refers to the process of sharing an arithmetic-logic-unit (ALU) under mutually-exclusive conditions. Consider the following `if` statement.

```
if MAX > 100 then
  JAM := SAM + BAM;
else
  JAM := SAM – CAM;
end if;
```

If no resource allocation is performed, the "+" and "–" operators get synthesized into two separate ALUs. However, if resource allocation is performed, only one ALU is necessary that performs both the "+" and "–" operations. This is because the two operators are used under mutually-exclusive conditions. A multiplexer is also generated; it is needed at the second port of the multiplexer to direct inputs *BAM* and *CAM*. Figure 4-2 shows the hardware synthesized for the `if` statement when no resource allocation is performed. Figure 4-3 shows the same example when resource allocation is performed.

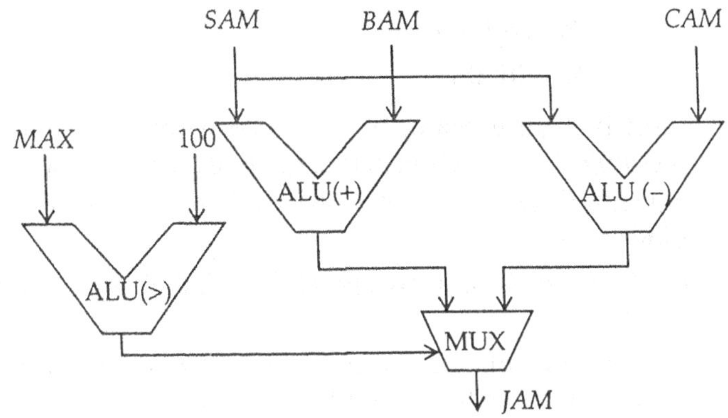

Figure 4-2 Without resource allocation.

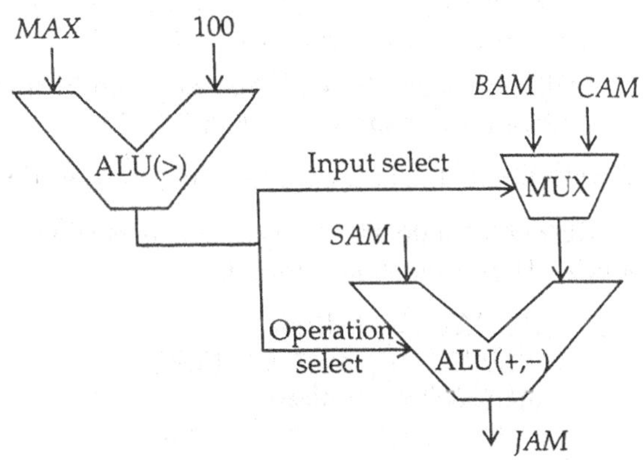

Figure 4-3 With resource allocation.

Notice that with sharing an ALU, a multiplexer has been introduced at one of the inputs of the ALU that contributes to the path delay. However, the amount of logic generated has been reduced due to sharing. This is again a trade-off that a designer has to make. In timing-critical designs, it may be better if no resource sharing is performed.

There are other variations of sharing that a synthesis tool may automatically enforce. Operators that are usually shared are:

i. relational operators
ii. addition

iii. subtraction

iv. multiplication

v. division

Usually it is not worthwhile to generate an ALU that does an addition and a multiplication. Multiplication and division operators are typically shared amongst themselves. When sharing with other operators, the following possibilities exist:

a. Same operator, same operands: definitely must share. Example: $A + B, A + B$

b. Same operator, one different operand: trade-off, since one multiplexer will be introduced. Example: $A + B, A + C$

c. Same operator, different operands: trade-off since two multiplexers are introduced. Example: $A + B, C + D$

d. Different operators, same operand: useful to share. Example: $A + B, A - B$

e. Different operators, one different operand: trade-off since one multiplexer introduced. Example: $A + B, A - C$

f. Different operators, different operands: trade-off since two multiplexers introduced. Example: $A + B, C - D$

Possibility **a** is the best case to share followed by **d**, (**b**, **e**) and (**c**, **f**).

Resource allocation may also be performed manually by rewriting the model. Here is such an example.

```
if SHREG = '0' then
  DATAOUT := ADL + CSN;
elsif RDN = '1' then
  DATAOUT := RDN + WRN;
else
  DATAOUT := ADL + RDN;
end if;

-- After manual resource allocation:
if SHREG = '0' then
  ARG1 := ADL;
  ARG2 := CSN;
elsif RDN = '1' then
  ARG1 := RDN;
  ARG2 := WRN;
else
  ARG1 := ADL;
  ARG2 := RDN;
```

```
end if;

DATAOUT := ARG1 + ARG2;
```

The modified model uses only one adder and the multiplexers at the input ports of the adder are implied by the `if` statement. The original example may synthesize with three adders.

4.2 Conversion Functions

VHDL is a strongly-typed language. Consequently, it is important to keep track of types in expressions and assignments. Conversion functions are often used to convert values from one type to another to maintain type compatibility. Here is an example.

```
function "+" (L, R: BIT_VECTOR) return BIT_VECTOR;

function TO_BITVECTOR (ARG, LEN: INTEGER)
    return BIT_VECTOR;
. . .
signal ZUT, TAR: BIT_VECTOR (3 downto 0);
. . .
ZUT <= TAR + TO_BITVECTOR (2, TAR'LENGTH);
```

Notice that it is not possible to simply write "*TAR* + 2" since the "+" operator is overloaded on both its operands to be of type *BIT_VECTOR*. Therefore to be type compatible, the conversion function *TO_BITVECTOR* is used.

The type conversion function really does not represent any hardware from a synthesis viewpoint, since the intention is simply to add the number 2 to *TAR*. The conversion function is introduced as a consequence of VHDL typing rules.

One way to avoid performing such a type conversion is to use the signed and unsigned types when performing arithmetic operations. In the above example, if signals *ZUT* and *TAR* are declared to be of type *UNSIGNED* (from package *NUMERIC_STD*), then a type conversion function is not necessary as shown below. This is because an overloaded "+" operator is predefined in the package *NUMERIC_STD* for operands of type *UNSIGNED* and an integer.

```
library IEEE; use IEEE.NUMERIC_STD.all;
. . .
```

```
signal ZUT, TAR: UNSIGNED (3 downto 0);
. . .
ZUT <= TAR + 2;
```

Here is another example of a conversion function usage.

```
function TO_BIT (ARG: BOOLEAN) return BIT;
variable CAR, BAR: BIT_VECTOR (0 to 3);
variable ZAB: BIT;
. . .
ZAB := TO_BIT (CAR > BAR);
```

The result of the relational operator is of type *BOOLEAN*. However, per VHDL rules, it is illegal to assign a boolean value to a variable of type *BIT*. Therefore, a conversion function is necessary. Again, in terms of hardware, it really does not represent extra logic since the logic clearly implies to connect the output of the comparator to *ZAB*.

Since conversion functions do not represent hardware, it is important to find out the built-in conversion functions provided by a synthesis tool and use only these where necessary. In such cases, no extra logic is synthesized for the conversion functions.

4.3 Type *INTEGER*

The VHDL predefined type *INTEGER* represents a minimum of 32 bits in hardware (since the minimum defined range of type *INTEGER* is $-(2^{31}-1)$ to $+(2^{31}-1)$). In many modeling situations, it is not necessary to model an integer as 32 bits. Here is an example of such an usage.

```
variable TIN: INTEGER;
. . .
TIN := TO_INTEGER (R_BUS(0 to 7));
NIB := TIN + 16;
```

Variable *TIN* is declared to be of type *INTEGER*. However, the only assignment to it is that of an 8-bit bus. Therefore, it would be helpful (to the synthesis tool) to limit the range of the integer also to a 8-bit range with a declaration such as:

```
variable TIN: INTEGER range 0 to 255;
```

A synthesis tool may generate 32 bits for *TIN* and realize that only the first 8 bits are used and then discard the rest. However, this is extra work for the synthesis tool to perform. Not only that, by specifying the integer constraint explicitly, a VHDL simulator can make sure that the integer value never exceeds the range.

Now consider the second assignment statement. A synthesis tool might generate a 32-bit adder first (since variable *TIN* is of size 32) and later realize that this was not necessary since the higher level bits were not used. Again by specifying a constraint with the type *INTEGER* for variable *TIN*, we are saving precious synthesis time, and in addition, we are placing additional constraints that can be checked for violations during a simulation.

The recommendation therefore is to use the unbounded type *INTEGER* only where necessary. In most of the cases, it would be better to specify a range constraint with the type *INTEGER*.

4.4 Common Subexpressions

It is very useful in practice to identify common subexpressions and to reuse computed values where possible. Here is a simple example.

```
variable RUN: . . .
. . .
RUN := R1 + R2;
. . .
CAR := R3 – (R1 + R2);
-- Assume that the second assignment is executed every time the first
-- statement is executed. Note that this assumption may not be true if
-- either of the statements is within an if or a case statement.
```

If a synthesis tool does not identify common subexpressions, two adders would be generated, each computing the same result, that of *R1* + *R2*. A logic optimization tool may or may not be able to identify such common logic, thus leading to larger designs. Therefore it is useful to identify common subexpressions and to reuse the computed values. For the previous example, we could replace the second assignment by:

```
CAR := R3 – RUN;
```

If the first assignment were a signal assignment (*RUN* would then have to be declared as a signal), such as:

```
signal RUN: . . .
. . .
RUN <= R1 + R3;
```

then a temporary variable will have to be introduced such as:

```
TEMP := R1 + R2;
RUN <= TEMP;
. . .
CAR := R3 – TEMP;
```

The problem of identifying common subexpressions becomes more important if larger blocks such as multipliers are used.

4.5 Moving Code

It may so happen that within a loop statement, there is an expression whose value does not change through every iteration of the loop. Also typically a synthesis tool handles a for-loop by unrolling the loop the specified number of times. In such a case, redundant code is introduced for the expression whose value is invariant of the loop index. Again a logic optimizer may or may not be smart enough to optimize such logic. Performing the optimizations at a higher level, that is, within the model, would help the optimizer in working on more critical pieces of the code. Here is an example of such a for-loop.

```
CAR := . . .
. . .
for COUNT in 1 to 5 loop
  . . .
  TIP := CAR – 6;
  -- Assumption: CAR is not assigned a new value within the loop.
  . . .
end loop;
```

The right-hand-side expression in the assignment statement value is invariant of the loop index, that is, the value computed in variable *TIP* is independent of the loop index. However, a synthesis tool may generate five subtracters, one for each loop iteration, thus generating extra logic. In this case, only one subtracter is really necessary.

The best way to handle this case is to move the loop-invariant expression out of the loop. This also improves simulation efficiency. This is shown in the following example.

```
CAR := . . .
. . .
TEMP:= CAR - 6;    -- A temporary variable is introduced.

for COUNT in 1 to 5 loop
  . . .
  TIP := TEMP;
  -- Assumption: CAR is not assigned a new value within the loop.
  . . .
end loop;
```

Such movement of code may have to be performed by the designer to produce more efficient code.

4.6 Common Factoring

Common factoring is the extraction of common subexpressions in mutually-exclusive branches of an `if` or a `case` statement. Here is an example.

```
if TEST then
  AX := A and (B + C);
else
  BY := (B + C) or T;
end if;
```

The expression "*B*+*C*" is computed in mutually-exclusive branches of an `if` statement. However, instead of the synthesis tool generating two adders, it is useful to factor out the expression and place it before the `if` statement. This is shown next.

```
TEMP := B + C;        -- A temporary variable is introduced.

if TEST then
  AX := A and TEMP;
else
  BY := TEMP or T;
end if;
```

By performing this common factoring, less logic is synthesized (in the above example, only one adder gets synthesized) so that a logic optimizer may concentrate on optimizing more critical areas.

4.7 Commutativity and Associativity

In certain cases, it might be necessary to perform commutative operations before performing some of the earlier mentioned optimizations. Here is an example where performing a commutative operation before common subexpression identification helps in identifying common subexpressions.

```
RUN := R1 + R2;
...
CAR := R3 – (R2 + R1);
```

Applying commutativity rules to the expression "*R2* + *R1*" helps in identifying the common subexpression "*R1* + *R2*" that is also used in the first assignment.

Similarly, associativity rules can be applied before using any of the earlier described optimizations. Here is an example.

```
LAM := A + B + C;
...
BAM := C + A – B;
```

Notice that applying associativity and commutativity rules on the expression in the first statement identifies "*C* + *A*" as a common subexpression. After subexpression identification, the example appears like this.

```
TEMP := C + A;          -- A temporary variable is introduced.
LAM := TEMP + B;
BAM := TEMP – B;
```

If associativity and commutativity are not used, a synthesis tool may generate three adders and one subtracter; after subexpression identification, it may generate only two adders and one subtracter, thus providing increased savings in logic.

4.8 Other Optimizations

There are two other optimizations that usually a synthesis tool would have no problem handling. These are

i. Dead-code elimination

ii. Constant folding

These optimizations are usually performed by a synthesis system and a designer does not have to worry about it. These optimizations are nonetheless explained below.

Dead code elimination deletes code that never gets executed. For example,

```
if 2 > 4 then
  OLI := SDY and RDY;
end if;
```

Clearly, there is no need to synthesize an and gate since the assignment statement will never get executed and represents dead code.

Constant folding implies to compute constant expressions during compile time as opposed to implementing logic and then letting a logic optimizer try getting rid of the logic. Here is a simple example.

```
constant FAC: INTEGER := 4;
. . .
YAK := 2 ** FAC;
```

Constant folding computes the value of the right-hand-side expression during compile time and assigns the value to *YAK*. No hardware need be generated. This leads to savings in logic optimization time.

4.9 Flip-flop and Latch Optimizations

4.9.1 Avoiding Flip-flops

It is important to understand the flip-flop inference rules of a synthesis tool. These rules may vary from one synthesis tool to another. If the inference rules are not followed, a synthesized netlist may have many more flip-flops than are really necessary. Here is a case in point.

```
signal PS: INTEGER range 0 to 1;
signal ZOUT: BIT_VECTOR(0 to 3);
signal CLK: BIT;
. . .
process
begin
  wait until CLK = '1';

  case PS is
    when 0 =>
      PS <= 1;
      ZOUT <= "0100";
    when 1 =>
      PS <= 0;
      ZOUT <= "0001";
  end case;
end process;
```

Here the intention appears to be to store the value of signal *PS* in a flip-flop (rising-edge triggered). After synthesis, not only is there a flip-flop for PS, there are also four flip-flops for the signal *ZOUT*. This is because *ZOUT* is also a signal and it is being assigned under the control of a clock. It may or may not be the intention to generate flip-flops for the signal *ZOUT*. If not, then a `case` statement needs to be written in a separate process in which the signal *ZOUT* is assigned, this time not under the control of the clock. The modified example that generates only one flip-flop is shown next.

```
process
begin
  wait until CLK = '1';

  case PS is
    when 0 =>
      PS <= 1;
    when 1 =>
      PS <= 0;
  end case;
end process;

process (PS)
begin
  case PS is
    when 0 =>
      ZOUT <= "0100";
```

```
      when 1 =>
        ZOUT <= "0001";
    end case;
  end process;
```

4.9.2 Avoiding Latches

A variable or a signal that does not have a value specified in all branches of a `case` or an `if` statement can lead to a latch being built. This is because in VHDL, a variable (defined within a process) or a signal infer memory, and thus if a variable or a signal is not assigned a value in all branches of a condition, the value needs to be saved in memory. Here is an example.

```
process (PROBE, CNT)
  variable LUCK: BIT;
begin
  if PROBE = '1' then
    LUCK := CNT;
  end if;
  . . .
end process;
```

What is the value of *LUCK* when *PROBE* is '0'? It must be the old value of *LUCK*. Thus the value of *LUCK* needs to be saved; a latch is created for this variable.

The best way to avoid latches is to first determine from the synthesis tool how many latches have been inferred. A designer now needs to go back and check if each latch inferred really needs to be a latch. In many cases, a designer never intended for a latch or the designer forgot to specify values under all conditions. The best rule is to check the latches that get synthesized and go back and determine why each latch got synthesized and fix code if necessary to avoid latches.

Here are two ways of avoiding a latch for the above example. In the first approach, define a value for the variable in the `else` branch as well.

```
process (PROBE, CNT)
  variable LUCK: BIT;
begin
  if PROBE = '1' then
    LUCK := CNT;
  else                       -- Else clause added.
    LUCK := '0';
```

```
    end if;
    ...
end process;
```

In the second approach, initialize the value of the variable before the `if` statement.

```
process (PROBE, CNT)
  variable LUCK: BIT;
begin
  LUCK := '0';              -- Value of variable is initialized.

  if PROBE = '1' then
    LUCK := CNT;
  end if;
  ...
end process;
```

4.10 Design Size

Small Designs Synthesize Fastei

Experimental studies have shown that logic circuits of size between 2000 to 5000 gates are best handled by a logic optimizer. This implies that in the VHDL model, process statements must not be inordinately long. Design should be structured into multiple processes or multiple design entities.

Unfortunately, to date no correlation has been found between the gates produced and the number of lines of VHDL code. A 2500-gate circuit could have been synthesized from a 10-line VHDL code (may have a for-loop) or by 10,000 lines of VHDL code (maybe from a large `case` statement with simple assignments).

Synthesis run-times, mainly logic optimization, are exponential with design size. Thus it is critical to keep the sizes of subblocks within a design small.

Hierarchy

It is useful to retain the hierarchy of a VHDL model in terms of processes and blocks. This enables a hierarchy of subcircuits to be produced by the synthesis tool that a logic optimizer can effectively handle.

Quite often, a synthesis tool might automatically preserve the hierarchy of a large datapath operator. For example,

```
...
ZIM := RIM + SIM;        -- RIM and SIM are 16-bits.
...
```

In this case, a synthesis tool may preserve the 16-bit adder as a separate hierarchy.

Macros as Structure

Synthesis is not the right mechanism to build a memory such as a ROM or a RAM. RAMs are usually available predefined in a technology library. When a component such as a RAM is required, it is better to treat this as a component, instantiate this in the model, and then synthesize. A synthesis tool merely creates a black box for the RAM into which the designer would later link in the RAM component.

Similar actions may be necessary if a designer has a statement of the form:

```
CRY := BRY * TRY;        -- 16-bit arguments.
```

and expects the synthesis tool to implement an efficient multiplier. The designer may have a better designed multiplier. Again in this case, it is better for the designer to instantiate a multiplier as a component, rather than expressing the multiplication operator which, upon synthesis, may or may not produce an efficient multiplier.

4.11 Using Parenthesis

When writing VHDL code, the designer must be aware of the logic structure being generated. One such important point is the use of parenthesis. Here is an example.

RESULT <= RHI + RLO – PHY_DATA + MAC_RESET;

A synthesis tool when synthesizing the right-hand side-expression follows the VHDL rules for expression evaluation, that is, left to right, and builds a circuit as shown in Figure 4-4. The logic structure generated may end up having a

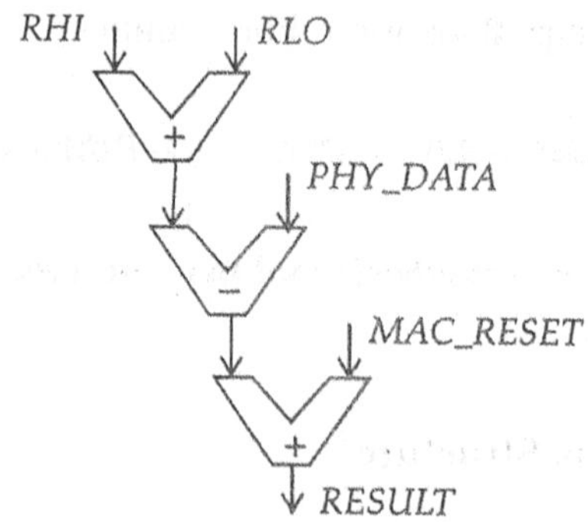

Figure 4-4 Without using parenthesis.

longer critical path. A better alternative is to use parenthesis, such as:

RESULT <= (RHI + RLO) – (PHY_DATA – MAC_RESET);

which results in a smaller critical path. The synthesized circuit is shown in Figure 4-5. Using parenthesis may also help identify opportunities for identi-

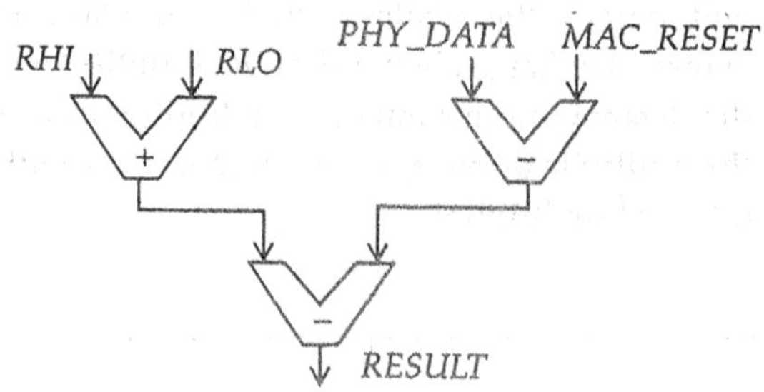

Figure 4-5 After using parenthesis.

fying common subexpressions.

Recommendation: Use parenthesis liberally in an expression to control the structure of the synthesized logic.

4.12 Building with Predefined Blocks

A typical synthesis system provides a number of built-in building blocks, for example, a "+" generates an adder, and a construct such as "*SELECT_VALUE* := *MUX* (*ADDRESS*), where *MUX* is an array" generates a multiplexer. Sometimes a block is required that is slightly different from the one provided by the system. An example of this is that of building a 4-bit adder with both carry-in and carry-out. Here is a VHDL model that can be used to build the required adder using the built-in "+" adder. The advantage of such modeling is that other optimizations can be applied on the predefined blocks, such as resource allocation.

```
library IEEE;
use IEEE.STD_LOGIC_1164.all, IEEE.NUMERIC_STD.all;
package EXTENDED is
  procedure ADD_CARRY_IO (A, B: in UNSIGNED;
                          CIN: in STD_LOGIC;
                          signal SUM: out UNSIGNED;
                          signal COUT: out STD_LOGIC);
end EXTENDED;

package body EXTENDED is
  procedure ADD_CARRY_IO (A, B: in UNSIGNED;
                          CIN: in STD_LOGIC;
                          signal SUM: out UNSIGNED;
                          signal COUT: out STD_LOGIC) is
    variable A_TMP, B_TMP, SUM_TMP:
        UNSIGNED (A'LENGTH+1 downto 0);
  begin
    assert A'LENGTH = B'LENGTH
      report "ADD_CARRY_IO: Operand sizes do not match."
      severity ERROR;

    A_TMP := '0' & A & CIN;
    B_TMP := '0' & B & '1';
    SUM_TMP := A_TMP + B_TMP;
    SUM <= SUM_TMP (A'LENGTH downto 1);
```

```
    COUT <= SUM_TMP (A'LENGTH+1);
  end ADD_CARRY_IO;
end;

library IEEE;
use IEEE.STD_LOGIC_1164.all, IEEE.NUMERIC_STD.all;
use WORK.EXTENDED.all;
entity BIG_BLOCK is
  port (ZA, ZB: in UNSIGNED (0 to 3);
        ZCIN: in STD_LOGIC;
        ZSUM: out UNSIGNED (0 to 3);
        ZCOUT: out STD_LOGIC);
end;

architecture PROC_CALL of BIG_BLOCK is
begin
  ADD_CARRY_IO (A => ZA, B => ZB, CIN => ZCIN,
          SUM => ZSUM, COUT => ZCOUT);
end PROC_CALL;
```

4.13 Using One Adder

Consider the following code.

```
signal SUM: UNSIGNED (4 downto 0);
signal OPD1, OPD2: UNSIGNED (3 downto 0);
signal CIN: STD_LOGIC;
. . .
SUM <= OPD1 + OPD2 + CIN;
```

Synthesis may generate two adders for the signal assignment statement (some synthesis systems may recognize this expression and generate only one adder with a carry-in). However, if the goal is to produce only one adder and be portable, the code could be modified as follows. In this case, only one adder will get synthesized.

```
library IEEE;
use IEEE.STD_LOGIC_1164.all;
use IEEE.NUMERIC_STD.all;
entity ONE_ADDER is
  port (OPD1, OPD2: in UNSIGNED (3 downto 0);
        CIN: in STD_LOGIC;
```

```
    RESULT: out UNSIGNED (4 downto 0));
end;

architecture BEHAVIOR of ONE_ADDER is
  signal T1, T2, TR: UNSIGNED (5 downto 0);
begin
  T1 <= '0' & OPD1 & CIN;
  T2 <= '0' & OPD2 & '1';
  TR <= T1 + T2;
  RESULT <= TR (5 downto 1);
end;
```

❑

Chapter 5

Verification

Having synthesized a VHDL behavioral model into a netlist, it is important to verify the functionality of the synthesized netlist to ensure it still matches the intended functionality. This step is important since a synthesis system may make certain assumptions or interpretations of the VHDL code that may not match those intended by the model writer.

In this chapter, we assume that this verification step is performed using simulation which verifies the functionality between the behavioral model and the synthesized netlist. We illustrate some cases of simulation mismatches that might possibly occur, describe their cause, and provide recommendations on avoiding these.

5.1 Entity Interface

In this chapter, we assume that the synthesis process produces a synthesized netlist in VHDL as shown in Figure 5-1. A VHDL netlist is a collection of component instances interconnected by signals. When describing a netlist in VHDL, it is necessary to associate type information with each signal as well. For example, should the type of the signal be? *BIT*, *STD_ULOGIC*, *STD_LOGIC* or *MVL7*? This is a design modeling choice; that is, it depends on how many values are to be used in simulation to model a signal. In this chapter, we assume that type *STD_ULOGIC* is used as a basic type for all signals in a netlist.

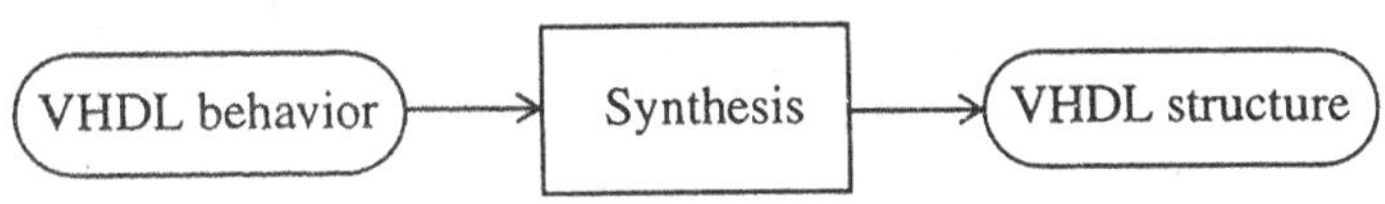

Figure 5-1 A netlist is produced from synthesis.

Having selected a type for modeling a signal in a netlist, there might be a potential conflict with the behavioral entity if it uses different types. Here is an example of such an entity declaration.

```
library ATTLIB;
use ATTLIB.MVL_PACKAGE.all;
entity DIV is
  port (CK, RESET, TESTN : in MVL;
        ENA : out MVL);
end DIV;

library IEEE;
use IEEE.STD_LOGIC_1164.all;
entity DIV_STR is
  port (CK, RESET, TESTN: in STD_ULOGIC;
        ENA: out STD_ULOGIC);
end DIV_STR;
```

Since the stimulus was originally defined for the behavioral entity (it generates *MVL* values), the stimulus file also has to be suitably modified so that it can be applied to the structural entity. We shall later see that writing a VHDL test bench for verification eases this problem a little since conversion functions can be used in the test bench.

Similar problems occur if the behavioral entity has ports of any type other than the *STD_ULOGIC*, for example, a record type, integer type, or a boolean type.

5.2 A Test Bench

One approach to verifying functionality is to simulate the VHDL structural model with the same set of stimulus as used during behavioral simulation, save the results in a results file and compare to see if the results are identical. The stimulus file may have to be modified if a port type in the behavioral model is any other than type *STD_ULOGIC*. This scenario is shown in Figure 5-2.

Another approach is to write a test bench; a test bench is a model written in VHDL that applies stimulus, compares the output responses, and reports any simulation mismatches. Conversion functions are used within the test bench to convert stimulus values to type *STD_ULOGIC*. Figure 5-3 shows such a scenario. A test bench for a model called *DIV* is shown next. The stimulus is read from a vector file "INPUTS.VEC"; its contents are of the form:

```
T'100
T'000
T'101
. . .
```

```
library IEEE;
use IEEE.STD_LOGIC_1164.all, IEEE.NUMERIC_STD.all;
use STD.TEXTIO.all;
entity DIV_TB is end;

use WORK.TSG_VHDL.all;
architecture TEST_BENCH of DIV_TB is
  -- Component declarations:
  component DIV port (
    CK: in STD_ULOGIC;
    RESET: in STD_ULOGIC;
    TESTN: in STD_ULOGIC;
```

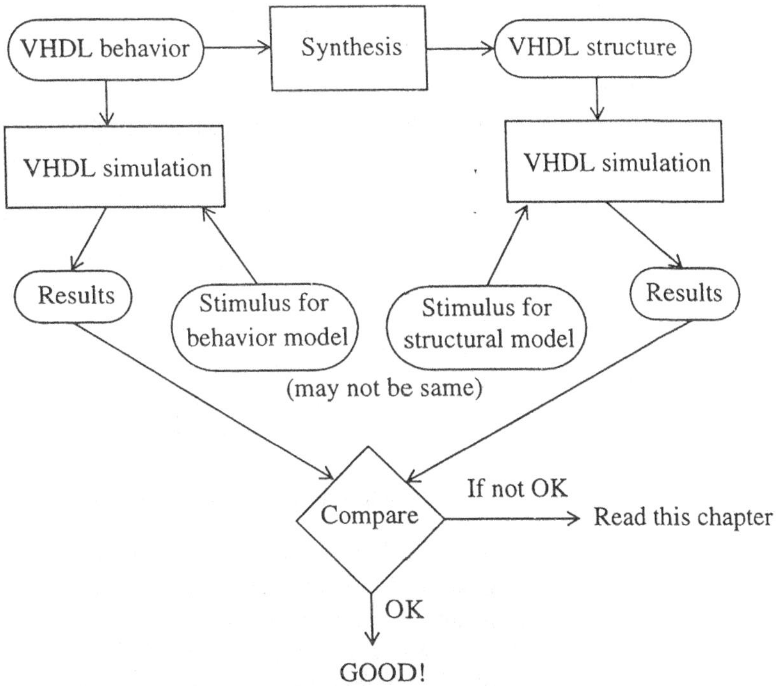

Figure 5-2 Verification by simulation.

```
   ENA: out STD_ULOGIC
); end component;   -- The behavioral component.

component DIV_STR port (
   CK: in STD_ULOGIC;
   RESET: in STD_ULOGIC;
   TESTN: in STD_ULOGIC;
   ENA: out STD_ULOGIC
); end component;        -- The structural component.

-- Configuration specifications:
for all: DIV use entity WORK.DIV;
for all: DIV_STR use configuration WORK.DIV_STR_STR_CON;

-- Input and output signals:
signal CK_BEH_IN: STD_ULOGIC;
signal RESET_BEH_IN: STD_ULOGIC;
```

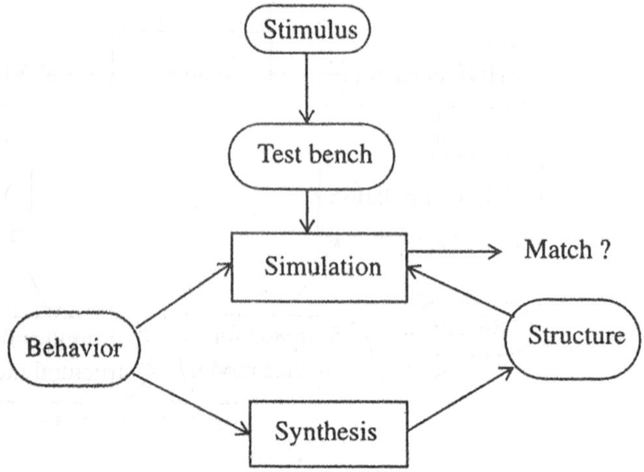

Figure 5-3 Using a common test bench.

```
  signal TESTN_BEH_IN: STD_ULOGIC;
  signal ENA_BEH_OUT: STD_ULOGIC;
  signal CK_STR_IN: STD_ULOGIC;
  signal RESET_STR_IN: STD_ULOGIC;
  signal TESTN_STR_IN: STD_ULOGIC;
  signal ENA_STR_OUT: STD_ULOGIC;
begin
  -- Component instantiations:
  BEH: DIV port map (CK_BEH_IN, RESET_BEH_IN,
            TESTN_BEH_IN, ENA_BEH_OUT);
  STR: DIV_STR port map (CK_STR_IN, RESET_STR_IN,
            TESTN_STR_IN, ENA_STR_OUT);

  -- Read vector file and compare:
  process
    file VEC_FILE: TEXT is in "INPUTS.VEC";
    variable IN_BUF, OUT_BUF: LINE;
    variable TOT_VECTORS: NATURAL;
  begin
    while not ENDFILE (VEC_FILE) loop
      IN_BUF := null;
      READLINE (VEC_FILE, IN_BUF);

      -- Skip iteration if not a Tquote vector in file:
      if IN_BUF(1 to 2) /= "T ' " then
```

```
      next;
    end if;

    TOT_VECTORS := TOT_VECTORS + 1;
    -- Get vector starting from index 3:
    CK_BEH_IN <= TO_STDULOGIC (IN_BUF(3));
    RESET_BEH_IN <= TO_STDULOGIC (IN_BUF(4));
    TESTN_BEH_IN <= TO_STDULOGIC (IN_BUF(5));
    CK_STR_IN <= TO_STDULOGIC (IN_BUF(3));
    RESET_STR_IN <= TO_STDULOGIC (IN_BUF(4));
    TESTN_STR_IN <= TO_STDULOGIC (IN_BUF(5));

    wait for 1 ns;     -- Wait for logic to settle.

    -- Compare outputs:
    if
      NOT_EQUALS (ENA_BEH_OUT, ENA_STR_OUT)
    then
      WRITE (OUT_BUF, STRING'("**** MISMATCH " &
        "ERROR: Outputs do not match on vector "));
      WRITE (OUT_BUF, TOT_VECTORS);
      WRITE (OUT_BUF, STRING'(" at time "));
      WRITE (OUT_BUF, NOW);
      WRITE (OUT_BUF, STRING'(":  ("));
      WRITE (OUT_BUF, TO_CHARACTER (ENA_BEH_OUT));
      WRITE (OUT_BUF, STRING'(" <---> "));
      WRITE (OUT_BUF, TO_CHARACTER (ENA_STR_OUT));
      WRITE (OUT_BUF, STRING'(")"));
      WRITELINE (OUTPUT, OUT_BUF);
    end if;
  end loop;

  report "Completed running testbench"
    severity NOTE;

  wait;              -- Done verification.
 end process;
end;
```

Note the use of conversion functions to convert stimulus values to type *STD_ULOGIC* and also their use in converting the observed results of the behavioral model into type *STD_ULOGIC* so that a comparison can be made. The function *NOT_EQUALS* returns false if the two operands are the same or if either is an 'X' or an 'U'. This test bench model prints all mismatch violations that occur.

In the following sections, we see examples of how mismatches may occur.

5.3 Delays in Assignment Statements

Delays specified in a behavioral model may potentially cause a mismatch in simulation results. Here is an example of a behavioral model and its synthesized netlist.

```
library IEEE;
use IEEE.NUMERIC_STD.all;
entity ADDER is
  port (A, B: in UNSIGNED(0 to 3);
        C: out UNSIGNED (0 to 3));
end;

architecture TEST of ADDER is
begin
  C <= A + B after 5 ns;
end TEST;

-- The synthesized netlist is:
library IEEE, SYNTH;
use IEEE.STD_LOGIC_1164.all, SYNTH.GENERIC_COMP.all;
entity ADDER is
  port (A0, A1, A2, A3, B0, B1, B2, B3: in STD_ULOGIC;
        C0, C1, C2, C3: out STD_ULOGIC);
end ADDER;

architecture ADDER_STR of ADDER is
  signal C2_1, S248, S310, S241, S244, S295, S299, S242, S243, S291,
       S237, S238, S239, S240, S334, S235, S236: STD_ULOGIC;
begin
  C0_1: OAI21 port map (C2_1, S248, S310, C0);
  S310_1: ND2 port map (S248, C2_1, S310);
  S248_1: XOR2 port map (A0, B0, S248);
  C2_2: AOI22 port map (S241, S244, A1, B1, C2_1);
  C1_1: OAI22 port map (S295, S244, S299, S241, C1);
  S299_1: INRB port map (S244, S299);
  S244_1: OAI22 port map (B1, S242, A1, S243, S244);
```

```
S243_1: INRB port map (B1, S243);
S242_1: INRB port map (A1, S242);
S295_1: INRB port map (S241, S295);
S241_1: OAI22 port map (S291, S237, S238, S239, S241);
S291_1: INRB port map (S240, S291);
C2_1: OAI21 port map (S237, S240, S334, C2);
S334_1: ND2 port map (S237, S240, S334);
S240_1: OAI22 port map (B2, S238, A2, S239, S240);
S239_1: INRB port map (B2, S239);
S238_1: INRB port map (A2, S238);
S237_1: ND2 port map (A3, B3, S237);
C3_1: OAI22 port map (B3, S235, A3, S236, C3);
S236_1: INRB port map (B3, S236);
S235_1: INRB port map (A3, S235);
end ADDER_STR;
```

If the vectors from a stimulus file were applied, say every 1 ns, and all the components in the netlist represent behavioral models with no delay, the results from the behavior and structure model will be skewed. The correct approach in such a case is:

i. either to delete all delays from the behavioral model (which may be too much to ask for!)

ii. or to apply the stimulus with a period greater than 5 ns: a much better rule.

Thus to avoid delays in a behavioral model from causing simulation mismatches, the maximum delay in a behavioral model must be computed. The stimulus application time must be greater than this maximum delay.

When delays are present in the models for the library components, these delays must also be considered in determining the stimulus period.

5.4 Unconnected Ports

It could happen that a structural model has a component with an unconnected input port. Such a case is shown in the following example.

```
entity AOI22 is
  port (A, B, D: in BIT;
        Z: out BIT);
end AOI22;
```

```
architecture TEST of AOI22 is
begin
  process (A, B, D)
    variable T1, T2, C: BIT;
  begin
    T1 := A and B;
    T2 := C and D;          -- Note that C is not assigned anywhere.
    Z <= not (T1 or T2);
  end process;
end;

-- Its synthesized netlist is:
library IEEE;
use IEEE.STD_LOGIC_1164.all;
entity AOI22_STR is
  port (A, B, D: in STD_ULOGIC;
        Z: out STD_ULOGIC);
end AOI22_STR;

architecture AOI22_STR of AOI22_STR is
  component AND2
    port (INPUT_1, INPUT_2: in STD_ULOGIC;
          OUTPUT_1: out STD_ULOGIC);
  end component;

  component INRB
    port (INPUT_1: in STD_ULOGIC;
          OUTPUT_1: out STD_ULOGIC);
  end component;

  component OR2
    port (INPUT_1, INPUT_2: in STD_ULOGIC;
          OUTPUT_1: out STD_ULOGIC);
  end component;

  signal T1_1, T2_1, T2_0 : STD_ULOGIC;
begin
  S0_1: AND2 port map (INPUT_1=>A, INPUT_2=>B,
             OUTPUT_1=> T1_1);
  S1_1: AND2 port map (INPUT_1=>open, INPUT_2=>D,
             OUTPUT_1=> T2_1);
  S2_1: OR2 port map (INPUT_1=>T1_1, INPUT_2=> T2_1,
```

```
                OUTPUT_1=>T2_0);
    S3_1: INRB port map (INPUT_1=>T2_0, OUTPUT_1=>Z);
  end AOI22_STR;
    -- Note: A logic optimizer has not yet been used; it could
    -- potentially remove such a gate.
```

In order for the entity *AOI22_STR* to compile, a default value must be specified for the first port of component *AND2*. Question is, what must be its value? '0', '1', or 'U'? During behavioral simulation (that is, in the simulation of entity *AOI22*), the value of *C* used is a '0'; this is the leftmost value of type *BIT*. Therefore in structural simulation (simulation of entity *AOI22_STR*) as well, the default value of the port for component *AND2* must be set to '0', otherwise a simulation mismatch may occur. The correct component declaration to be used for component *AND2* is:

```
component AND2
  port (INPUT_1, INPUT_2: in STD_ULOGIC := '0';
      OUTPUT_1: out STD_ULOGIC);
end component;
```

Recommendation: A good synthesis system will issue warning messages about a value used before being defined (such as variable *C* in the entity *AOI22*). Heed these warnings.

5.5 Signals vs. Variables

If a signal is used instead of a variable to hold a temporary value in a set of sequential statements, simulation mismatches can occur as shown in the following example.

```
MIX_UP: process (CCK)
begin
  if CCK'EVENT and CCK = '1' then
    SPI_PLD <= PI_PLD;
  end if;

  ICA_SRN <= SPI_PLD;
end process;
```

SPI_PLD is a signal that is assigned a value in an `if` statement and its value is later assigned to signal *ICA_SRN*. Mismatches will potentially occur since changes to *SPI_PLD* do not propagate to *ICA_SRN* at the same time. This behavior does not occur in the corresponding structural model; the output of the flip-flop *SPI_PLD* is connected directly to signal *ICA_SRN*.

If the correct intention was to use *SPI_PLD* as a temporary, then *SPI_PLD* should be made a variable. Alternately, the signal *SPI_PLD* could be put on the sensitivity list of the process or the signal assignment could be moved out of the process as shown next.

```
SIG_OUT : process (CCK)
begin
  if CCK'EVENT and CCK = '1' then
    SPI_PLD <= PI_PLD;
  end if;
end process;

ICA_SRN <= SPI_PLD;
```

If the intention of the original process (process *MIX_UP*) was for signal *SPI_PLD* to be assigned a value on the rising clock edge and for signal *ICA_SRN* to be assigned a value at the falling clock edge, then for the model to be correctly synthesizable, it needs to be rewritten as follows.

```
BRK_A : process (CCK)
begin
  if CCK'EVENT and CCK = '1' then        -- Rising edge.
    SPI_PLD <= PI_PLD;
  end if;
end process;

BRK_B : process (CCK)
begin
  if CCK'EVENT and CCK = '0' then        -- Falling edge.
    ICA_SRN <= SPI_PLD;
  end if;
end process;
```

Here is another example.

```
process (RESET, CCK, ZT)
begin
  if CCK'EVENT and CCK = '1' then
    DZ(0) <= ZT;

    for J in 0 to 2 loop
      DZ(J+1) <= DZ(J);
    end loop;
```

```
    Z1 <= DZ(3);
  end if;

  ZOUT <= Z1;
end process;
```

There are three dangerous conflicts here. Signal *DZ*(0) (also *DZ*(1) and *DZ*(2)) is being assigned and then used. Signal *DZ*(3) is being assigned and then used. Signal *Z1* is assigned and then used. *DZ* and *Z1* should be modeled as variables if mismatches are to be avoided.

Recommendation: Check to see if there are any signals that are being assigned and then later read in the process. To prevent mismatches, it is better to model such temporaries as variables.

5.6 Variables and Latches

In Chapter 3, we described rules for inferring latches for variables. We also described an exception to the rule, that is, a variable does not infer a latch if it is used as a temporary. However, there are a few other cases where a variable is not inferred a latch, even though it appears from the code sequence that it should be.

Let us consider the first case.

```
signal CTL : BOOLEAN;
signal JRQ: BIT;
. . .
P1: process (CTL)
  variable DBX: BIT;
begin
  if CTL then
    DBX := JRQ;
  else
    DBX := DBX;
  end if;
end process;
```

In this process, variable *DBX* is assigned in all branches of the `if` statement. However, data flow analysis reveals that the value of *DBX* needs to be saved (since its value is used before an assignment when *CTL* is false). In this case, a synthesis system may produce a warning message about variable *DBX* being used before its assignment and also about a potential simulation mismatch.

Let us reiterate the rule for inferring latches once more:

i. A variable is assigned in a conditional (`if` or a `case` statement).
ii. Variable is NOT assigned in all branches of the conditional.
iii. Value of variable needs to be saved between multiple invocations of the process.

All the three conditions must be satisfied before a variable is inferred as a latch. In process *P1*, *DBX* violates rule (ii). Therefore no latch is produced for *DBX*.

Here is another example.

```
P2: process (CTL)
  variable DBX, BDY: BIT;
begin
  if CTL then
    DBX := JRQ;
  else
    DBX := BDY;
  end if;

  BDY := DBX;
end process;
```

In this process, it appears that there should be a latch for either *DBX* or *BDY*. There is no latch for *DBX* since it violates rule (ii). There is no latch for *BDY* since it violates rule (i). Simulation semantics however indicate that value for *BDY* needs to be saved. A synthesis system in this case may not produce a latch; instead it may issue a warning message about *BDY* being used before its definition and in addition, produce a warning message about a potential for simulation mismatch.

In the following process, no latch is produced for *DBX* since it violates rule (ii) but a latch is produced for *BDY*.

```
P3: process (CTL)
  variable DBX, BDY: BIT;
begin
  if CTL then
    DBX := JRQ;
  else
    DBX := BDY;
```

```
    end if;

    if JRQ = '1' then
      BDY := DBX;
    end if;
  end process;
```

What about the following process?

```
P4: process (CTL)
  variable DBX, BDY: BIT;
begin
  if CTL then
    DBX := JRQ;
  else
    DBX := BDY;
  end if;

  if JRQ = '1' then
    BDY := DBX;
  else
    BDY := '1';
  end if;
end process;
```

There are no latches for *DBX* and *BDY*. However simulation semantics indicate that *BDY* needs to be saved. A synthesis system may not produce a latch; it may generate a warning about the variable being used before its definition and that for a potential for a simulation mismatch.

5.7 Inertial and Transport Delays

Delays are often ignored by a synthesis system. The fact that it is ignored may simply cause simulation results to differ between the synthesized netlist and the behavior model. A case in point.

```
LX <= '1' after 3 ns;

if COND then
  LX <= transport '0' after 5 ns;
  . . .
```

Behavioral simulation shows a value of '1' on signal *LX* after 3 ns and the value going to '0' after 5 ns if the condition *COND* is true. However, since a synthesis system ignores delays, if *COND* is true, the net effect is as if '0' is assigned to *LX* and the appropriate hardware gets synthesized to reflect this. Notice that if the synthesized netlist is simulated, the value of signal *LX* will not go to '1' if *COND* is true.

Recommendation: Avoid inserting delays into a behavioral model that is to be synthesized. If necessary, lump total delays for a signal in one place.

5.8 Resolution Function

A synthesis system may treat a resolution function in a different way than that specified by the function itself. For example, any resolution function specified in a signal declaration may be ignored and a global option may be specified on how to treat signals that are driven by more than one source. Since the synthesis system treats the resolution function as a special case, simulation mismatches can potentially occur.

Here is an example.

```
signal Z: WIRED_OR BIT;
. . .
Z <= TO_BIT (CLY);
. . .
Z <= LA or BL;
```

In behavioral simulation, the values of the two drivers for signal Z are passed to the *WIRED_OR* resolution function and its return value becomes the effective value for signal Z.

However, assuming that an "and drivers" option is specified, the synthesized netlist will connect the drivers of signal Z using an and gate. This is shown in Figure 5-4. This functionality is different from the functionality of the behavioral model and simulation mismatches may occur.

Recommendation: Avoid having two or more drivers for a signal, thus obviating the need for a resolution function. If a resolution function is necessary, use only one type of resolution function in a behavioral model and specify the same or its equivalent as an option to the synthesis system.

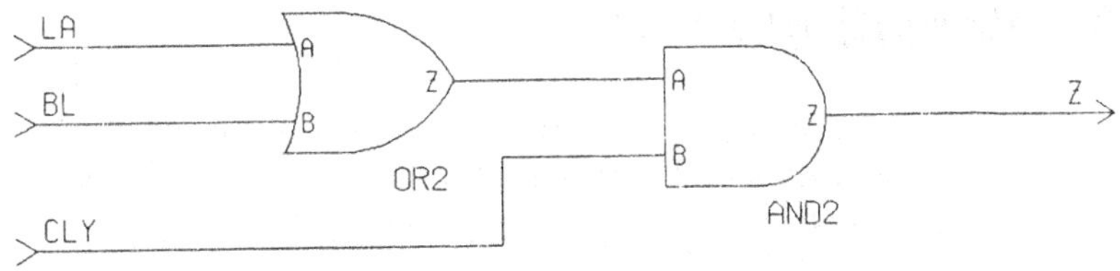

Figure 5-4 Inserting an explicit gate for modeling a resolution function.

5.9 Built-in Types and Functions

A synthesis system typically supports two types of built-in functions:

i. conversion functions

ii. arithmetic functions

Conversion functions are used to convert values from one type to another type. These functions merely transfer data from one type to another (so as to conform to VHDL's strong typing rules) and are not meant to be synthesized as hardware logic; a synthesis system often recognizes these functions as built-ins and does not generate any extra logic; that is, the conversion function body is not synthesized. Examples of conversion functions are:

function *TO_INTEGER* (*ARG*: *BIT_VECTOR*) **return** *INTEGER*;
function *TO_STDLOGICVECTOR* (*ARG*: *INTEGER*;
 SIZE: *NATURAL*) **return** *STD_LOGIC_VECTOR*;

Arithmetic functions of certain predefined types are similarly built-in into a synthesis system. Examples are:

function "+" (*L*, *R*: *UNSIGNED*) **return** *UNSIGNED*;
function "–" (*L*: *SIGNED*; *R*: *INTEGER*) **return** *SIGNED*;

When using such built-in arithmetic functions, care must be taken in modifying the body of the arithmetic function. Otherwise, it could lead to simulation mismatches; the synthesis system may synthesize the built-in function, whereas during behavioral simulation, the function body is simulated.

Recommendation: Find out the built-in functions provided by a synthesis system and use these. Do not modify the built-in functions. If a change is necessary, create a separate package and then use the function from this package.

5.10 Sensitivity List

Quite often, a synthesis system ignores a sensitivity list of a process during synthesis. This can lead to simulation mismatches if proper care is not taken in modeling. Here is a simple example.

```
SENSE: process (RD)
begin
  GT <= RD and CK;
end process;
```

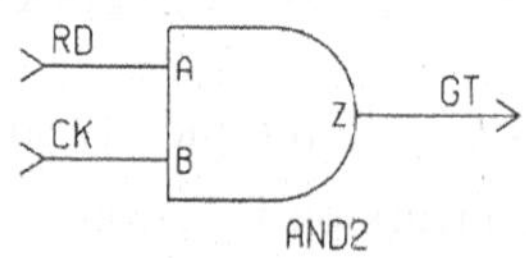

Figure 5-5 Netlist is sensitive to both signals *RD* and *CK*.

The synthesized structural model, as shown in Figure 5-5, evaluates on all changes of signals *RD* and *CK*, while the behavioral model executes only on changes to signal *RD*.

Here is another example of a process with an incomplete sensitivity list that causes simulation mismatches.

```
signal VAL: UNSIGNED (MAXSIZE–1 downto 0);
signal COUNTER: UNSIGNED (VAL'LEFT downto 0);
. . .
CNT_PRC: process (RESET, CCK, ENA)
begin
  COUNT (COUNTER, CCK, RESET, ENA);
  VAL <= COUNTER;
end process;
```

In this example, the signal *COUNTER* is not in the sensitivity list of the process and thus any changes made by procedure *COUNT* to signal *COUNTER* do not affect the value of *VAL*. Signal *VAL* gets updated with the value of *COUNTER* next time when there is an event on signal *RESET*, *CCK* or *ENA*. In this example, the signal assignment statement must be moved outside the process so that any changes of value on *COUNTER* gets automatically updated into *VAL*. Alternately, *COUNTER* could also have been placed in the sensitivity list of the process (this could potentially create extra simulation cycles).

Here is another example of a process with an incomplete sensitivity list that may cause simulation mismatches.

```
signal RST: BIT;
signal PBUS, TREG: STD_LOGIC_VECTOR (3 downto 0);
. . .
process (RST)
begin
  if RST = '1' then
    TREG <= (others => '0');
  else
    TREG <= PBUS;
  end if;
end process;
```

The signal *PBUS* is not in the sensitivity list of the process. However in the synthesized netlist, any changes on *PBUS* will propagate into *TREG* if the `if` condition is false. This is not consistent with the behavioral model and thus a simulation mismatch occurs.

Recommendation: For a process without a `wait` statement, include all signals read in the process in the sensitivity list of the process.

5.11 Initialization

VHDL provides a convenient way to specify the initial state of a circuit (reminder: a state of a circuit may be modeled using a variable or a signal). The initial state can be specified by specifying an initial value for the variable or the signal in its declaration. Unfortunately, such an initialization is not supported by most synthesis systems, since no reset signal is specified. A simulator has no problem in initializing the state by using the initial value; however, in hardware, registers usually start in an unknown state when they are powered on.

A synthesis system may ignore initial values specified for a variable or a signal in its declaration. This can cause a mismatch in simulation results. Here is an example that illustrates this problem. In this example, the state of the circuit is stored in the signal *SPEED_STATE*.

```
library IEEE;
use IEEE.STD_LOGIC_1164.all;
entity CAR_CTRL is
  port (ACCELERATOR,
       BRAKE,
       CLK: in STD_LOGIC;
       SPEED: out STD_LOGIC_VECTOR(1 downto 0));
end CAR_CTRL;

architecture CAR_CTRL of CAR_CTRL is
     signal SPEED_STATE: STD_LOGIC_VECTOR (1 downto 0)
       := "00";
begin
  process (CLK)
  begin
    if CLK = '1' and CLK'EVENT then
      if BRAKE = '1' then
        case SPEED_STATE is
          when "00" =>
            SPEED_STATE <= "00";
          when "01" =>
            SPEED_STATE <= "00";
          when "10" =>
            SPEED_STATE <= "01";
          when "11" =>
            SPEED_STATE <= "10";
          when others =>
            null;
        end case;
      elsif ACCELERATOR = '1' then
        case SPEED_STATE is
          when "00" =>
            SPEED_STATE <= "01";
          when "01" =>
            SPEED_STATE <= "10";
          when "10" =>
            SPEED_STATE <= "11";
          when "11" =>
            SPEED_STATE <= "11";
          when others =>
            null;
        end case;
      else
```

```
        null;                -- Speed does not change.
      end if;
    end if;
  end process;

  SPEED <= SPEED_STATE;
end CAR_CTRL;
```

If a synthesis system ignores the initial value of signal *SPEED_STATE* (which is usually the case), the flip-flops generated for the signal *SPEED_STATE* do not get initialized to their initial value. This can be seen from the following synthesized netlist. The synthesized netlist is also shown in a schematic form in Figure 5-6.

```
library IEEE;
use IEEE.STD_LOGIC_1164.all;
entity CAR_CTRL_STR is
  port (ACCELERATOR, BRAKE, CLK: in STD_LOGIC;
      SPEED: out STD_LOGIC_VECTOR(1 downto 0));
end CAR_CTRL_STR;

library SYNTH;
use SYNTH.GENERIC_COMP.all;
architecture CAR_CTRL_STR of CAR_CTRL_STR is
  signal SPEED_1: STD_LOGIC_VECTOR(1 downto 0);
  signal DSPEED_STATE0_1, DSPEED_STATE1_1, NET, NET0,
        S219, S225, S281, S224, S231, S280, S222, S279, S278
        : STD_LOGIC;
begin
  S0_E_1: FD1S3AX port map (D=>DSPEED_STATE0_1, CK=>CLK,
          Q=>SPEED_1(0), QN=>NET);
  S1_E_1: FD1S3AX port map (D=>DSPEED_STATE1_1, CK=>CLK,
          Q=>SPEED_1(1), QN=>NET0);
  DSPEED_STATE1_2: OAI222 port map (A1=>S219, A2=>S225,
          B1=>S281, B2=>S224, C1=>NET0, C2=>S231,
          Z=>DSPEED_STATE1_1);
  S281_1: INRBH port map (A=>S280, Z=>S281);
  S280_1: OAI211 port map (A1=>SPEED_1(1), A2=>NET, B=>S225,
          C=>S222, Z=> S280);
  DSPEED_STATE0_2: OAI222 port map (A1=>NET, A2=>S231,
          B1=>S279, B2=>S224, C1=>S219, C2=>S222,
          Z=>DSPEED_STATE0_1);
  S224_1: ND2 port map (A=>ACCELERATOR, B=>S219, Z=>S224);
```

```
S219_1: INRBH port map (A=>BRAKE, Z=>S219);
S279_1: INRBH port map (A=>S278, Z=>S279);

S278_1: OAI211 port map (A1=>SPEED_1(1), A2=>SPEED_1(0),
        B=>S225, C=>S222, Z=>S278);
S222_1: ND2 port map (A=>SPEED_1(1), B=>NET, Z=>S222);
S225_1: ND2 port map (A=>SPEED_1(0), B=>SPEED_1(1),
        Z=>S225);
S231_1: OR2 port map (A=>BRAKE, B=>ACCELERATOR,
        Z=>S231);
SPEED(1) <= SPEED_1(1);
SPEED(0) <= SPEED_1(0);
end CAR_CTRL_STR;
```

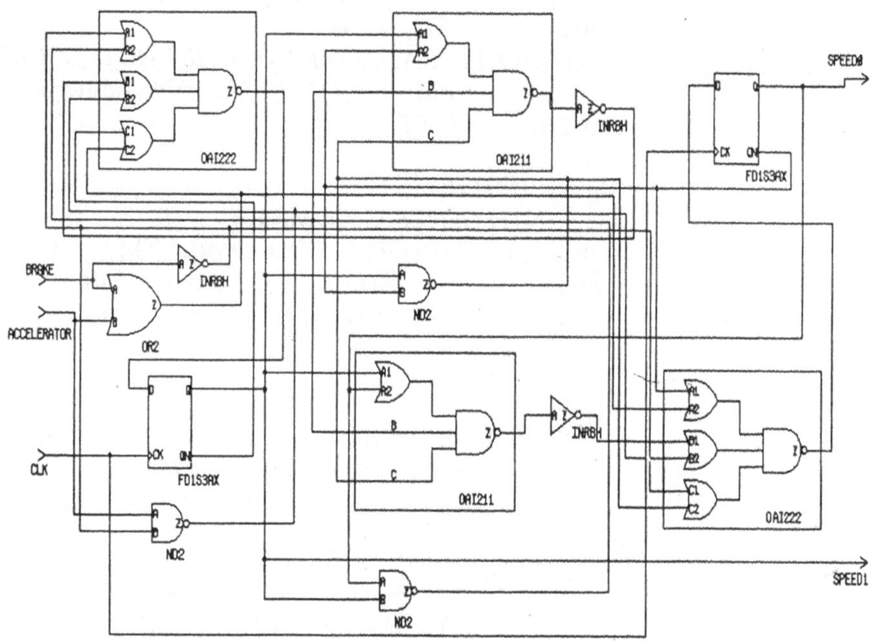

Figure 5-6 A car controller with no explicit reset.

Thus while the behavioral model starts with an initial value of "00" for *SPEED_STATE*, the structural model behaves differently, that is, the flip-flops get initialized to "UU", unless the synthesized netlist is manually modified by assigning an initial value for the flip-flops. This is shown in the following skeleton code of the synthesized netlist.

```
architecture CAR_CTRL_STR of CAR_CTRL_STR is
  signal SPEED_1: STD_ULOGIC_VECTOR(1 downto 0) := "00";
  signal DSPEED_STATE0_1,
  . . .
```

The recommended approach is to explicitly model the initial value as part of the behavior, as is shown in the following modified model. A new signal, *RESET*, needs to be introduced.

```
library IEEE;
use IEEE.STD_LOGIC_1164.all;
entity CAR_CTRL is
  port (ACCELERATOR,
        BRAKE,
        CLK,
        RESET: in STD_LOGIC;
        SPEED: out STD_LOGIC_VECTOR(1 downto 0));
end CAR_CTRL;

architecture RESETABLE_CAR_CTRL of CAR_CTRL is
    signal SPEED_STATE: STD_LOGIC_VECTOR (1 downto 0);
begin
  process (CLK, RESET)
  begin
    if RESET = '1' then          -- Asynchronous reset.
      SPEED_STATE <= (others => '0');
    elsif CLK = '1' and CLK'EVENT then
      if BRAKE = '1' then
        case SPEED_STATE is
          when "00" =>
            SPEED_STATE <= "00";
          when "01" =>
            SPEED_STATE <= "00";
          when "10" =>
            SPEED_STATE <= "01";
          when "11" =>
            SPEED_STATE <= "10";
          when others =>
            null;
        end case;
      elsif ACCELERATOR = '1' then
        case SPEED_STATE is
          when "00" =>
            SPEED_STATE <= "01";
```

```
            when "01" =>
              SPEED_STATE <= "10";
            when "10" =>
              SPEED_STATE <= "11";
            when "11" =>
              SPEED_STATE <= "11";
            when others =>
              null;
          end case;
        else
          null;                -- Speed does not change
        end if;
      end if;
    end process;

    SPEED <= SPEED_STATE;
  end RESETABLE_CAR_CTRL;
```

A generic description of a car controller appears in the next chapter.

5.12 Using Attribute *ENUM_ENCODING*

Consider the following model that uses a signal of an enumeration type. The encoding for the enumeration literals of the enumeration type are explicitly specified using the attribute *ENUM_ENCODING*.

```
architecture ENCODING of ENGINE is
  type CAR_SPEED is (STOP, SLOW, MEDIUM, FAST);
  signal SPEED: CAR_SPEED;
  attribute ENUM_ENCODING: BOOLEAN;
  attribute ENUM_ENCODING of CAR_SPEED: type
            is "1000 0100 0010 0001";
begin
  process . . .
  begin
    . . .
    if SPEED > SLOW then
      BRAKE <= TRUE;
    else
      BRAKE <= FALSE;
    end if;
```

```
    ...
  end process;
end ENCODING;
```

The attribute *ENUM_ENCODING* is a special attribute recognized by a synthesis system; it is not necessarily recognized by every simulation system. Consequently, during behavioral simulation, the condition *SPEED > SLOW* will be true for *SPEED* values of *MEDIUM* or *FAST*. However, in the synthesized netlist, *STOP* (with value "1000") is greater than *SLOW* (with value "0100"), thus causing simulation mismatches.

Recommendation: When using attribute *ENUM_ENCODING*, avoid using relational operators <, <=, >, >=, since the values of these depend on the encoding of the states, which may not be understood by a simulation system.

Chapter 6

Modeling Hardware Elements for Synthesis

In Chapter 3, we looked at the synthesis of VHDL into gates. In this chapter we continue to describe the synthesis process by starting with the familiar elements that a logic designer uses and show how to describe these in VHDL. Some of the examples are similar to the ones in Chapter 3, but a number of other aspects of synthesis are brought out. As before, we show both the VHDL input to synthesis and the schematic for the output circuitry.

This chapter also provides a number of VHDL synthesis examples. These models illustrate the usage of VHDL constructs collectively to model a design that can be synthesized.

6.1 Modeling a Wire

A wire can be modeled using a signal. A variable can also be used to model a wire; however, multiple assignments to the same variable are considered as different instances of a wire. Consider the following model of a 2-by-1 multiplexer with an enable signal.

```
library IEEE;
use IEEE.STD_LOGIC_1164.all;
entity MUX2x1 is
  port (A, B, SEL, ENA: in STD_LOGIC;
        ZQ: out STD_LOGIC);
end MUX2x1;

architecture SIG_WIRES of MUX2x1 is
  signal TRA, TRB, TOR: STD_LOGIC;
begin
  TRA <= A and SEL;
  TRB <= B and (not SEL);
  TOR <= TRA or TRB;
  ZQ <= TOR when ENA = '1' else 'Z';
end SIG_WIRES;
```

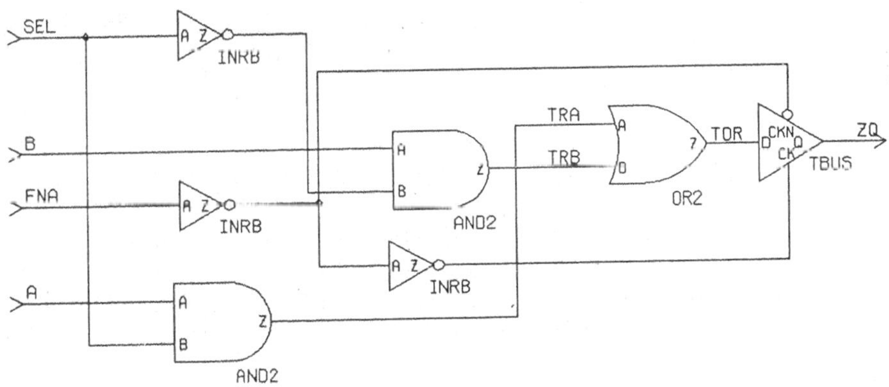

Figure 6-1 A signal becomes a wire.

In this case, signals *TRA*, *TRB*, and *TOR* are wires. Figure 6-1 shows the synthesized netlist. Here is the same example, but this time, variables are used.

```
architecture VAR_WIRES of MUX2x1 is
begin
  process (A, B, SEL, ENA)
    variable TA, TB: STD_LOGIC;
  begin
    TA := A and SEL;
    TB := B and (not SEL);
    TA := TA or TB;

    if ENA = '1' then
      ZQ <= TA;
    else
      ZQ <= 'Z';
    end if;
  end process;
end VAR_WIRES;
```

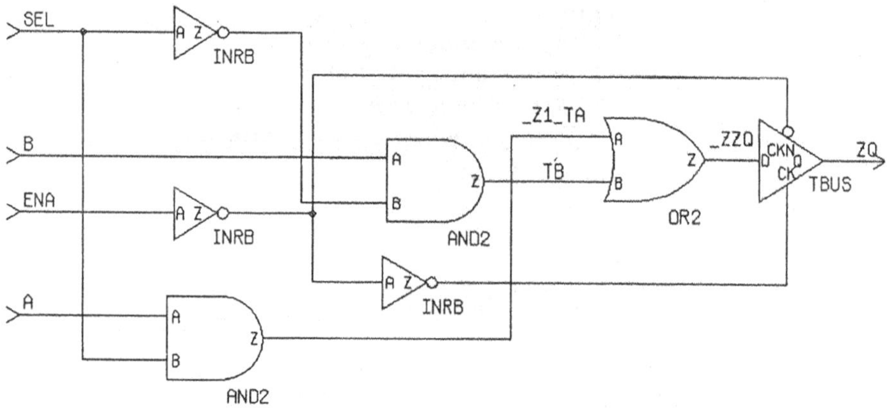

Figure 6-2 A variable is also a wire.

TA and *TB* are variables in the process. Variable *TA* is assigned twice. However the different assignments are considered as different instances of a wire. The synthesized netlist is shown in Figure 6-2.

6.2 Modeling Combinational Logic

The best way for describing combinational logic is to use concurrent signal assignment statements. A process statement can also be used to describe combinational logic; however, the synthesized logic may not be apparent from the description. If combinational logic is described using concurrent signal assignment statements, the synthesized logic is implicit in the description. Consider the model of a built-in self-test cell.

```
library IEEE;
use IEEE.STD_LOGIC_1164.all;
entity BIST_CELL is
  port (B0, B1, D0, D1: in STD_LOGIC;
       Z: out STD_LOGIC);
end BIST_CELL;

architecture CONC_SIG of BIST_CELL is
  signal S1, S2, S3, S4: STD_LOGIC;
begin
  S1 <= B0 nand D1;
  S2 <= D0 nand B1;
  S3 <= S2 nor S1;
  S4 <= S2 and S1;
  Z <= S4 nor S3;
end CONC_SIG;
```

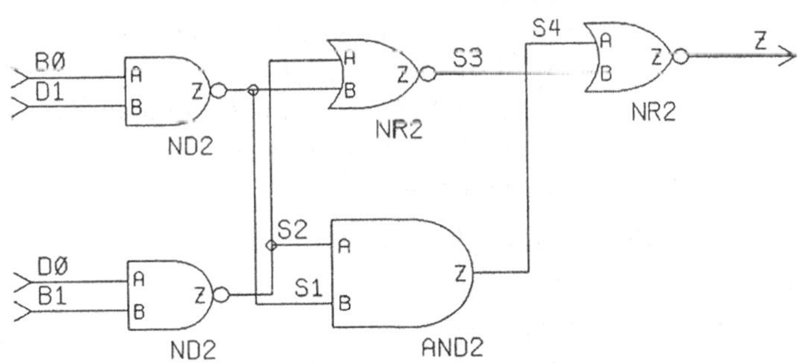

Figure 6-3 Combinational logic from concurrent signal assignments.

The synthesized circuit is shown in Figure 6-3. Notice the structure of the synthesized circuit is very similar to that of the concurrent signal assignment statements. Here is the same model, but this time the cell is described using a process statement.

```
architecture PROCESS_EX of BIST_CELL is
begin
  process (B0, D0, B1, D1)
    variable S1, S2: STD_LOGIC;
  begin
    S1 := B0 nand D1;
    S2 := D0 nand B1;
    S1 := S2 nor S1;
    S2 := S2 and S1;
    Z <= S1 nor S2;
  end process;
end PROCESS_EX;
```

Notice that variables *S1* and *S2* are used as temporaries in more than one place and do not represent one wire. The synthesized circuit still remains the same as that shown in Figure 6-3; however, the one-to-one mapping between the variables in the process and the nets in the synthesized structure is not present.

6.3 Modeling Sequential Logic

The behavior of sequential logic can be described by using a process statement of a special form. This is of the form:

```
process
begin      -- First statement has to be a wait statement.
  wait until clock_edge;
  -- Synchronous logic described here since all statements execute
  -- only if clock edge occurs.
end process;
```

where *clock_edge* is one of

```
clock_name = logic-0
clock_name = logic-1
RISING_EDGE (clock_name)
FALLING_EDGE (clock_name)
```

The last two forms of clock edge can only be used if the clock signal is of type *STD_ULOGIC* or *STD_LOGIC*. Here is an example of such a process.

```
library IEEE;
use IEEE.STD_LOGIC_1164.all;
entity PICK_ONE is
  port (A, B, CLK, CTRL: in STD_LOGIC;
       Z: out STD_LOGIC);
end;

architecture SYNC of PICK_ONE is
begin
  process
  begin
    wait until CLK = '0';

    if CTRL = '1' then
      Z <= A;
    else
      Z <= B;
    end if;
  end process;
end SYNC;
```

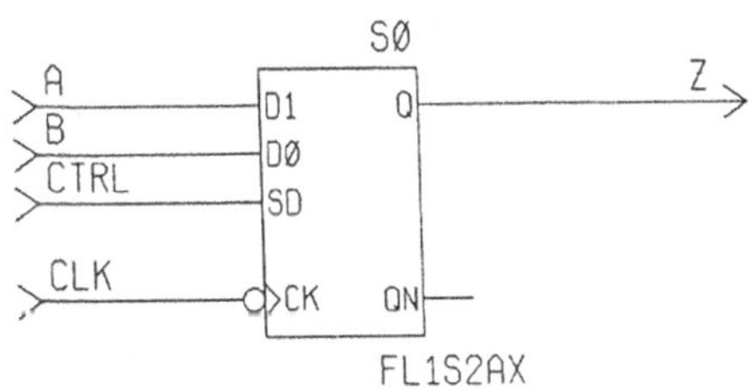

Figure 6-4 Sequential logic synthesized using a special process statement.

The assignment to signal Z happens only at the falling edge of a clock. The synthesized circuit is shown in Figure 6-4. Signal *Z* is inferred to be a falling-edge-triggered flip-flop. The flip-flop shown in the figure has a data-select, that is, the signal *CTRL* selects either *A* or *B* as the data for the flip-flop.

6.4 Modeling a Flip-flop

A flip-flop can be modeled using a signal or a variable.

6.4.1 From a Signal

If a signal is assigned a value under the control of a clock edge, a flip-flop is generated.

```
entity FLIP_FLOP is
  port (CLK: in BIT;
        CURRENT_STATE: in INTEGER range 0 to 15;
        NEXT_STATE: out INTEGER range 0 to 15);
end FLIP_FLOP;

architecture INFER of FLIP_FLOP is
begin
  process
  begin
    wait until CLK = '1';        -- Rising clock edge.
    NEXT_STATE <= CURRENT_STATE;
  end process;
end INFER;
```

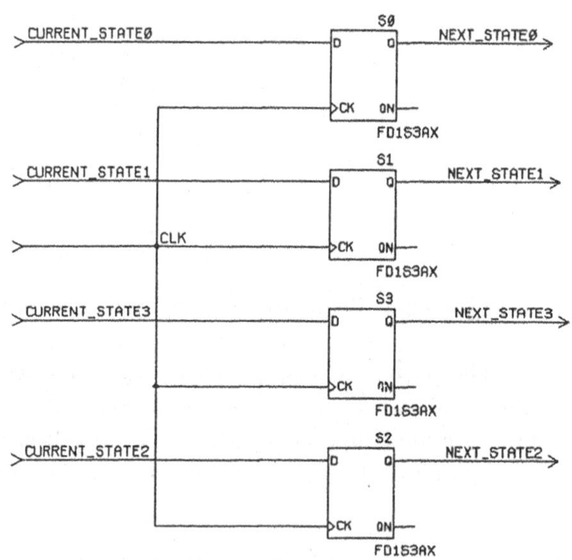

Figure 6-5 Flip-flops inferred from a signal assigned under clock control.

In this example, signal *NEXT_STATE* is assigned a value only if there is a rising edge on signal *CLK*. Thus, four rising-edge-triggered flip-flops (need to store values 0 through 15) are inferred for signal *NEXT_STATE*. This is shown in Figure 6-5.

If a falling-edge-triggered flip-flop needs to be inferred, then the `wait` statement needs to be replaced by the following `wait` statement.

```
wait until CLK = '0';
```

6.4.2 From a Variable

A variable assigned under the control of a clock may or may not be inferred a flip-flop. This depends on whether the value of the variable is defined and then used, or if it is used first and then defined. In the former case, no flip-flop need be inferred, while in the latter case, a flip-flop has to be inferred. Let us look at the case where a variable is defined before use and it is assigned a value under the control of a clock.

```
process
  variable TEMP: INTEGER range 0 to 15;
begin
  wait until CLK = '1';
  TEMP := CURRENT_STATE;
  NEXT_STATE <= TEMP;
end process;
```

No flip-flops are inferred for variable *TEMP* since a value is assigned to the variable and used immediately in the same clock edge. The synthesized circuit is the same as the one shown in Figure 6-5. Now let us consider the case where a variable is used before its assignment that occurs under the control of a clock.

```
VAR_FF: process
  variable TEMP: INTEGER range 0 to 15;
begin
  wait until CLK = '0';
  NEXT_STATE <= TEMP;
  TEMP := CURRENT_STATE;
end process;
```

In this case, falling-edge-triggered flip-flops are inferred for variable *TEMP* as well since its value needs to be saved between clock edges. The synthesized circuit is shown in Figure 6-6.

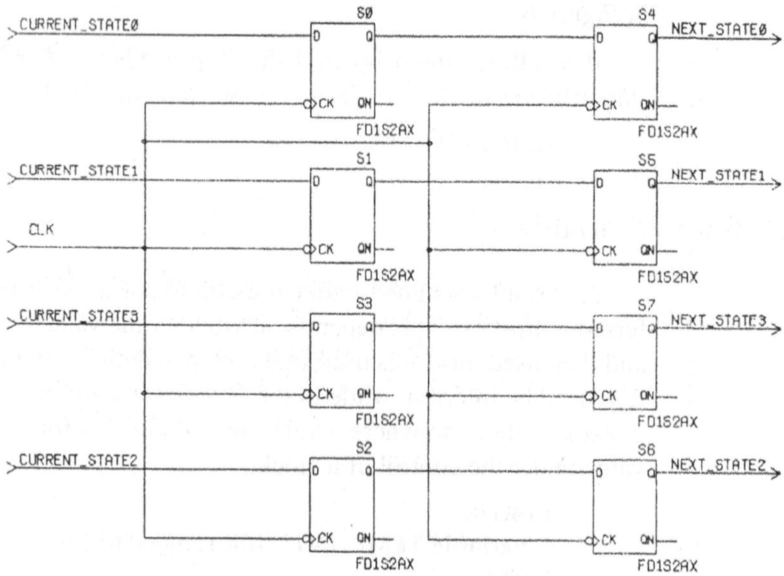

Figure 6-6 A variable is also inferred as a flip-flop.

6.5 Flip-flop with Asynchronous Preset and Clear

To model a flip-flop with asynchronous preset and clear, a special form of the `if` statement is required. This is of the form:

if *condition1* **then**
  -- *Asynchronous-logic-1*
elsif *condition2* **then**
  -- *Asynchronous-logic-2*
...
elsif *clock_edge* **then**
  -- *Synchronous-logic*
end if;

where *clock_edge* is one of

clock_name = *clock_value* **and** *clock_name*'*EVENT*
clock_name = *clock_value* **and** (**not** *clock_name*'*STABLE*)
RISING_EDGE (*clock_name*)
FALLING_EDGE (*clock_name*)

where *clock_value* is either a logic-0 (to indicate a falling edge) or a logic-1 (to indicate a rising edge). The last two functions can be used only if the clock signal is of type *STD_ULOGIC* or *STD_LOGIC*.

The special `if` statement can have any number of `elsif` branches, with each branch describing asynchronous logic behavior except for the last `elsif` branch. The last `elsif` branch describes synchronous logic behavior and must have a clock edge as the branch condition. Note that this special `if` statement has no `else` branch. Here is an example of inferring a flip-flop with asynchronous preset and clear.

```
entity ASYNC_FLIP_FLOP is
  port (CLK, RESET, SET: in BIT;
        CURRENT_STATE: in INTEGER range 0 to 15;
        NEXT_STATE: out INTEGER range 0 to 15);
end ASYNC_FLIP_FLOP;

architecture INFER of ASYNC_FLIP_FLOP is
begin
  process (RESET, SET, CLK, CURRENT_STATE)
  begin
    if RESET = '0' then
      NEXT_STATE <= 12;          -- "1100"          -- Stmt A
    elsif SET = '0' then
      NEXT_STATE <= 5;           -- "0101"          -- Stmt B
    elsif CLK = '0' and CLK'EVENT then
      NEXT_STATE <= CURRENT_STATE;                  -- Stmt C
    end if;
  end process;
end INFER;
```

Since signal *NEXT_STATE* is assigned a value under the control of a clock edge (Stmt *C*) and it is also assigned asynchronously (Stmt *A* and *B*), a falling-edge-triggered flip-flop with asynchronous preset and clear is synthesized. This is shown in Figure 6-7. Note that four flip-flops are required. The first flip-flop (the leftmost bit of *NEXT_STATE*) has both asynchronous preset and clear terminals since it needs to be preset on signal *RESET* and cleared on signal *SET*. Similarly, the fourth flip-flop has both asynchronous preset and clear terminals since it needs to be preset on signal *SET* and cleared on signal *RESET*. The second flip-flop has only a preset terminal since a '1' is asynchronously assigned in both the conditions, while the third flip-flop has only a clear terminal since a '0' is assigned under both the conditions.

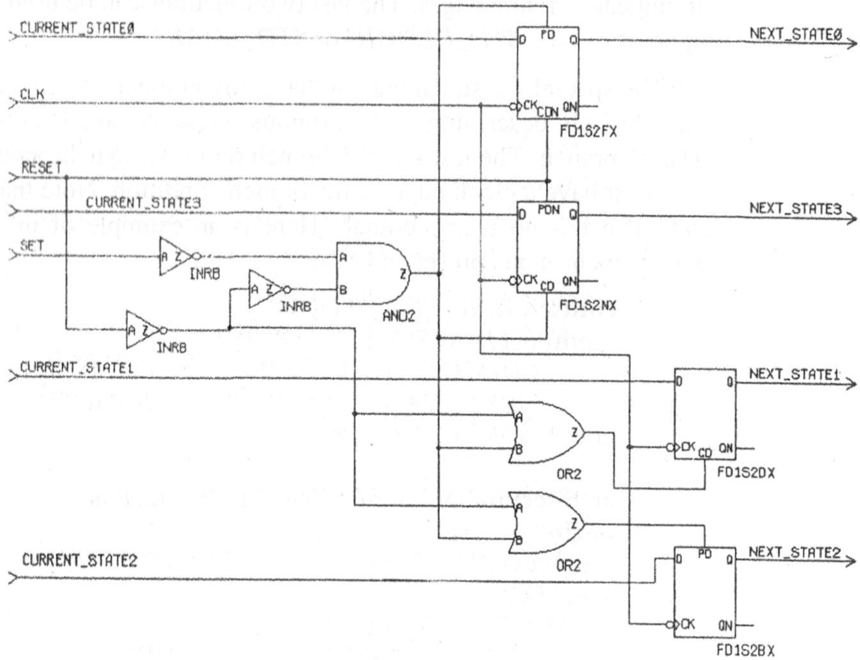

Figure 6-7 Flip-flops with asynchronous preset and clear.

6.6 Flip-flop with Synchronous Preset and Clear

Let us first look at an example.

```
entity SYNC_FLIP_FLOP is
  port (CLK, RESET, SET: in BIT;
        CURRENT_STATE: in INTEGER range 0 to 15;
        NEXT_STATE: out INTEGER range 0 to 15);
end SYNC_FLIP_FLOP;

architecture IS_IT_SYNC of SYNC_FLIP_FLOP is
begin
  process
  begin
    wait until CLK = '0';
```

```
      if RESET = '0' then
        NEXT_STATE <= 12;                -- "1100"
      elsif SET = '0' then
        NEXT_STATE <= 5;                 -- "0101"
      else
        NEXT_STATE <= CURRENT_STATE;
      end if;
    end process;
  end IS_IT_SYNC;
```

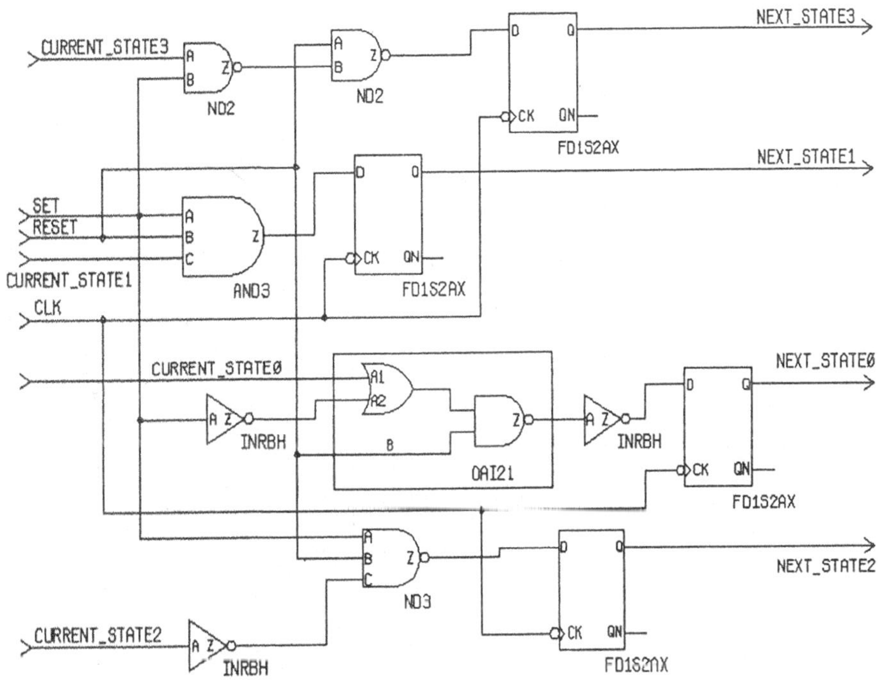

Figure 6-8 Not synchronous preset and clear flip-flop.

From this example, it appears that all the inputs to *NEXT_STATE*, the value 12, the value 5, and the signal *CURRENT_STATE*, should be multiplexed using appropriate select lines into the D-input of the inferred flip-flops for signal *NEXT_STATE*. This is shown in Figure 6-8. So then, how can we infer flip-flops with synchronous preset and clear? A synthesis tool may provide an option under which synchronous preset and clear flip-flops are generated. A synthesized netlist for the above entity using synchronous preset and clear flip-flops is shown in Figure 6-9. Notice that the first and fourth flip-flops are synchronous preset and clear falling-edge-triggered flip-flops while the second flip-flop is a synchronous preset falling-edge-triggered flip-flop and the third flip-flop is a synchronous clear falling-edge-triggered flip-flop.

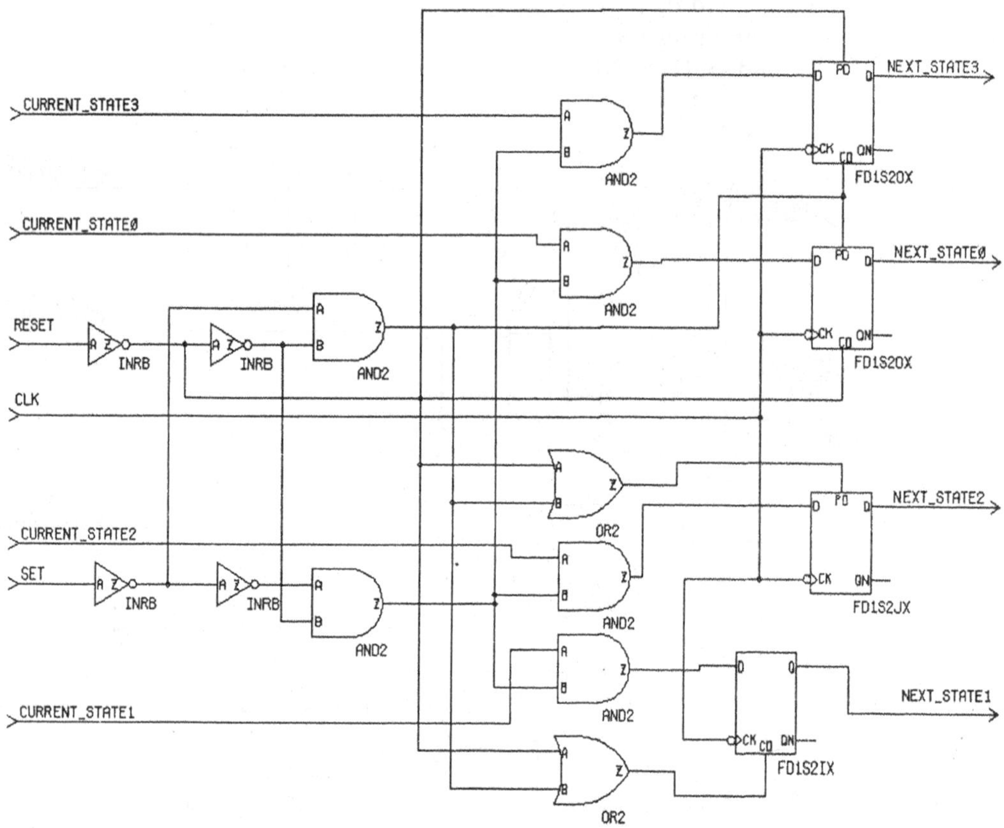

Figure 6-9 Flip-flops with synchronous preset and clear.

6.7 Modeling a Latch

A level-sensitive flip-flop or a latch can be inferred by using an incompletely specified `if` statement or a `case` statement, that is, if a signal is not assigned a value in all branches of an `if` or a `case` statement, a latch is inferred for that signal. Here is an example.

```
entity LEVEL_FF is
  port (CLK: in BIT;
        CURRENT_STATE: in INTEGER range 0 to 15;
        NEXT_STATE: out INTEGER range 0 to 15);
end;

architecture INFER of LEVEL_FF is
begin
  process (CLK, CURRENT_STATE)
  begin
    if CLK = '1' then
      NEXT_STATE <= CURRENT_STATE;
    end if;
  end process;
end INFER;
```

The signal *NEXT_STATE* is assigned a value only when signal *CLK* has the value '1'. If *CLK* is '0', *NEXT_STATE* retains its previous value, thus inferring a latch. The synthesized netlist is shown in Figure 6-10.

A variable is also inferred as a latch if it is incompletely assigned in a conditional statement (`if` statement or a `case` statement). This is shown in the following process. The synthesized circuit is the same as that shown in Figure 6-10.

```
NOT_ASSIGN: process (CLK, CURRENT_STATE)
  variable TEMP: INTEGER range 0 to 15;
begin
  if CLK = '1' then
    TEMP := CURRENT_STATE;
  end if;

  NEXT_STATE <= TEMP;
end process;
```

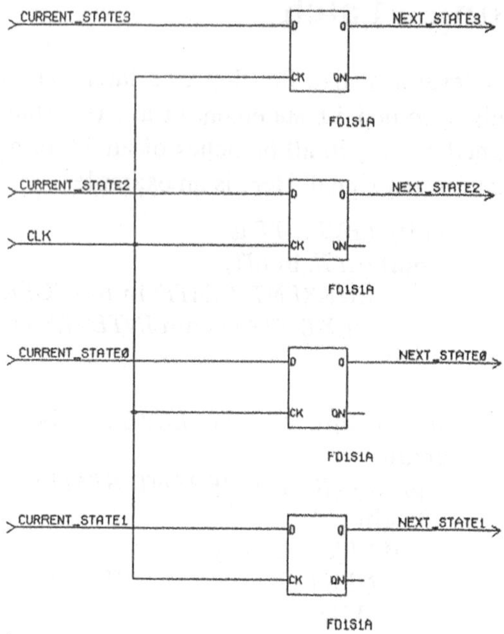

Figure 6-10 An incompletely specified condition infers a latch.

However, if a variable is defined and used within a conditional branch, no latch inference is necessary as shown in the following process. This is because the value of variable *TEMP* need not be saved between level changes of signal *CLK*.

```
NO_LATCH: process (CLK, CURRENT_STATE)
  variable TEMP: INTEGER range 0 to 15;
begin
  if CLK = '1' then
    TEMP := CURRENT_STATE;
    NEXT_STATE <= TEMP;
  end if;
end process;
```

If a variable is used before its definition, then a latch is inferred. Here is such a process. The synthesized circuit is shown in Figure 6-11.

```
-- Variable used before its definition:
VAR_LATCH: process (CLK, CURRENT_STATE)
  variable TEMP: INTEGER range 0 to 15;
begin
  if CLK = '1' then
    NEXT_STATE <= TEMP;
    TEMP := CURRENT_STATE;
  end if;
end process;
```

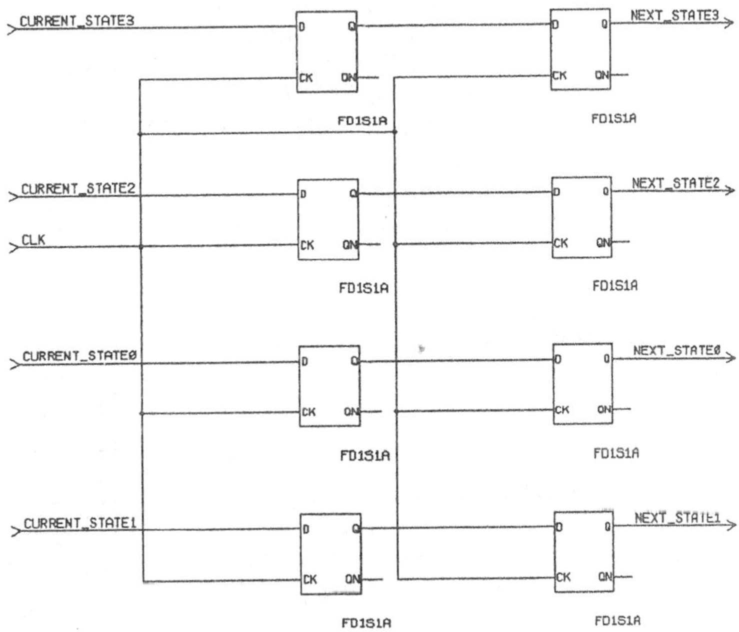

Figure 6-11 A variable used before being assigned in a conditional.

6.8 Latch with Asynchronous Preset and Clear

If a signal is assigned in multiple branches of a conditional statement, bits that are '1' get assigned to the preset terminal while those with '0' get assigned to a latch with a clear terminal. This is shown in the following example. The synthesized netlist is shown in Figure 6-12.

```
entity ASYNC_LATCH is
  port (CLK, RESET, SET: in BIT;
        CURRENT_STATE: in INTEGER range 0 to 15;
        NEXT_STATE: out INTEGER range 0 to 15);
end ASYNC_LATCH;

architecture ASYNC of ASYNC_LATCH is
begin
  process (RESET, SET, CLK, CURRENT_STATE)
  begin
    if RESET = '0' then
      NEXT_STATE <= 12;        -- "1100"
    elsif SET = '0' then
      NEXT_STATE <= 5;         -- "0101"
    elsif CLK = '0' then
      NEXT_STATE <= CURRENT_STATE;
    end if;
  end process;
end ASYNC;
```

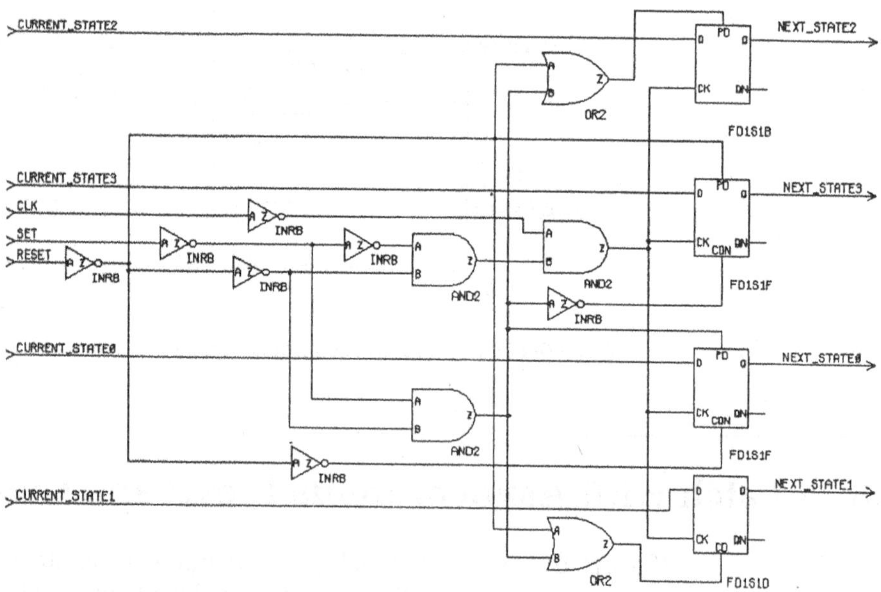

Figure 6-12 Latch with asynchronous preset and clear.

The first and the fourth latches have both preset and clear terminals since a '1' and a '0' are assigned under different conditions. The second latch has a preset terminal only while the third latch has an asynchronous clear terminal only.

6.9 Modeling a Memory

A memory is best modeled as a component. Typically, synthesis tools are not efficient in designing a memory. More traditional techniques are usually used to build a memory. Once having built this component, it can then be instantiated in a synthesis model as a component using the component instantiation statement.

```
    component ROM
      port (CK, OUT_ENA: in STD_LOGIC;
            ADDR: in STD_LOGIC_VECTOR (M-1 downto 0);
            Q, QN: out STD_LOGIC_VECTOR (N-1 downto 0));
    end component;

    signal CLK, ENA: STD_LOGIC;
    signal ABUS: STD_LOGIC_VECTOR (M-1 downto 0);
    signal DBUS: STD_LOGIC_VECTOR (N-1 downto 0);
  begin
    R1: ROM (CK => CLK, OUT_ENA => ENA, ADDR => ABUS,
             Q => DBUS, QN => open);
```

A register file can be modeled as a two-dimensional array of signals which can then be synthesized. Here is an example of a generic register file.

```
library IEEE; use IEEE.STD_LOGIC_1164.all;
entity RF_MODEL is
  generic (N: POSITIVE := 2; M: POSITIVE := 2);
  port (CLK, RW: in STD_LOGIC;
        INDEX: in INTEGER range 1 to N;
        DATA_IN: in STD_LOGIC_VECTOR(1 to M);
        DATA_OUT: out STD_LOGIC_VECTOR(1 to M));
end RF_MODEL;
```

```
architecture RF_BEH of RF_MODEL is
   type RF_TYPE is array (1 to N) of STD_LOGIC_VECTOR(1to M);
   signal REG_FILE: RF_TYPE;
begin
   process
   begin
      wait until CLK = '0';
      if RW = '1' then
         DATA_OUT <= REG_FILE (INDEX);
      else
         REG_FILE(INDEX) <= DATA_IN;
      end if;
   end process;
end RF_BEH;
```

A synthesized netlist for a 2-by-2 register file is shown in Figure 6-13. Note that there are a total of six flip-flops, four for the register file *REG_FILE* and two for *DATA_OUT.*

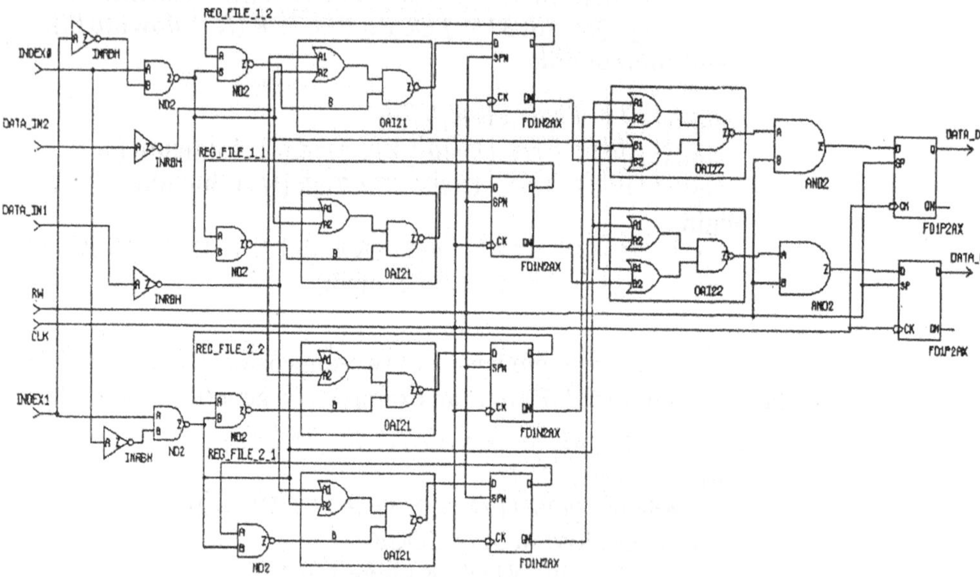

Figure 6-13 A 2-by-2 register file.

6.10 Using a Pre-built Component

There are times when a designer wants the synthesis tool to use a pre-built component instead of the one generated by the synthesis tool. In such a case, the best way is to instantiate the pre-built component as a component in the design.

Here is a 3-bit up-down counter that shows how a pre-built D-type flip-flop is used along with its remaining behavior. The key statements that are necessary to be added are the component instantiation statements and the component declaration. With such a model, a synthesis tool retains the pre-built component in the synthesized design to achieve the desired result. This is shown in the synthesized netlist that appears in Figure 6-14.

```
library IEEE;
use IEEE.STD_LOGIC_1164.all;
entity UPC is
  port (CK, CUCD, PC: in STD_LOGIC;
      Q0, Q1, Q2: out STD_LOGIC);
end UPC;

architecture SPECIAL of UPC is
  signal QN0, QN1, QN2, BIT01, BIT11,
         BIT12, BIT13, BIT21: STD_LOGIC;
  signal TQ0, TQ1: STD_LOGIC;

  component SPECIAL_FF
    port (D, CLK, PRECLR: in STD_LOGIC;
         Q, QBAR: out STD_LOGIC);
  end component;
begin
  Q0 <= TQ0;
  Q1 <= TQ1;

  BIT01 <= CUCD xor TQ0;
  BIT11 <= BIT01 xor QN1;
  BIT12 <= CUCD xor TQ1;
  BIT13 <= BIT01 or BIT12;
  BIT21 <= BIT13 xor QN2;

  LQ0: SPECIAL_FF port map (QN0, CK, PC, TQ0, QN0);
  LQ1: SPECIAL_FF port map (BIT11, CK, PC, TQ1, QN1);
```

```
    LQ2: SPECIAL_FF port map (BIT21, CK, PC, Q2, QN2);
end SPECIAL;
```

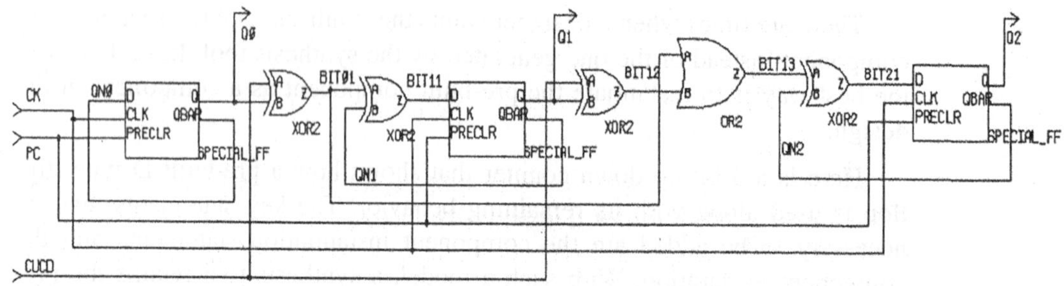

Figure 6-14 Using a special flip-flop.

6.11 Writing Boolean Equations

Boolean equations represent combinational logic. One approach for modeling boolean equations is by using concurrent signal assignment statements. Here is an example of a Gray code to binary code convertor using boolean equations. Figure 6-15 shows the synthesized logic. The truth table for the convertor is as follows.

A B C	Binary Code
0 0 0	0 0 0
0 0 1	0 0 1
0 1 1	0 1 0
0 1 0	0 1 1
1 1 0	1 0 0
1 1 1	1 0 1
1 0 1	1 1 0
1 0 0	1 1 1

```
entity GRAY_TO_BINARY1 is
  port (A, B, C: in BIT;
        BC0, BC1, BC2: out BIT);
end GRAY_TO_BINARY1;

architecture BOOLEAN_LOGIC of GRAY_TO_BINARY1 is
  signal NOTA, NOTB, NOTC: BIT;
begin
  NOTC <= not C;
```

```
   NOTB <= not B;
   NOTA <= not A;

   BC0 <= (A and B and NOTC) or (A and B and C) or
          (A and NOTB and C) or (A and NOTB and NOTC);
   BC1 <= (NOTA and B and C) or (NOTA and B and NOTC) or
          (A and NOTB and C) or (A and NOTB and NOTC);
   BC2 <= (NOTA and NOTB and C) or (NOTA and B and NOTC) or
          (A and B and C) or (A and NOTB and NOTC);
end BOOLEAN_LOGIC;
```

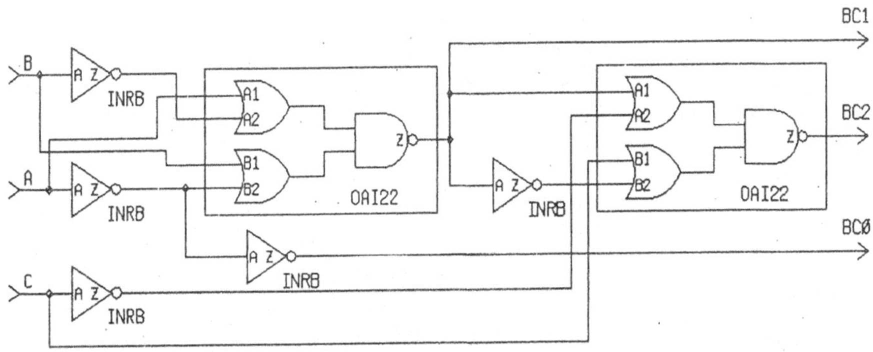

Figure 6-15 Gray to binary logic (after logic optimization).

Here are two other ways of modeling the gray-to-binary code converte The first approach uses a constant *GRAY2BINARY* to store the truth table.

```
library IEEE;
use IEEE.STD_LOGIC_1164.all;
use IEEE.NUMERIC_STD.all;
entity GRAY_TO_BINARY2 is
  port (GRAY: in STD_LOGIC_VECTOR(2 downto 0);
        BIN: out STD_LOGIC_VECTOR(2 downto 0));
end GRAY_TO_BINARY2;

architecture CONSTANT_TABLE of GRAY_TO_BINARY2 is
  type TABLE_TYPE is array (0 to 7)
    of STD_LOGIC_VECTOR(2 downto 0);
  constant GRAY2BINARY: TABLE_TYPE :=
    ("000", "001", "011", "010", "111", "110", "100", "101");
begin
```

```
    BIN <= GRAY2BINARY(TO_INTEGER(UNSIGNED(GRAY)));
end CONSTANT_TABLE;
```

In the next approach, the truth table for the gray-to-binary code converter is described using a selected signal assignment.

```
entity GRAY_TO_BINARY3 is
    port (A, B, C: in BIT;
            BC0, BC1, BC2: out BIT);
end GRAY_TO_BINARY3;

architecture SEL_SIG of GRAY_TO_BINARY3 is
  signal GRAY, BIN: BIT_VECTOR(2 downto 0);
begin
  GRAY <= A & B & C;
  BC2 <= BIN(2);
  BC1 <= BIN(1);
  BC0 <= BIN(0);

  with GRAY select
    BIN <= "000" when "000",
           "001" when "001",
           "010" when "011",
           "011" when "010",
           "100" when "110",
           "101" when "111",
           "110" when "101",
           "111" when "100";
end SEL_SIG;
```

See the section on "Modeling Combinational Logic" for more examples.

6.12 Modeling a Finite State Machine

6.12.1 Moore FSM

In a Moore finite state machine, the output of the circuit is dependent only on the state of the machine and not on its inputs. This is described pictorially in Figure 6-16. Since the outputs are dependent only on the state, a good way to describe a Moore machine is to use a process statement with a `case` statement. The `case` statement is used to switch between the various states and the output logic for each state is described in the appropriate branch. Either an `if` statement with a clock expression can be used around the `case` statement or a `wait` statement that triggers on every clock edge can be used as the first statement within the process. This models the condition of a finite state machine going from state to state synchronously on every clock edge. The machine state itself could be implemented as a variable or as a signal.

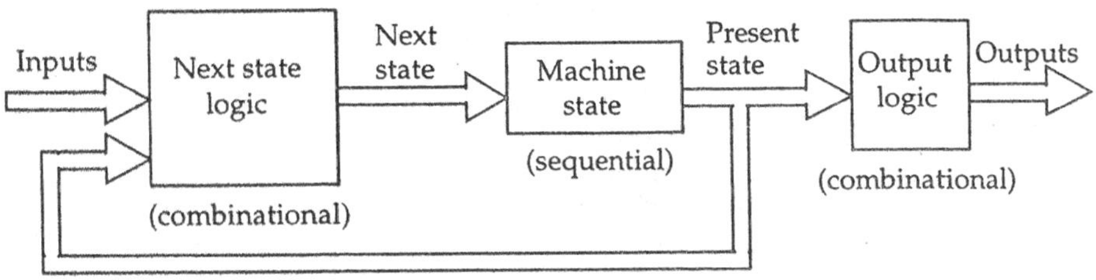

Figure 6-16 A Moore finite state machine.

Here is an example of a Moore finite state machine. A signal *MOORE_STATE* is used to model the machine state which can have either of the four states. The `wait` statement indicates that the state transitions occur synchronously on every rising clock edge.

```
library IEEE;
use IEEE.STD_LOGIC_1164.all;
entity MOORE is
  port (A, CLK: in STD_LOGIC;
       Z: out STD_LOGIC);
end MOORE;

architecture FSM_EXAMPLE of MOORE is
  type STATE_TYPE is (S0, S1, S2, S3);
  signal MOORE_STATE: STATE_TYPE;
begin
  process
  begin
    wait until CLK='1';

    case MOORE_STATE is
      when S0 =>
        Z <= '1';
```

```
                if A = '0' then
                    MOORE_STATE <= S0;
                else
                    MOORE_STATE <= S2;
                end if;
            when S1 =>
                Z <= '0';

                if A = '0' then
                    MOORE_STATE <= S0;
                else
                    MOORE_STATE <= S2;
                end if;
            when S2 =>
                Z <= '0';

                if A = '0' then
                    MOORE_STATE <= S2;
                else
                    MOORE_STATE <= S3;
                end if;
            when S3 =>
                Z <= '1';

                if A = '0' then
                    MOORE_STATE <= S1;
                end if;
        end case;
    end process;
end FSM_EXAMPLE;
```

When this model is synthesized, three flip-flops are inferred; two to hold the value of the machine state (signal *MOORE_STATE*) and one for the output *Z*. The synthesized netlist is shown in Figure 6-17. States are encoded using sequential state assignment. This can be changed by using the attribute *ENUM_ENCODING*; such an example is shown in the next section.

The state *MOORE_STATE* can also be modeled using a variable in the above example. In terms of synthesis results, the resulting netlist is the same. However, simulation run time may be impacted. Here is another architecture body for the entity *MOORE* that declares *MOORE_STATE* as a variable.

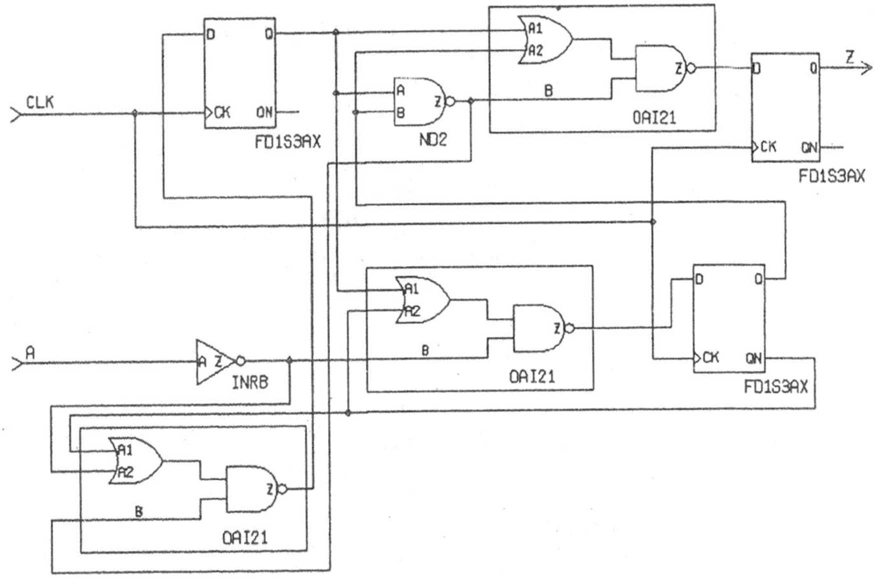

Figure 6-17 The synthesized netlist for the Moore FSM model.

```
architecture VARIABLE_STATE of MOORE is
begin
  process
    type STATE_TYPE is (S0, S1, S2, S3);
    variable MOORE_STATE: STATE_TYPE;
  begin
    wait until CLK = '1';

    case MOORE_STATE is
      when S0 =>
        Z <= '1';

        if A = '0' then
          MOORE_STATE := S0;
        else
          MOORE_STATE := S2;
        end if;
      when S1 =>
        Z <= '0';

        if A = '0' then
          MOORE_STATE := S0;
```

```
            else
              MOORE_STATE := S2;
            end if;
          when S2 =>
            Z <= '0';

            if A = '0' then
              MOORE_STATE := S2;
            else
              MOORE_STATE := S3;
            end if;
          when S3 =>
            Z <= '1';

            if A = '0' then
              MOORE_STATE := S1;
            end if;
        end case;
      end process;
    end FSM_EXAMPLE;
```

6.12.2 Mealy FSM

In a Mealy finite state machine, the output is dependent both on the machine state as well as on the inputs to the finite state machine. This is shown pictorially in Figure 6-18. Notice that in this case, outputs can change asynchronously with respect to clock.

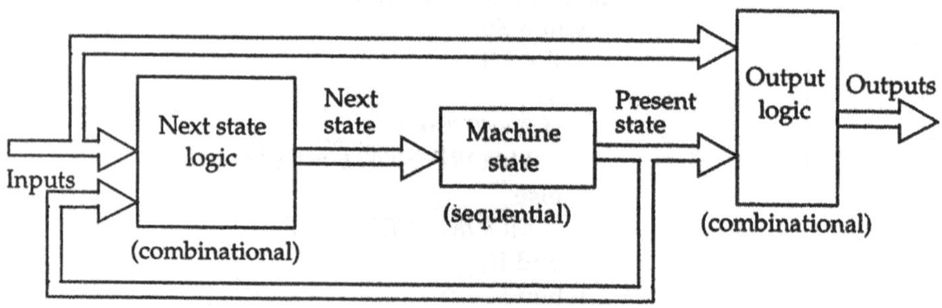

Figure 6-18 A Mealy finite state machine.

One of the best ways of describing a Mealy finite state machine is by using two processes, one for describing the synchronous logic, and one for describing the combinational logic (this includes both next state logic and output logic). It is necessary to do this since any changes on inputs directly affect the outputs of the process used to describe the combinational logic. Since there are two processes, the state of the machine has to be modeled using a signal.

Here is an example of a Mealy finite state machine. Signal *MEALY_STATE* holds the machine state, while signal *NEXT_STATE* is used to pass information from the combinational logic process to the sequential logic process. In this example, instead of using sequential state assignment, the state values are explicitly assigned using the attribute *ENUM_ENCODING*; state *ST0* has the value "1111", state *ST1* has the value "1101", and so on.

```
package NEWPACK is
  type MEALY_TYPE is (ST0, ST1, ST2, ST3);
  attribute ENUM_ENCODING: STRING;
  attribute ENUM_ENCODING of MEALY_TYPE: type
      is "1111 1101 1001 1000";
end NEWPACK;

use WORK.NEWPACK.all;
entity MEALY is
  port (A, CLK: in BIT;
        Z: out BIT);
end;

architecture MEALY_FSM of MEALY is
  signal MEALY_STATE, NEXT_ST: MEALY_TYPE;
begin
  SEQ_LOGIC: process (CLK)
  begin
    if CLK = '1' and (not CLK'STABLE) then
      MEALY_STATE <= NEXT_ST;
    end if;
  end process;

  COMB_LOGIC: process (MEALY_STATE, A)
  begin
    case MEALY_STATE is
      when ST0 =>
        if A = '1' then
          Z <= '1';
```

```
          NEXT_ST <= ST3;
        else
          Z <= '0';
          NEXT_ST <= ST0; -- Assignment is redundant from
            -- simulation point of view but necessary for synthesis,
            -- else latches are inferred for signal NEXT_ST.
        end if;
      when ST1 =>
        if A = '1' then
          Z <= '1';
          NEXT_ST <= ST0;
        else
          Z <= 0';
          NEXT_ST <= ST1;
        end if;
      when ST2 =>
        if A = '0' then
          Z <= '0';
          NEXT_ST <= ST2;
        else
          Z <= '1';
          NEXT_ST <= ST1;
        end if;
      when ST3 =>
        if A = '0' then
          Z <= '0';
          NEXT_ST <= ST2;
        else
          Z <= '1';
          NEXT_ST <= ST1;
        end if;
      end case;
  end process;
end;
```

Four flip-flops are inferred to hold the value of the signal *MEALY_STATE* with the specified state assignment. Figure 6-19 shows the synthesized netlist for this example.

An alternate way of modeling either the Mealy finite state machine or the Moore finite state machine is to use three processes, one for the next state generation logic, one for the output logic and one for the machine state. Here is the entity *MEALY* described using three processes.

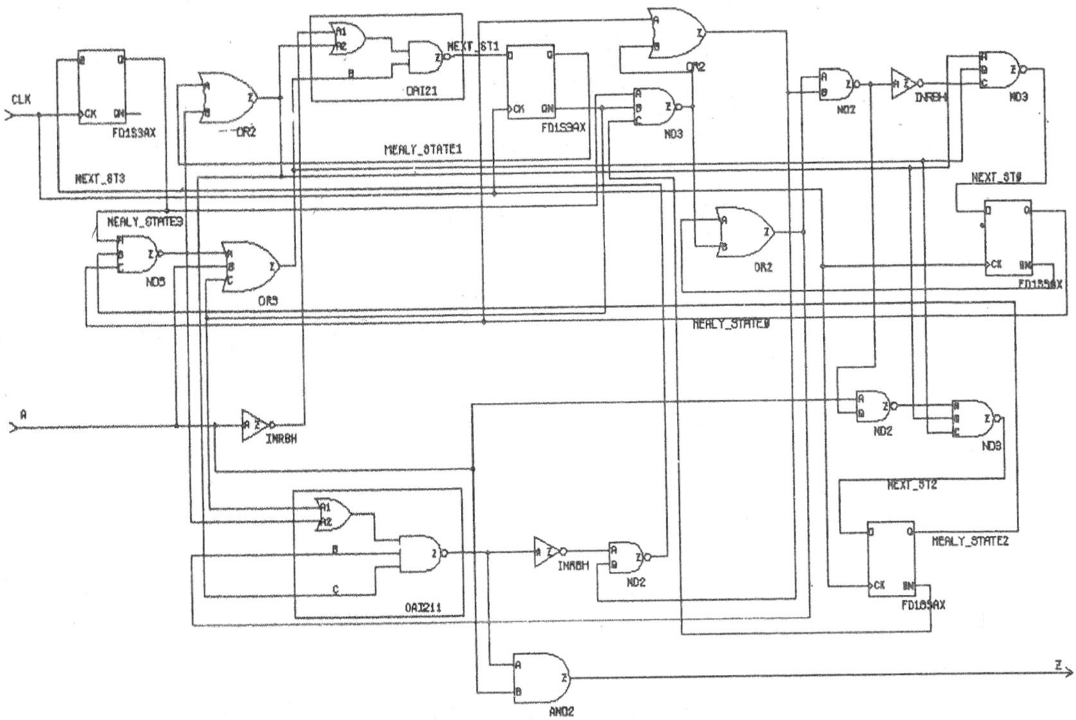

Figure 6-19 The synthesized netlist for the Mealy FSM example.

```
architecture MEALY_FSM_THREE_PROCESSES of MEALY is
  signal MEALY_STATE, NEXT_ST: MEALY_TYPE;
begin
  MACHINE_STATE: process (CLK)
  begin
    if CLK = '1' and (not CLK'STABLE) then
      MEALY_STATE <= NEXT_ST;
    end if;
  end process;

  OUTPUT_LOGIC: process (MEALY_STATE, A)
  begin
    case MEALY_STATE is
      when ST0 =>
        if A = '1' then
          Z <= '1';
        else
```

```
          Z <= '0';
        end if;
      when ST1 =>
        if A = '1' then
          Z <= '1';
        else
          Z <= '0';
        end if;
      when ST2 =>
        if A = '0' then
          Z <= '0';
        else
          Z <= '1';
        end if;
      when ST3 =>
        if A = '0' then
          Z <= '0';
        else
          Z <= '1';
        end if;
    end case;
  end process;

  NEXT_STATE_LOGIC : process (MEALY_STATE, A)
  begin
    case MEALY_STATE is
      when ST0 =>
        if A = '1' then
          NEXT_ST <= ST3;
        else
          NEXT_ST <= ST0; -- Assignment is redundant from
            -- simulation point of view but necessary for synthesis,
            -- else latches are inferred for signal NEXT_ST.
        end if;
      when ST1 =>
        if A = '1' then
          NEXT_ST <= ST0;
        else
          NEXT_ST <= ST1;
        end if;
      when ST2 =>
        if A = '0' then
          NEXT_ST <= ST2;
```

```
        else
          NEXT_ST <= ST1;
        end if;
      when ST3 =>
        if A = '0' then
          NEXT_ST <= ST2;
        else
          NEXT_ST <= ST1;
        end if;
      end case;
  end process;
end;
```

Readability and functionality of the finite state machine appears more clearer in this model.

6.12.3 Encoding States

There are many ways to model the machine states of a finite state machine. Described here are some of the most common ones. The *MOORE* entity described earlier is used as an example in describing these encodings.

Using Integer Types

The simplest way is to assign integer values to states.

```
signal MOORE_STATE: INTEGER range 0 to 3;
. . .
case MOORE_STATE is
  when 0 => . . .
    MOORE_STATE <= 2;
    . . .
  when 1 =>
    . . .
end case;
```

Using Constant Declarations

Another option is to declare constants and use these in the case statement.

```
constant S0: NATURAL := 0;
constant S1: NATURAL := 1;
```

```
constant S2: NATURAL := 2;
constant S3: NATURAL := 3;

signal MOORE_STATE: INTEGER range 0 to 3;
. . .
case MOORE_STATE is
  when S0 => . . .
    MOORE_STATE <= S2;
    . . .
  when S1 =>
    . . .
end case;
```

The advantage of this approach is that the state encodings are described explicitly in one place and can be changed easily. If either the constant declarations or the integer values are used directly, a synthesis system will generate the minimum number of bits needed to encode the integer value. In the above example, only two bits are needed for state encoding since the maximum integer value is 3.

What if a different encoding needs to be specified, for example, 1-shift encoding? This can be done by describing each state as a vector of bits.

```
constant S0: STD_LOGIC_VECTOR := "000";
constant S1: STD_LOGIC_VECTOR := "001";
constant S2: STD_LOGIC_VECTOR := "010";
constant S3: STD_LOGIC_VECTOR := "100";

signal MOORE_STATE: STD_LOGIC_VECTOR (0 to 2);
. . .
case MOORE_STATE is
  when S0 => . . .
    MOORE_STATE <= S2;
    . . .
  when S1 =>
    . . .
end case;
```

In this case, the number of bits required for state encoding is dictated by the number of bits in the constant which in this example is 3 bits.

Using Enumeration Types

VHDL also provides enumeration types which can very conveniently be used in describing the states of a finite state machine.

```
type FSM_STATES is (S0, S1, S2, S3);

signal MOORE_STATE: FSM_STATES;
...
case MOORE_STATE is
  when S0 => . . .
    MOORE_STATE <= S2;
    ...
  when S1 =>
    ...
end case;
```

Notice that in this case, no explicit encoding for the enumeration types is specified. So what is the value used for each state? Each enumeration literal is encoded to correspond to its position number in the enumeration type, that is, literal *S0* is encoded with value 0, *S1* with 1, *S2* with 2 and *S3* with 3. Thus two bits will be used for holding the state value.

How can this encoding be changed? This can be done using the *ENUM_ENCODING* attribute. Using this attribute, each state is explicitly encoded as a bit string. Here is an example.

```
type FSM_STATES is (S0, S1, S2, S3);

signal MOORE_STATE: FSM_STATES;

attribute ENUM_ENCODING: STRING;
attribute ENUM_ENCODING of FSM_STATES:
    type is "000 001 011 111";
...
case MOORE_STATE is
  when S0 => . . .
    MOORE_STATE <= S2;
    ...
  when S1 =>
    ...
end case;
```

Since each state is encoded as three bits, three flip-flops are inferred for this example.

The above techniques show how states can be explicitly or implicitly encoded. Other synthesis systems may provide an option for performing automated state assignment.

6.12.4 Another Example

Here is an example of a 3-bit Gray code up-down counter modeled as a finite state machine. The counter counts up when signal *UP_DOWN* is high, else it counts down. If signal *ENABLE* is low, counting is disabled. If signal *RESET* is high, the counter is reset to zeros. The state diagram is shown in Figure 6-20.

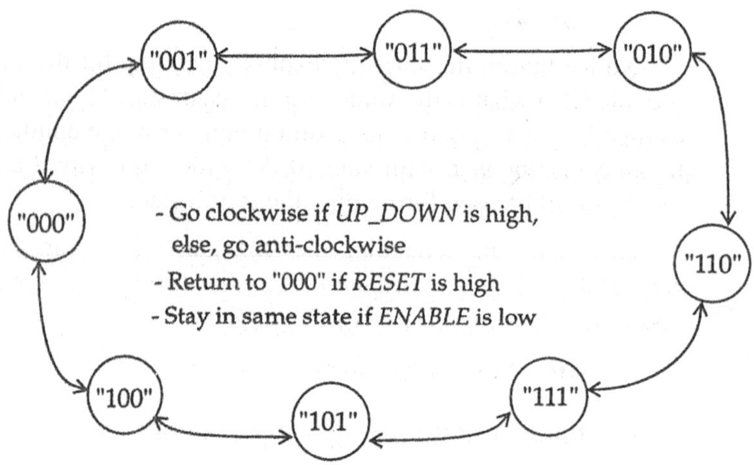

Figure 6-20 State diagram for a 3-bit Gray code up-down counter.

Here is the model for this counter. An array of an array, *GRAY_CODE*, holds the encodings of the Gray code sequence. The state of the finite state machine is stored in the signal *BINARY_INDEX* which is incremented or decremented in a binary sequence. Based on the binary value in *BINARY_INDEX*, the corresponding value is selected from the constant *GRAY_CODE*. Three asynchronous clear rising-edge-triggered flip-flops are synthesized for this model corresponding to the signal *BINARY_INDEX*. A multiplexer then selects the Gray code from the binary index based on the output values of the flip-flops.

```
library IEEE;
use IEEE.STD_LOGIC_1164.all;
use IEEE.NUMERIC_STD.all;
entity GRAY_FSM is
  port (CLK, RESET, ENABLE, UP_DOWN: in STD_LOGIC;
       GRAY_CNT: out STD_LOGIC_VECTOR(0 to 2));
end GRAY_FSM;

architecture CONSTANTS of GRAY_FSM is
  type CON_ARRAY is array (0 to 7) of
    STD_LOGIC_VECTOR(0 to 2);
  constant GRAY_CODE: CON_ARRAY
    := ("000", "001", "011", "010", "110", "111", "101", "100");
  signal BINARY_INDEX: UNSIGNED(0 to 2);
begin
  process (CLK, RESET, ENABLE, UP_DOWN)
  begin
    if RESET = '0' then
      BINARY_INDEX <= "000";
    elsif CLK = '1' and CLK'EVENT then
      if ENABLE = '1' then
        if UP_DOWN = '1' then
          BINARY_INDEX <= BINARY_INDEX + 1;
        else
          BINARY_INDEX <= BINARY_INDEX - 1;
        end if;
      end if;
    end if;
  end process;

  GRAY_CNT <= GRAY_CODE (TO_INTEGER(BINARY_INDEX));
end CONSTANTS;
```

The above approach of storing the Gray code encodings in a constant can be used to transform a binary number to any user-specific encoding simply by changing the encodings in the constant declaration (such as for *GRAY_CODE*). Another alternate way of modeling a Gray code counter is described in section 6.16.4.

The synthesized netlist for the entity *GRAY_FSM* is described next.

```
library SYNTH;
use SYNTH.GENERIC_COMP.all;
architecture GRAY_FSM_STRUTURE of GRAY_FSM is
```

```
    signal BINARY_INDEX2, v_I0_v_S12_1, BINARY_INDEX1,
        v_I0_v_S18_1, BINARY_INDEX0, v_I0_v_S24_1, NET, NET0,
        NET1, S362, S365, S348, S345, S342, S351, S368, S163, S339,
        S239, S359: STD_LOGIC;
begin
  L1: FL1S3EX port map (D0=>BINARY_INDEX2,
      D1=>v_I0_v_S12_1, CK=>CLK, SD=>ENABLE,
      CDN=>RESET, Q=>BINARY_INDEX2, QN=>NET);
  L2: FL1S3EX port map (D0=>BINARY_INDEX1,
      D1=>v_I0_v_S18_1, CK=>CLK, SD=>ENABLE,
      CDN=>RESET, Q=>BINARY_INDEX1, QN=>NET0);
  L3: FL1S3EX port map (D0=>BINARY_INDEX0,
      D1=>v_I0_v_S24_1, CK=>CLK, SD=>ENABLE,
      CDN=>RESET, Q=>BINARY_INDEX0, QN=> NET1);
  GRAY_CNT0: INRB port map (A=>NET1, Z=>GRAY_CNT(0));
  GRAY_CNT1: OAI22 port map (A1=>S362, A2=>NET1,
      B1=>BINARY_INDEX0, B2=> S365, Z=>GRAY_CNT(1));
  S365_1: NR2 port map (A=>S348, B=>S345, Z=>S365);
  S362_1: NR2 port map (A=>S342, B=>S351, Z=>S362);
  GRAY_CNT2: INRB port map (A=>S368, Z=>GRAY_CNT(2));
  L4: OAI22 port map (A1=>S163, A2=>NET1,
      B1=>BINARY_INDEX0, B2=>S339, Z=>v_I0_v_S24_1);
  S163_1: INRB port map (A=>S339, Z=>S163);
  S339_1: OAI22 port map (A1=>UP_DOWN, A2=>S342, B1=>S348,
      B2=>S239, Z=> S339);
  L5: OAI22 port map (A1=>UP_DOWN, A2=>S359, B1=>S368,
      B2=> S239, Z=>v_I0_v_S18_1);
  S239_1: INRB port map (A=>UP_DOWN, Z=>S239);
  S368_1: NR2 port map (A=>S351, B=>S345, Z=>S368);
  S345_1: NR2 port map (A=>NET0, B=>BINARY_INDEX2,
      Z=>S345);
  S351_1: NR2 port map (A=>NET, B=>BINARY_INDEX1, Z=>S351);
  S359_1: NR2 port map (A=>S342, B=>S348, Z=>S359);
  S348_1: NR2 port map (A=>NET0, B=>NET, Z=>S348);
  S342_1: NR2 port map (A=>BINARY_INDEX1,
      B=>BINARY_INDEX2, Z=>S342);
  L6: INRB port map (A=>BINARY_INDEX2, Z=>v_I0_v_S12_1);
end GRAY_FSM_STR;
```

6.13 Modeling an Universal Shift Register

Here is a synthesis model of a 3-bit universal shift register. The universal shift register performs the following functions:

i. hold value
ii. shift left
iii. shift right
iv. load value

This universal register can be used as a serial-in, serial-out shift register, parallel-in, serial-out shift register, serial-in, parallel-out shift register, and as a parallel-in, parallel-out shift register. Here is the state table for the 3-bit universal shift register.

Function	*Inputs* (*S0 S1*)	*Next state* (*Q*[2]	*Q*[1]	*Q*[0])
Hold	0 0	*Q*[2]	*Q*[1]	*Q*[0]
Shift left	0 1	*Q*[1]	*Q*[0]	*RIN*
Shift right	1 0	*LIN*	*Q*[2]	*Q*[1]
Load	1 1	*PAR_IN*[2]	*PAR_IN*[1]	*PAR_IN*[0]

The synthesis model follows. The synthesized netlist is shown in Figure 6-21.

```
library IEEE;
use IEEE.STD_LOGIC_1164.all;
entity UNIV_SHIFT_REG is
  generic (WIDTH: POSITIVE := 3);
  port ( CLK, CLR, LIN, RIN, S0, S1: in STD_LOGIC;
        PAR_IN: in STD_LOGIC_VECTOR(WIDTH-1 downto 0);
        Q: buffer STD_LOGIC_VECTOR(WIDTH-1 downto 0));
end UNIV_SHIFT_REG;

architecture BEHAVIOR of UNIV_SHIFT_REG is
begin
  process (CLK, CLR)
    subtype TWO_BIT is STD_LOGIC_VECTOR (0 to 1);
  begin
    if CLR = '0' then
      Q <= (others => '0');
    elsif RISING_EDGE (CLK) then
      case TWO_BIT ' (S0 & S1) is
```

```
                when "00" =>
                  null;
                when "01" =>
                  Q <= Q(WIDTH-2 downto 0) & RIN;
                when "10" =>
                  Q <= LIN & Q(WIDTH-1 downto 1);
                when "11" =>
                  Q <= PAR_IN;
                when others =>
                    null;
              end case;
            end if;
          end process;
        end BEHAVIOR;
```

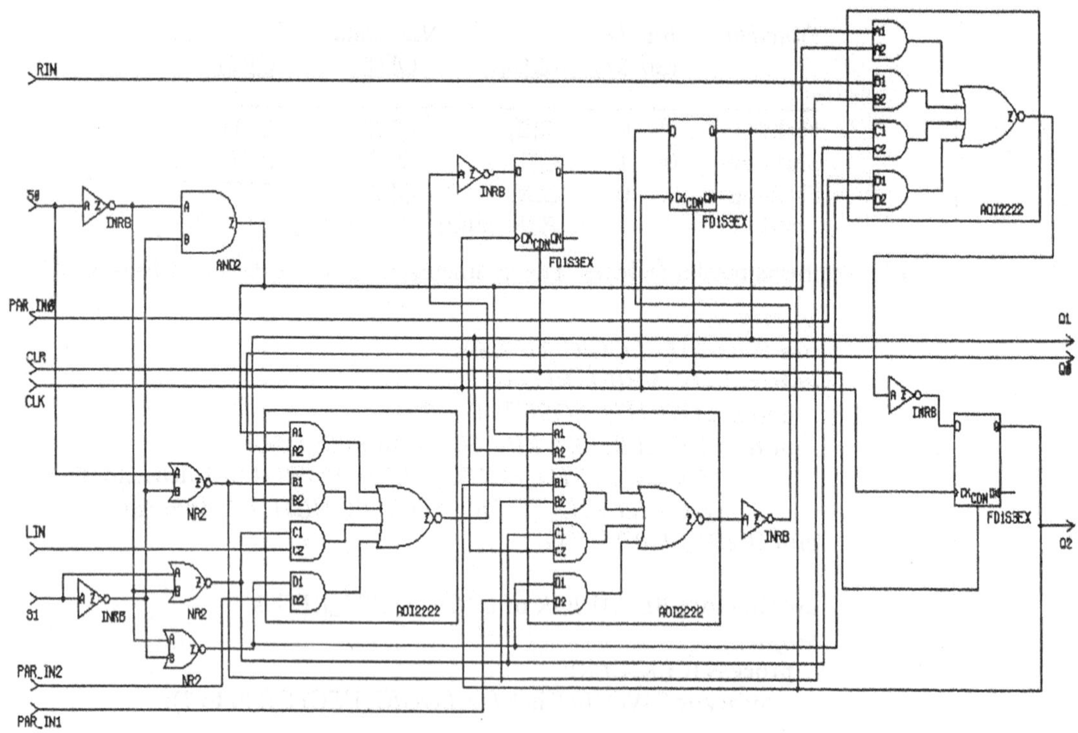

Figure 6-21 A 3-bit universal shift register.

6.14 A Generic Parallel to Serial Converter

Here is an example of a generic *N*-bit parallel to serial converter. Parallel data is loaded in when signal *DATA_RDY* is '1'. Each bit is shifted out serially on the rising edge of the clock.

```
library IEEE;
use IEEE.STD_LOGIC_1164.all;
entity PARALLEL2SERIAL is
  generic (N: POSITIVE := 3);
  port (PAR_DATA: in STD_LOGIC_VECTOR(1 to N);
      CLK, DATA_RDY: in STD_LOGIC;
      SER_OUT: out STD_LOGIC);
end;

architecture SHIFT of PARALLEL2SERIAL is
  signal SAVE_REG: STD_LOGIC_VECTOR (1 to N);
begin
  process (CLK, DATA_RDY, PAR_DATA)
  begin
    if DATA_RDY = '1' then
      SAVE_REG <= PAR_DATA;
    elsif CLK'EVENT and CLK = '1' then
      SAVE_REG (1 to N–1) <= SAVE_REG (2 to N);
    end if;
  end process;

  SER_OUT <= SAVE_REG(1);
end;
```

The synthesized netlist for a 3-bit converter is shown in Figure 6-22. Note that *N* flip-flops are inferred in the model; these flip-flops save the parallel value read in.

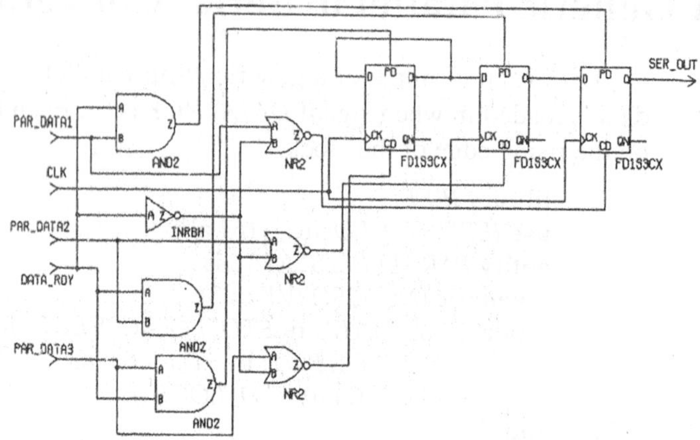

Figure 6-22 A 3-bit parallel to serial converter.

6.15 Modeling an ALU

6.15.1 A Generic ALU

Here is an example of a generic *N*-bit arithmetic-logic-unit that performs an exclusive-or, less than, and an increment-by-1 operation.

```
library IEEE;
use IEEE.STD_LOGIC_1164.all;
use IEEE.STD_LOGIC_ARITH.all;
entity FDS_ALU is
   generic (NBITS: POSITIVE := 5);
   port (A: in STD_LOGIC_VECTOR (NBITS-1 downto 0);
         B: in STD_LOGIC_VECTOR (NBITS-1 downto 0);
         SEL: in STD_LOGIC_VECTOR(3 downto 0);
         CMP: out STD_LOGIC;
         D: out STD_LOGIC_VECTOR (NBITS-1 downto 0));
end FDS_ALU;

architecture BEHAVIOR of FDS_ALU is
   constant OP_XOR: STD_LOGIC_VECTOR := "1111";
   constant OP_INCRA: STD_LOGIC_VECTOR := "1000";
```

```
  constant OP_LT: STD_LOGIC_VECTOR := "0011";
begin
  ALU_PROCESS:                -- Process label.
  process (A, B, SEL)
  begin
    case SEL is
      when OP_INCRA =>
        D <= STD_LOGIC_VECTOR(UNSIGNED(A) + 1);
        CMP <= 'X';
      when OP_XOR =>
        D <= A xor B;
        CMP <= 'X';
      when OP_LT =>
        if A < B then
          CMP <= '1';
        else
          CMP <= '0';
        end if;

        D <= (others => 'X');
      when others =>              -- Invalid selector input.
        CMP <= 'X';
        D <= (others => 'X');
    end case;
  end process ALU_PROCESS;
end BEHAVIOR;
```

The generic ALU can be synthesized for a different value of the generic by specifying the value of the generic when it is instantiated. This is shown in the following example for a 2-bit ALU. The synthesized netlist is shown in Figure 6-23.

```
library IEEE;
use IEEE.STD_LOGIC_1164.all;
entity ALU2BIT is
  port (A: in STD_LOGIC_VECTOR (NBITS–1 downto 0);
        B: in STD_LOGIC_VECTOR (NBITS–1 downto 0);
        SEL: in STD_LOGIC_VECTOR (3 downto 0);
        CMP: out STD_LOGIC;
        D: out STD_LOGIC_VECTOR (NBITS–1 downto 0));
end ALU2BIT;
```

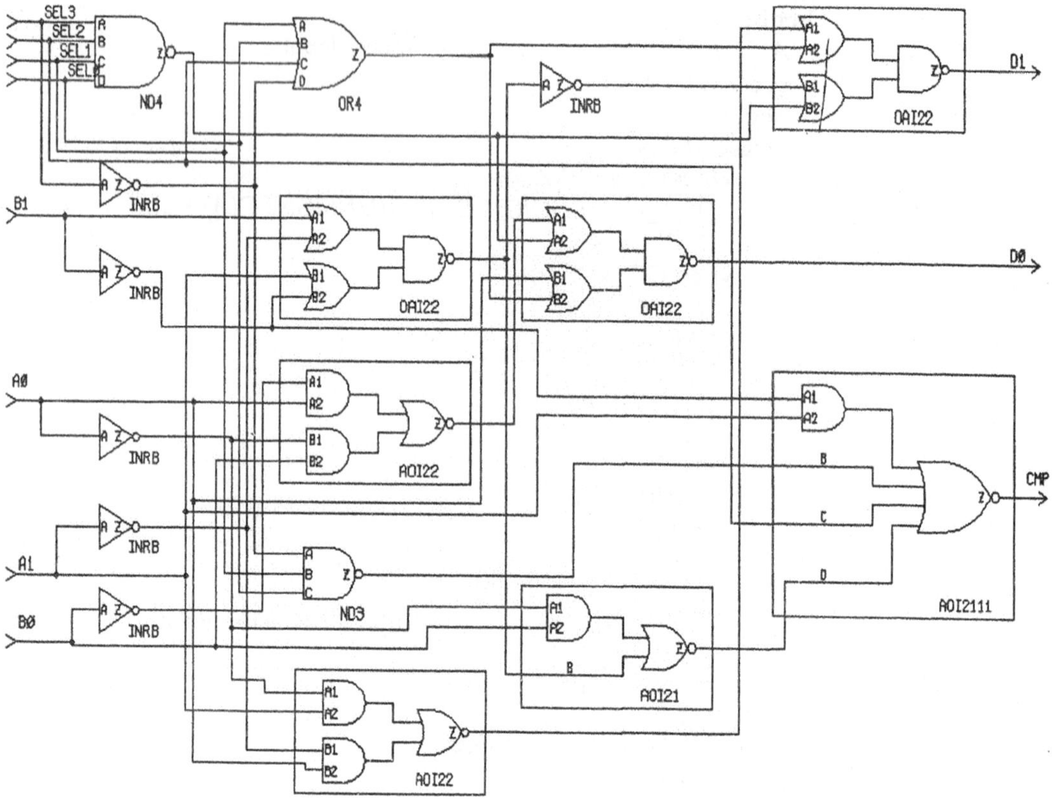

Figure 6-23 A 2-bit ALU.

```
architecture PART of ALU2BIT is
  component FDS_ALU
    generic (NBITS: POSITIVE);
    port (A: in STD_LOGIC_VECTOR (NBITS-1 downto 0);
          B: in STD_LOGIC_VECTOR (NBITS-1 downto 0);
          SEL: in STD_LOGIC_VECTOR (3 downto 0);
          CMP: out STD_LOGIC;
          D: out STD_LOGIC_VECTOR (NBITS-1 downto 0));
  end component;
begin
  NUM: FDS_ALU
        generic map (NBITS => 2)
        port map (A, B, SEL, CMP, D);
end PART;
```

6.15.2 A Simple ALU

Here is a model of a simple arithmetic-logic-unit. This logic unit performs four functions: `add`, `nand`, greater-than and `xor` of the signed operands. A selected signal assignment statement is used to model the arithmetic-logic-unit. Figure 6-24 shows the synthesized netlist.

```
package UTILS is
  type OP_TYPE is (ADD_OP, NAND_OP, GT_OP, XOR_OP);
end;

library IEEE;
use IEEE.STD_LOGIC_1164.all;
use IEEE.NUMERIC_STD.all, WORK.UTILS.all;
entity CUSTOM_ALU is
  generic (NBITS: POSITIVE := 2);
  port (A, B: in SIGNED (NBITS-1 downto 0);
        OP_CODE: in OP_TYPE;
        ZDATA: out SIGNED (NBITS-1 downto 0);
        ZCOMP: out BOOLEAN);
end CUSTOM_ALU;

architecture TEST of CUSTOM_ALU is
begin
  with OP_CODE select
    ZDATA <= A + B when ADD_OP,
             A nand B when NAND_OP,
             A xor B when XOR_OP,
             (others => 'X') when others;

  with OP_CODE select
    ZCOMP <= A > B when GT_OP,
             FALSE when others;
end TEST;
```

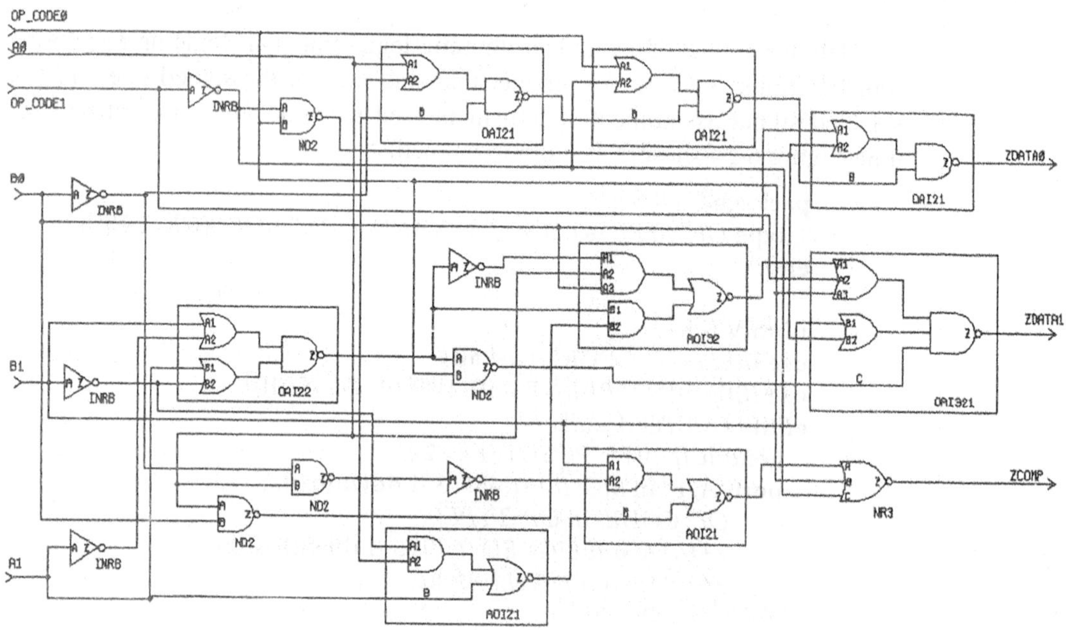

Figure 6-24 A 2-bit custom ALU.

6.16 Modeling a Counter

6.16.1 Ripple Counter

Here is a model for a generic *N*-bit binary ripple up-down counter with synchronous preset and preclear controls. The counting is synchronized to the rising edge of a clock. Figure 6-25 shows the synthesized netlist for a 2-bit ripple counter.

```
library IEEE;
use IEEE.STD_LOGIC_1164.all;
use IEEE.NUMERIC_STD.all;
entity RIPPLE_COUNTER is
   generic (NBITS: POSITIVE := 2);
   port (CK, CUCD, PC, CTLD: in STD_LOGIC;
         PI: in STD_LOGIC_VECTOR(0 to NBITS-1);
         Q: out STD_LOGIC_VECTOR(0 to NBITS-1);
```

```
    QN: out STD_LOGIC_VECTOR(0 to NBITS–1));
end RIPPLE_COUNTER;

architecture BEHAVIOR of RIPPLE_COUNTER is
begin
  COUNTER_PROCESS:
  process (CK)
    variable CNTR_VALUE: UNSIGNED(NBITS–1 downto 0);
  begin
    if RISING_EDGE(CK) then          -- Rising-edge-triggered.
      if PC = '1' then               -- Check preclear.
        CNTR_VALUE := (others => '0');
      else                       -- Actual counting or loading process.
        if CTLD = '0' then           -- Parallel loading.
          CNTR_VALUE := UNSIGNED(PI);
        else                         -- Beginning of counting part.
          if CUCD = '1' then         -- Count up.
            CNTR_VALUE := CNTR_VALUE + 1;
          else                       -- Count down.
            CNTR_VALUE := CNTR_VALUE – 1;
          end if;    -- The end of counting part.
        end if;      -- The end of parallel-loading routine.
      end if;        -- The end of check input.
    end if;          -- End of clock trigger.

    -- Output assignment:
    Q <= STD_LOGIC_VECTOR (CNTR_VALUE);
    QN <= not STD_LOGIC_VECTOR (CNTR_VALUE);
  end process COUNTER_PROCESS;
end BEHAVIOR;
```

6.16.2 Modulo-N Counter

Here is a model of a modulo-*N* binary up-counter. This counter has only a synchronous preclear control and all transitions occur on the rising clock edge. Figure 6-26 shows the synthesized netlist for a modulo-3 binary counter.

```
-- Number of bits in counter: NBITS
-- Modulo: UPTO
library IEEE;
use IEEE.STD_LOGIC_1164.all;
use IEEE.NUMERIC_STD.all;
entity MODULO_N is
```

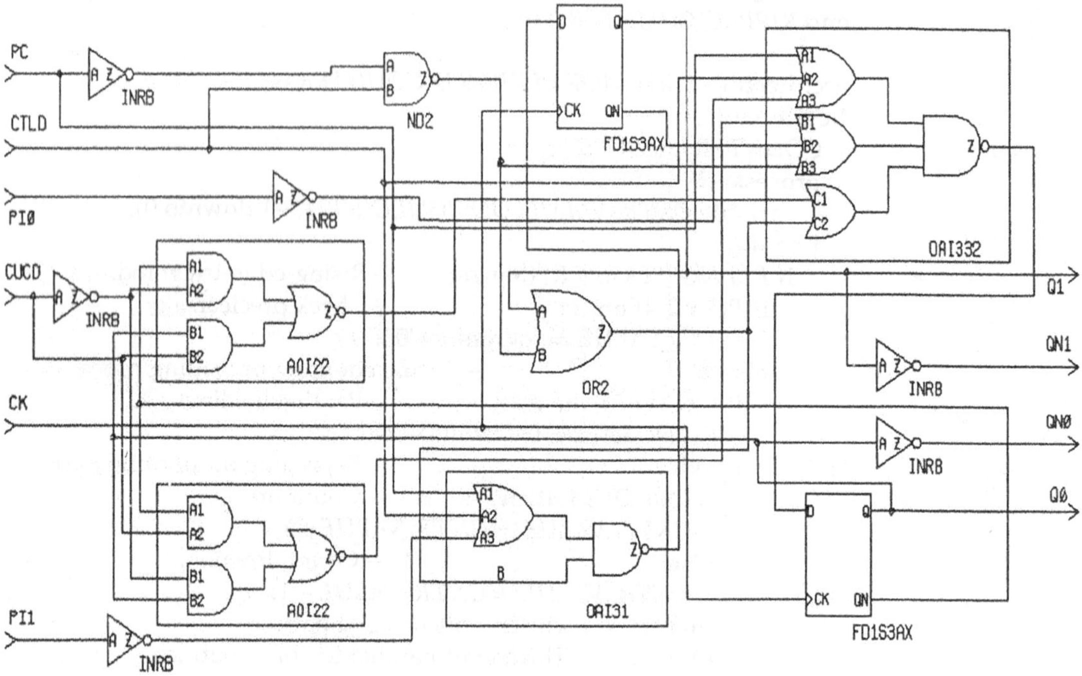

Figure 6-25 A 2-bit up-down, loadable, clearable ripple counter.

```
    generic (NBITS: POSITIVE := 2; UPTO: POSITIVE := 3);
    port (CK, PC: in STD_LOGIC;
          Q: out STD_LOGIC_VECTOR (0 to NBITS-1);
          QN: out STD_LOGIC_VECTOR (0 to NBITS-1));
end MODULO_N;

architecture BEHAVIOR of MODULO_N is
begin
    process (CK)
        variable CNTR_VALUE: UNSIGNED (NBITS-1 downto 0);
    begin
        if RISING_EDGE(CK) then              -- Rising-edge trigger.
            if PC = '1' then                 -- Check preclear.
                CNTR_VALUE := (others => '0');
            else                             Counting part.
                CNTR_VALUE := (CNTR_VALUE + 1) mod UPTO;
            end if;     -- The end of check input.
        end if;         -- End of clock trigger.
```

```
    -- Output assignment:
    Q <= STD_LOGIC_VECTOR (CNTR_VALUE);
    QN <= not STD_LOGIC_VECTOR (CNTR_VALUE);
  end process;
end BEHAVIOR;.
```

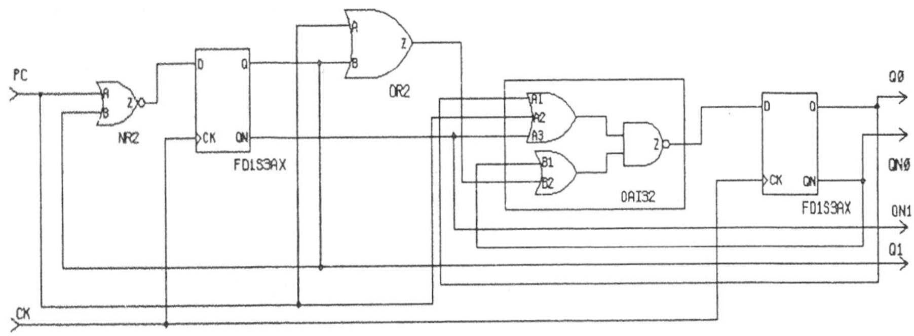

Figure 6-26 A modulo-3 binary counter.

6.16.3 Johnson Counter

A Johnson counter is a shift-type counter. Here is an example of a 3-bit Johnson counter stream:

000
001
011
111
110
100
000

The key to modeling a Johnson counter is to note that if the most significant bit (the leftmost bit) of the counter is a '1', then a '0' has to be shifted in from right; if the most significant bit is a '0', then a '1' has to be shifted in from the right. Here is the model for a generic *N*-bit Johnson counter with an asynchronous preclear control. Figure 6-27 shows the synthesized netlist for a 3-bit Johnson counter.

```
library IEEE;
use IEEE.STD_LOGIC_1164.all;
entity JOHNSON_COUNTER is
  generic (NBITS: POSITIVE := 3);
  port (CK, PC: in STD_LOGIC;
        Q: out STD_LOGIC_VECTOR (0 to NBITS-1));
end JOHNSON_COUNTER;

architecture BEHAVIOR of JOHNSON_COUNTER is
begin
  process (CK, PC)
    variable CNTR_VALUE: STD_LOGIC_VECTOR (0 to NBITS-1);
  begin
    if PC = '0' then                          -- Asynchronous preclear.
      CNTR_VALUE := (others => '0');
    elsif FALLING_EDGE (CK) then              -- Falling-edge trigger.
      CNTR_VALUE := CNTR_VALUE(1 to NBITS-1) &
            (not CNTR_VALUE(0));
    end if;

    Q <= CNTR_VALUE;
  end process;
end BEHAVIOR;
```

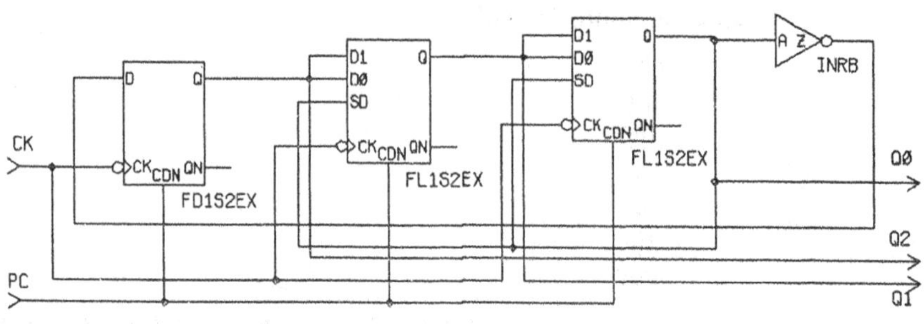

Figure 6-27 A 3-bit Johnson counter.

6.16.4 Gray Counter

A Gray counter is a binary counter with the following conversion logic:

1. The first Gray bit (the leftmost bit) is the same as the first binary bit.

ii. Exclusive-or each pair of adjacent bits to get the next Gray bit.

For example, a binary count of "1100" corresponds to a Gray count of "1010". Here is the VHDL model for a generic *N*-bit Gray up-counter with synchronous preclear. The synthesized netlist for a 3-bit Gray counter is shown in Figure 6-28.

```
library IEEE;
use IEEE.STD_LOGIC_1164.all;
use IEEE.NUMERIC_STD.all;
entity GRAY_COUNTER is
  generic (NBITS: POSITIVE := 3);
  port (CK, PC: in STD_LOGIC;
        Q: out STD_LOGIC_VECTOR (0 to NBITS–1);
        QN: out STD_LOGIC_VECTOR (0 to NBITS–1));
end GRAY_COUNTER;

architecture BEHAVIOR of GRAY_COUNTER is
begin
  COUNTER_PROCESS:
  process (CK)
    variable CNTR_VALUE: UNSIGNED (0 to NBITS–1);
    variable GRAY_CNT: STD_LOGIC_VECTOR (0 to NBITS–1);
  begin
    if RISING_EDGE(CK) then  -- Rising-edge trigger.
      if PC = '1' then       -- Check preclear.
        CNTR_VALUE := (others => '0');
      else
        CNTR_VALUE := CNTR_VALUE + 1;
      end if;                -- The end of check input.
    end if;                  -- End of clock trigger.

    -- Output assignment: convert from binary to Gray:
    GRAY_CNT(0) := CNTR_VALUE(0);

    for K in 1 to NBITS–1 loop
      GRAY_CNT (K) := CNTR_VALUE(K–1) xor CNTR_VALUE(K);
    end loop;

    Q <= GRAY_CNT;
    QN <= not GRAY_CNT;
  end process COUNTER_PROCESS;
end BEHAVIOR;
```

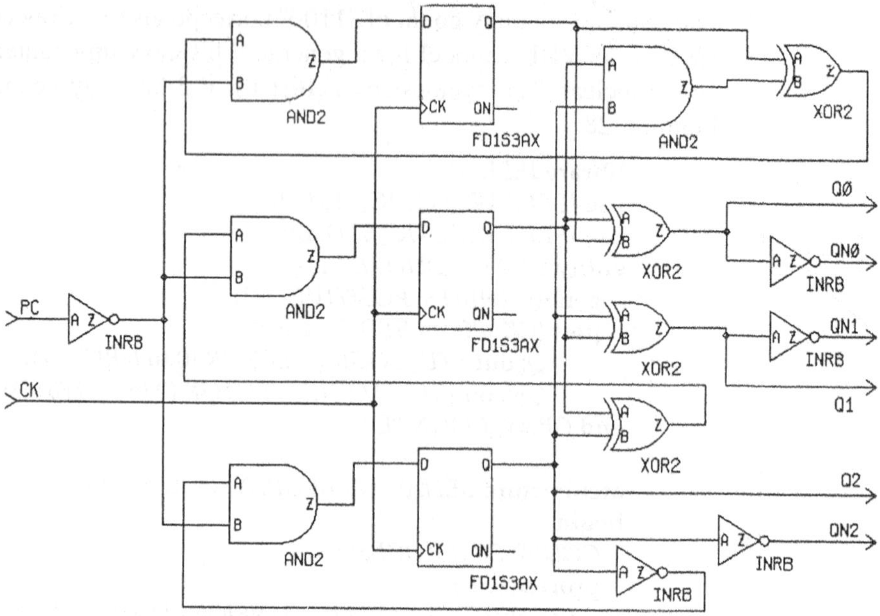

Figure 6-28 A 3-bit Gray counter.

6.17 Modeling a Generic Adder

Here is a model for a generic *N*-bit adder with carry input and output. The rightmost bit is the most significant bit. Figure 6-29 shows the synthesized netlist for a 3-bit adder with carry-in and carry-out.

```
library IEEE;
use IEEE.STD_LOGIC_1164.all;
entity ADD_CI_CO is
  generic (NBITS: POSITIVE := 3);
  port (A, B: in STD_LOGIC_VECTOR (1 to NBITS);
      CI: in STD_LOGIC;
      CO: out STD_LOGIC;
      S: out STD_LOGIC_VECTOR(1 to NBITS));
end ADD_CI_CO;
```

```
architecture BEHAVIOR of ADD_CI_CO is
  signal C: STD_LOGIC_VECTOR(1 to NBITS);
begin
  S <= (A xor B) xor (C(2 to NBITS) & CI);
  C <= ((A xor B) and (C(2 to NBITS) & CI)) or (A and B);
  CO <= C(1);
end BEHAVIOR;
```

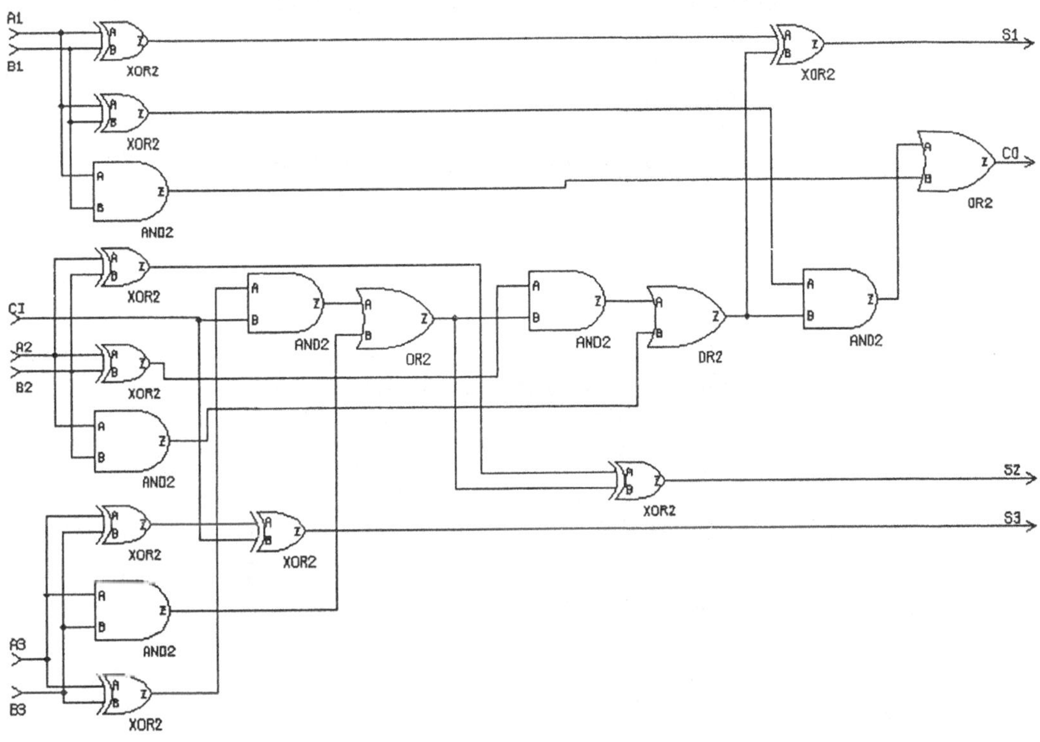

Figure 6-29 A 3-bit adder with carry-in and carry-out.

6.18 Modeling a Generic Comparator

Here is a model for a generic *N*-bit binary comparator. The input vectors are treated as unsigned quantities and a numerical comparison is made. Figure 6-30 shows the synthesized netlist for a 2-bit comparator.

```
library IEEE;
use IEEE.STD_LOGIC_1164.all, IEEE.NUMERIC_STD.all;
entity COMPARATOR is
  generic (NBITS: POSITIVE);
  port (A: in STD_LOGIC_VECTOR (0 to NBITS-1);
        B: in STD_LOGIC_VECTOR (0 to NBITS-1);
        EQ, GT, LT, NE, GE, LE: out STD_LOGIC);
end COMPARATOR;

architecture BEHAVIOR of COMPARATOR is
begin
  COMPARATOR_PROCESS:
  process (A, B)
  begin
    if UNSIGNED(A) > UNSIGNED(B) then
      EQ <= '0';
      GT <= '1';
      LT <= '0';
      NE <= '1';
      GE <= '1';
      LE <= '0';
    elsif UNSIGNED(A) < UNSIGNED(B) then
      EQ <= '0';
      GT <= '0';
      LT <= '1';
      NE <= '1';
      GE <= '0';
      LE <= '1';
    else
      EQ <= '1';
      GT <= '0';
      LT <= '0';
      NE <= '0';
      GE <= '1';
      LE <= '1';
    end if;
  end process COMPARATOR_PROCESS;
end BEHAVIOR;
```

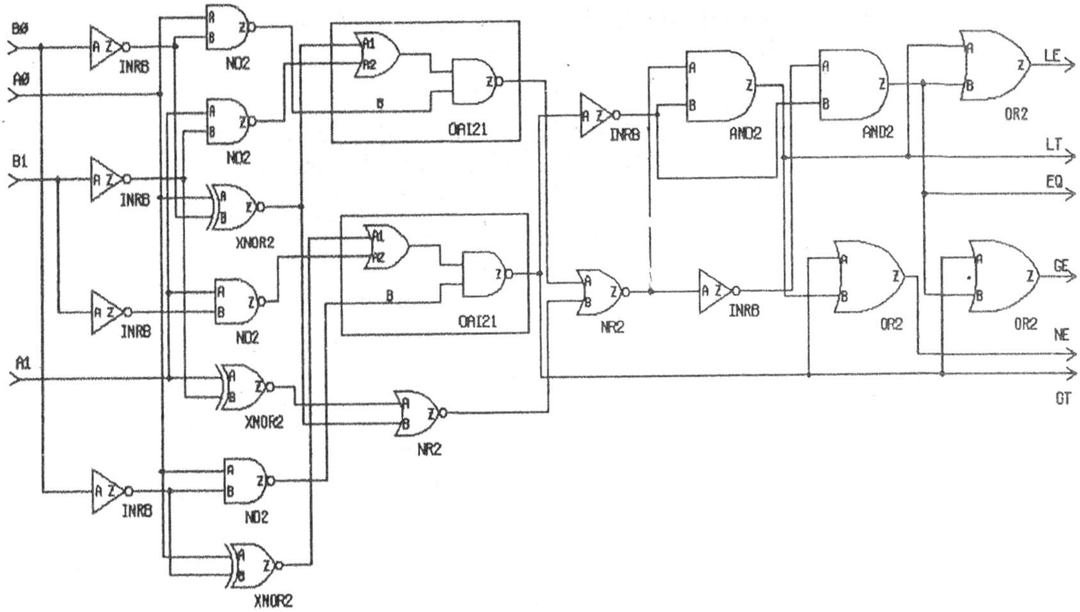

Figure 6-30 A 2-bit comparator.

6.19 Modeling a Generic Decoder

6.19.1 A Simple Decoder

Here is an example of a simple 2-by-4 decoder circuit. This is a combinational circuit modeled purely using concurrent signal assignment statements. The delays specified with the assignment statements are typically ignored by a synthesis system. Figure 6-31 shows the synthesized netlist.

```
library IEEE;
use IEEE.STD_LOGIC_1164.all;
entity DEC is
   port (A, B, ENABLE: in STD_LOGIC;
      Z0, Z1, Z2, Z3: out STD_LOGIC);
end DEC;
```

```
architecture DEC_DF of DEC is
  signal ABAR, BBAR: STD_LOGIC;
begin
  ABAR <= not A after 1 ns;
  BBAR <= not B after 1 ns;
  Z0 <= not (ENABLE and ABAR and BBAR) after 2 ns;
  Z1 <= not (ENABLE and ABAR and B) after 2 ns;
  Z2 <= not (ENABLE and A and BBAR) after 2 ns;
  Z3 <= not (ENABLE and A and B) after 2 ns;
end DEC_DF;
```

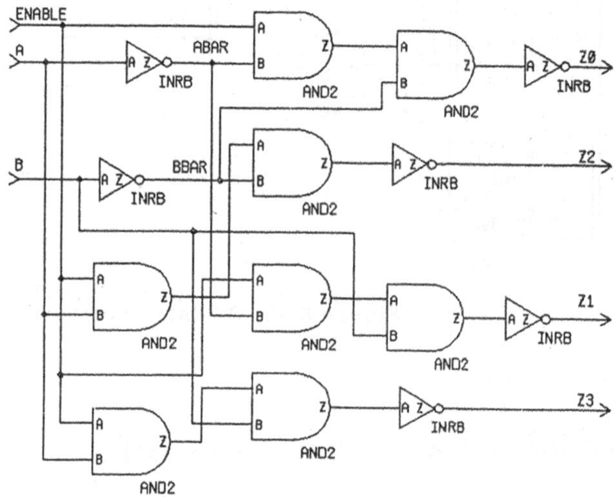

Figure 6-31 A simple 2-by-4 decoder.

6.19.2 Binary Decoder

Here is a model of a generic *N*-bit binary decoder. The synthesized circuit for a 2-bit binary decoder is shown in Figure 6-32.

```
library IEEE;
use IEEE.STD_LOGIC_1164.all; use IEEE.NUMERIC_STD.all;
entity BINARY_DECODER is
  generic (SBITS: POSITIVE := 2);
  port (S: in STD_LOGIC_VECTOR (0 to SBITS–1);
        Y: out STD_LOGIC_VECTOR (0 to 2**SBITS–1));
end BINARY_DECODER;
```

```
architecture BEHAVIOR of BINARY_DECODER is
begin
  DECODER_PROCESS:
  process (S)
  begin
    Y <= (others => '0');
    Y(TO_INTEGER(UNSIGNED(S))) <= '1';
  end process DECODER_PROCESS;
end BEHAVIOR;
```

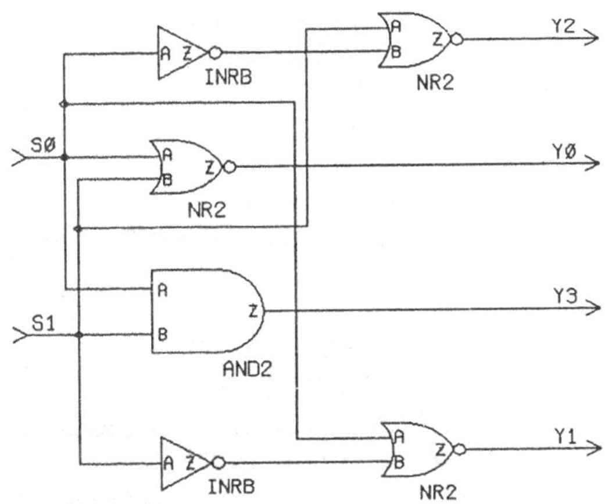

Figure 6-32 A 2-bit binary decoder.

6.19.3 Johnson Decoder

Here is a model of a generic *N*-bit Johnson decoder with an enable control. Figure 6-33 shows the synthesized netlist for a 3-bit Johnson decoder.

```
library IEEE;
use IEEE.STD_LOGIC_1164.all;
entity JOHNSON_DECODER is
  generic (NBITS: POSITIVE);
  port (S: in STD_LOGIC_VECTOR (0 to NBITS-1);
        EN: in STD_LOGIC;
        Y: out STD_LOGIC_VECTOR (0 to 2*NBITS-1));
end JOHNSON_DECODER;
```

```
architecture BEHAVIOR of JOHNSON_DECODER is
begin
  DECODER_PROCESS:
  process (S, EN)
    variable ADDRESS: INTEGER range 0 to 2*NBITS–1;
  begin
    if EN = '1' then          -- Enable signal.
      -- Calculate the output address.
      ADDRESS := 0;

      for K in 0 to NBITS–1 loop
        if S(K) = '1' then
          ADDRESS := ADDRESS + 1;
        end if;
      end loop;

      if S(0) = '1' then
        ADDRESS := 2 * NBITS – ADDRESS;
      end if;

      Y <= (others => '0');
      Y(ADDRESS) <= '1';
    elsif EN = '0' then       -- Enable signal is inactive.
      Y <= (others => '0');
    else                      -- Enable signal is unknown.
      Y <= (others => 'X');
    end if;                   -- End of enable.
  end process DECODER_PROCESS;
end BEHAVIOR;
```

6.20 Modeling a Multiplexer

6.20.1 A Simple Multiplexer

Here is a model of a 4-by-1 multiplexer circuit. In this case, a process statement has been used to model the combinational logic. Figure 6-34 shows the synthesized netlist.

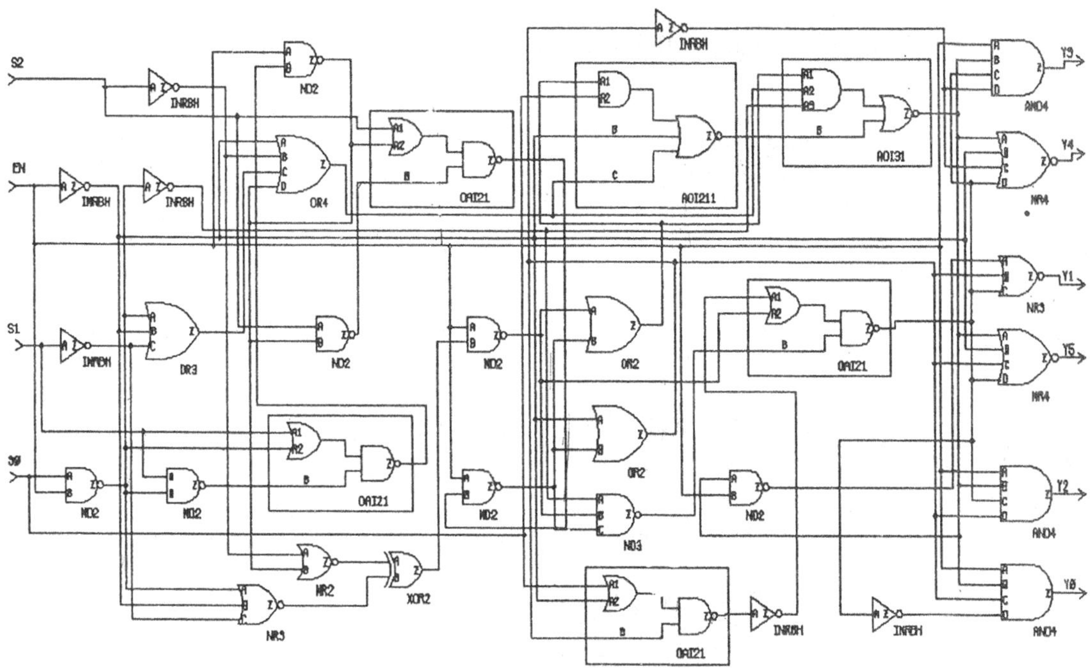

Figure 6-33 A 3-bit Johnson decoder.

```
library IEEE;
use IEEE.STD_LOGIC_1164.all;
entity MUX4x1 is
   port (D: in STD_LOGIC_VECTOR (0 to 3);
         S: in STD_LOGIC_VECTOR (0 to 1);
         Z: out STD_LOGIC);
end MUX4x1;

architecture SEQ_EX of MUX4x1 is
begin
   process (D, S)
   begin
      case S is
         when "00" =>
            Z <= D(0);
         when "01" =>
            Z <= D(1);
         when "10" =>
            Z <= D(2);
```

```
        when "11" =>
          Z <= D(3);
        when others =>
          Z <= 'X';
      end case;
    end process;
  end SEQ_EX;
```

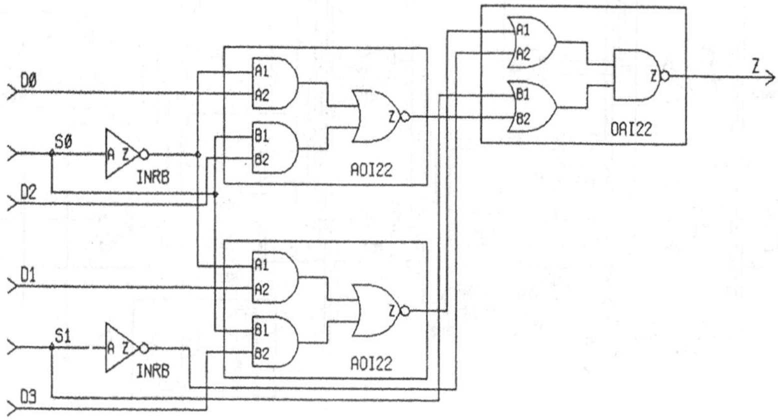

Figure 6-34 A 4-by-1 multiplexer.

An alternate way of modeling the simple multiplexer is shown in the following architecture body. The synthesized netlist is identical to the one shown in Figure 6-34.

```
architecture SIMPLER of MUX4x1 is
begin
  Z <= D(TO_INTEGER(UNSIGNED(S)));
end SIMPLER;
```

6.20.2 A Generic Multiplexer

Here is a model of a generic multiplexer. The number of bits per word and the number of words in the multiplexer are modeled as constants in a package. The multiplexer has inverted select lines, an enable signal, and the select lines are non-encoded. The inverted outputs are also provided. The synthesized netlist of a 2-by-2 (2 words of 2 bits per word) multiplexer is shown in Figure 6-35.

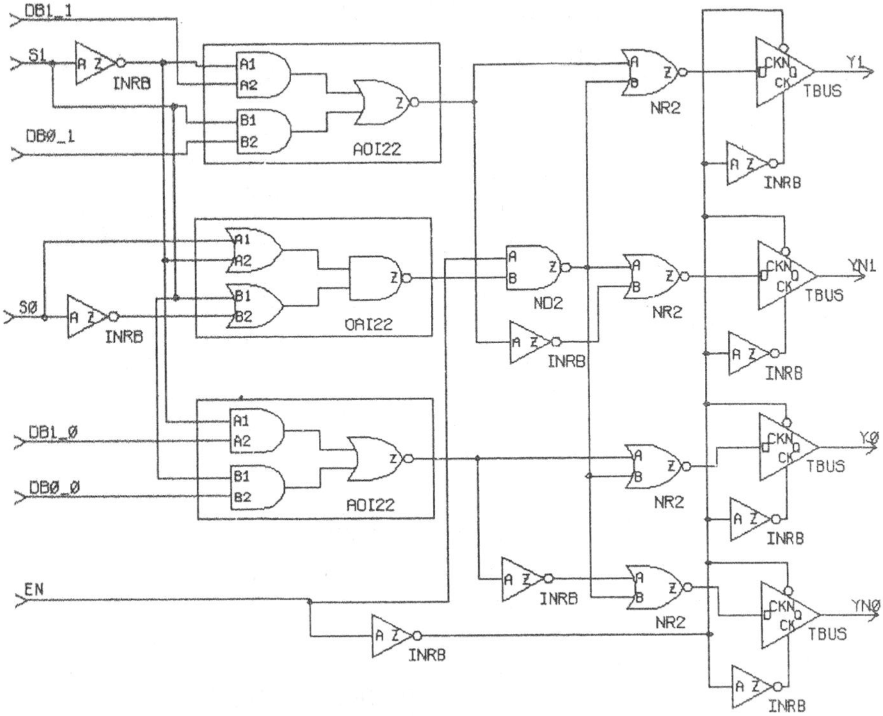

Figure 6-35 A 2-by-2 binary multiplexer.

```
library IEEE;
use IEEE.STD_LOGIC_1164.all;
package TYPES is
  constant NBITS: NATURAL := 2;
  constant WORDS: NATURAL := 2;
  type MUX_TYPE is array (WORDS–1 downto 0) of
      STD_LOGIC_VECTOR (NBITS–1 downto 0);
end;

use WORK.TYPES.all;
library IEEE;
use IEEE.STD_LOGIC_1164.all;
entity BINARY_MULTIPLEXER is
  port (DB: in MUX_TYPE;
      S: in STD_LOGIC_VECTOR (WORDS–1 downto 0);
      EN: in STD_LOGIC;
      Y: out STD_LOGIC_VECTOR (NBITS–1 downto 0);
```

```
    YN: out STD_LOGIC_VECTOR (NBITS-1 downto 0));
end BINARY_MULTIPLEXER;

architecture BEHAVIOR of BINARY_MULTIPLEXER is
begin
  MULTIPLEXER_PROCESS:
  process (DB, S, EN)
    procedure EXACT_ONE_ZERO_AND_POSITION_IN_VECTOR
        (INP: STD_LOGIC_VECTOR(WORDS-1 downto 0);
         VALID: out BOOLEAN;
         POSITION: out NATURAL) is
      variable NUMBER_OF_ZEROS:
        NATURAL range 0 to INP'LENGTH;
    begin
      NUMBER_OF_ZEROS := 0;

      for I in INP'RANGE loop
        if INP(I) = '0' then
          NUMBER_OF_ZEROS := NUMBER_OF_ZEROS + 1;
          POSITION := I;
        end if;
      end loop;

      VALID := NUMBER_OF_ZEROS = 1;
    end EXACT_ONE_ZERO_AND_POSITION_IN_VECTOR;

    variable POSITION: NATURAL;
    variable VALID: BOOLEAN;
    variable Y_TEMP: STD_LOGIC_VECTOR(NBITS-1 downto (
  begin
    if EN = '1' then
      EXACT_ONE_ZERO_AND_POSITION_IN_VECTOR
        (S, VALID, POSITION)·

      if VALID then
        Y_TEMP := DB(POSITION);
        Y <= Y_TEMP;
        YN <= not Y_TEMP;
      else
        Y <= (others => 'X');
        YN <= (others => 'X');
      end if;
    elsif EN = '0' then                -- When enable is inactive
```

```
    Y <= (others => 'Z');
    YN <= (others => 'Z');
  else                          -- When enable is unknown.
    Y <= (others => 'X');
    YN <= (others => 'X');
  end if;
 end process MULTIPLEXER_PROCESS;
end BEHAVIOR;
```

6.21 Modeling a Generic Parity Generator Circuit

Here is a model of a generic *N*-bit parity generator circuit. The model provides both an odd parity and an even parity output. Figure 6-36 shows the synthesized netlist of a 4-bit parity generator.

```
library IEEE;
use IEEE.STD_LOGIC_1164.all;
entity PARITY is
  generic (NBITS: POSITIVE := 4);
  port (D: in STD_LOGIC_VECTOR (NBITS-1 downto 0);
       ODF: out STD_LOGIC;
       EDF: out STD_LOGIC);
end PARITY;

architecture BEHAVIOR of PARITY is
begin
  PARITY_PROCESS:
  process (D)
    function NUMBER_OF_ONES
         (INP: in STD_LOGIC_VECTOR) return NATURAL is
      variable NMB: NATURAL range 0 to INP'LENGTH;
    begin
      NMB := 0;

      for K in INP'RANGE loop
        if INP(K) = '1' then
          NMB := NMB + 1;
        end if;
      end loop;

      return NMB;
```

```
    end NUMBER_OF_ONES;
  begin
    if (NUMBER_OF_ONES(D) rem 2) = 0 then
      ODF <= '1';
      EDF <= '0';
    else
      ODF <= '0';
      EDF <= '1';
    end if;
  end process PARITY_PROCESS;
end BEHAVIOR;
```

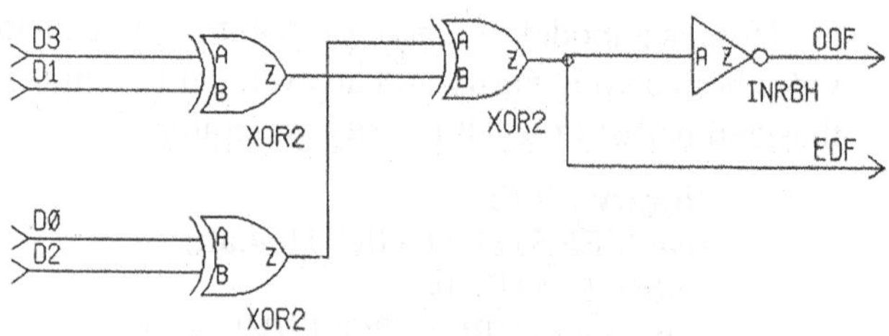

Figure 6-36 A 4-bit parity generator.

6.22 Modeling a Tri-state Gate

A tri-state gate is modeled by assigning a high-impedance value (Z) to a signal under the control of a condition. Here is an example.

```
library IEEE;
use IEEE.STD_LOGIC_1164.all;
entity TRISTATE is
  port (READ_STATE: in BOOLEAN;
        CPU_BUS: in STD_LOGIC_VECTOR (0 to 3);
        MAIN_BUS: out STD_LOGIC_VECTOR (0 to 3));
end TRISTATE;

architecture BANK of TRISTATE is
begin
  process (READ_STATE, CPU_BUS)
  begin
    if READ_STATE then        -- If CPU is in READ state.
```

```
      MAIN_BUS <= (others => 'Z');
    else
      MAIN_BUS <= CPU_BUS;
    end if;
  end process;
end BANK;
```

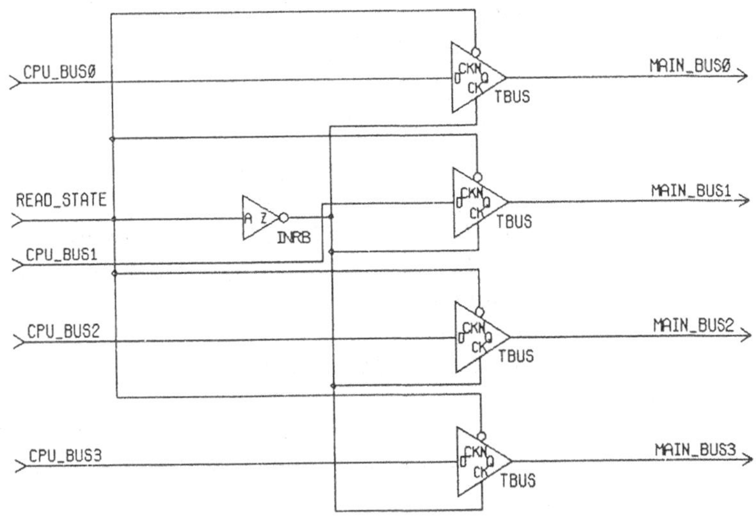

Figure 6-37 A bank of tri-state gates.

The synthesized netlist is shown in Figure 6-37. The signal *MAIN_BUS* is tristate'ed as long as *READ_STATE* is true. If *READ_STATE* is false, the value of *CPU_BUS* is assigned to *MAIN_BUS*.

6.23 A Count Three 1's Model

Here is a model that detects three 1's in an input data stream appearing on signal *DATA*. This signal is checked on every falling clock edge. If three consecutive 1's are found on the input, the output is set to *TRUE*, else it is set to *FALSE*.

```
entity COUNT3_1S is
  port (DATA, CLOCK, RESET: in BIT;
        SEQ_FOUND: out BOOLEAN);
```

```
end COUNT3_1S;

architecture SEQUENTIAL_BEHAVIOR of COUNT3_1S is
begin
  process
    constant PATTERN_SEARCHED_FOR:
      BIT_VECTOR (2 downto 0) := "111";
    variable PREVIOUS: BIT_VECTOR (2 downto 0);
  begin
    wait until CLOCK = '0';

    if RESET = '1' then
      PREVIOUS := "000";
      SEQ_FOUND <= FALSE;
    else
      PREVIOUS := PREVIOUS (1 downto 0) & DATA;
      SEQ_FOUND <= PREVIOUS = PATTERN_SEARCHED_FOR;
    end if;
  end process;
end SEQUENTIAL_BEHAVIOR;
```

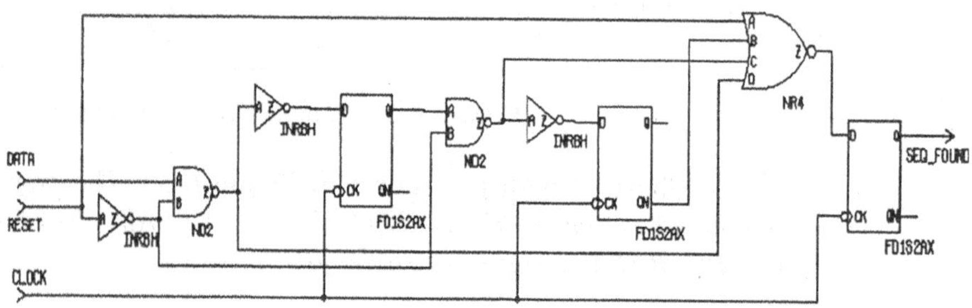

Figure 6-38 *COUNT3_1S* synthesized circuit.

Synthesis infers four flip-flops for this model, three for variable *PREVIOUS* and one for *SEQ_FOUND*. However, optimization reveals that one of the flip-flops for *PREVIOUS* is not necessary and hence it is removed. See Figure 6-38 for the synthesized netlist. In this model, the output is latched since it is assigned a value under the control of a clock edge. If a latched output is not desired, then the assignment to *SEQ_FOUND* must be done outside the process statement. Such an architecture is shown next.

```
architecture NO_LATCHED_OUTPUT of COUNT3_1S is
  constant PATTERN_SEARCHED_FOR:
    BIT_VECTOR (2 downto 0) := "111";
  signal PREVIOUS: BIT_VECTOR (2 downto 0);
begin
  process
  begin
    wait until CLOCK = '0';

    if RESET = '1' then
      PREVIOUS <= "000";
    else
      PREVIOUS <= PREVIOUS (1 downto 0) & DATA;
    end if;
  end process;

  SEQ_FOUND <= PREVIOUS = PATTERN_SEARCHED_FOR;
end NO_LATCHED_OUTPUT;
```

In this architecture, the output *SEQ_FOUND* is not latched. Synthesis infers three flip-flops for signal *PREVIOUS*; note that in this case, *PREVIOUS* is a signal and all the bit values need to be latched. The synthesized netlist for this architecture is shown in Figure 6-39.

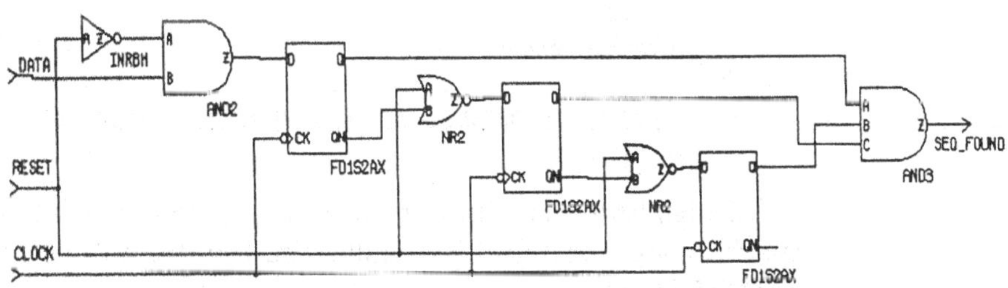

Figure 6-39 No latched output.

6.24 A Timer Model

In this model, the number of clock pulses (rising clock edge) is counted between the *START* and *STOP* signals. If the count equals 16, an overflow flag is set. Signal *RESET* going active low resets the counter to 0.

```
library IEEE;
use IEEE.STD_LOGIC_1164.all, IEEE.NUMERIC_STD.all;
entity TIMER is
  port (CLK, RESET: in STD_LOGIC;
        START, STOP: in BOOLEAN;
        OVERFLOW: out BOOLEAN;
        PULSE_COUNT: out UNSIGNED (3 downto 0));
end TIMER;

architecture PULSES of TIMER is
    signal PCNT: INTEGER range 0 to 15;
begin
  process (RESET, CLK)
  begin
    if RESET = '0' then
      PCNT <= 0;
      OVERFLOW <= FALSE;
    elsif CLK = '1' and CLK'EVENT then
      if START and (not STOP) then
        if PCNT = 15 then
          OVERFLOW <= TRUE;
        else
          PCNT <= PCNT + 1;
        end if;
      end if;
    end if;
  end process;

  PULSE_COUNT <= TO_UNSIGNED (PCNT, 4);
end PULSES;
```

The synthesized netlist is shown in Figure 6-40. Note that there are four asynchronous clear flip-flops synthesized for the pulse counter *CNT*, and one for *OVERFLOW*.

6.25 A Factorial Model

Here is a model that generates the factorial of a number given in *DATA*. The result is output in *FAC_OUT* and *EXP_OUT* as mantissa and exponent respectively. The exponent is base 2. The signal *RESET* causes the model to reset.

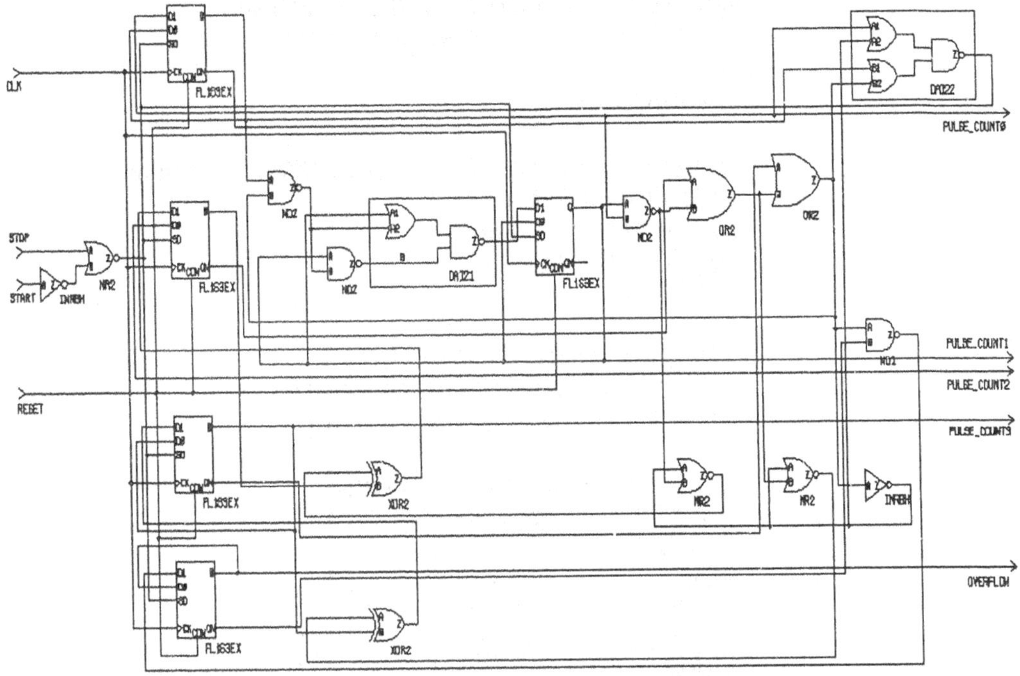

Figure 6-40 Netlist for timer circuit.

```
library IEEE;
use IEEE.STD_LOGIC_1164.all, IEEE.NUMERIC_STD.all;
entity FACEXP is
  port (RESET,                          -- Reset signal for calculation
        START,                          -- Start signal for calculation
        CLK: in STD_LOGIC;                          -- Clock signal
        DATA: in UNSIGNED (4 downto 0);             -- Input data
        DONE: out STD_LOGIC; -- Acknowledge signal for operation
        FAC_OUT,                                    -- Factorial
        EXP_OUT: out UNSIGNED (7 downto 0));        -- Exponent
end;

architecture FACEXP of FACEXP is
  signal STOP: STD_LOGIC;           -- Control signal for multiplication
  signal IN_LATCH: UNSIGNED (4 downto 0);   -- Input register
  signal EXPONENT,                          -- Exponent of result
         RESULT: UNSIGNED (7 downto 0);     -- Output register
begin
```

```
process
  variable RES_T, NXTRES_T, INL_T, NXTINL_T,
        EXP_T: INTEGER range 0 to 1024;
begin
  wait until CLK = '1';

  if ((START = '1') and (STOP = '1')) or (RESET = '1') then
    RESULT <= "00000001";
    EXPONENT <= (others => '0');
    IN_LATCH <= DATA;
    STOP <= '0';
  else
    RES_T := TO_INTEGER (RESULT);
    EXP_T := TO_INTEGER (EXPONENT);
    INL_T := TO_INTEGER (IN_LATCH);

    if (INL_T > 1) and (STOP = '0') then
      NXTRES_T := RES_T * INL_T;
      NXTINL_T := INL_T - 1;
    else
      NXTRES_T := RES_T;
      NXTINL_T := INL_T;
    end if;

    if INL_T <= 1 then
      STOP <= '1';
    end if;

    -- Normalization:
    for K in 1 to 5 loop
      if NXTRES_T > 256 then
        NXTRES_T := NXTRES_T / 2;
        EXP_T := EXP_T + 1;
      end if;
    end loop;

    RESULT <= TO_UNSIGNED (NXTRES_T, RESULT 'LENGTH);
    EXPONENT <= TO_UNSIGNED (EXP_T,
                        EXPONENT 'LENGTH);
    IN_LATCH <= TO_UNSIGNED (NXTINL_T,
                        IN_LATCH 'LENGTH);
  end if;
end process;
```

```
    DONE <= STOP;
    FAC_OUT <= RESULT;
    EXP_OUT <= EXPONENT;
  end FACEXP;
```

When synthesized, flip-flops are inferred for signals *IN_LATCH*, *RESULT*, *EXPONENT* and *STOP*.

6.26 A Car Controller Model

A generic model of a car controller is described here. The generic *N* models the number of steps allowed for the speed to increase (or decrease). If *BRAKE* is '1', then on every rising clock edge, the speed gradually decreases to 0. If *ACCELERATOR* is '1' and *BRAKE* is '0', then on every rising clock edge, the speed gradually increases by one step. The car speed is reset to 0 if *RESET* is '1'.

```
library IEEE;
use IEEE.STD_LOGIC_1164.all, IEEE.NUMERIC_STD.all;
entity CAR_CTR is
  generic (N: POSITIVE := 2);
  port ( ACCELERATOR, BRAKE, RESET, CLK: in STD_LOGIC;
         SPEED: out STD_LOGIC_VECTOR (N–1 downto 0));
end CAR_CTR;

architecture BEHAVIOR of CAR_CTR is
  signal SPEED_INTERNAL: UNSIGNED (N–1 downto 0);
begin
  process (CLK, RESET)
  begin
    if RESET = '1' then
      SPEED_INTERNAL <= (others => '0');
    elsif CLK = '1' and CLK'EVENT then
      if BRAKE = '1' then
        if SPEED_INTERNAL > 0 then
          SPEED_INTERNAL <= SPEED_INTERNAL – 1;
        end if;
      elsif ACCELERATOR = '1' then
        if SPEED_INTERNAL < 2 ** N–1 then
          SPEED_INTERNAL <= SPEED_INTERNAL + 1;
```

```
          end if;
        end if;
      end if;
    end process;

    SPEED <= STD_LOGIC_VECTOR(SPEED_INTERNAL);
  end BEHAVIOR;
```

The synthesized netlist for a car controller with $N = 2$ is shown in Figure 6-41. Note that there are two asynchronous clear flip-flops synthesized for signal *SPEED_INTERNAL*.

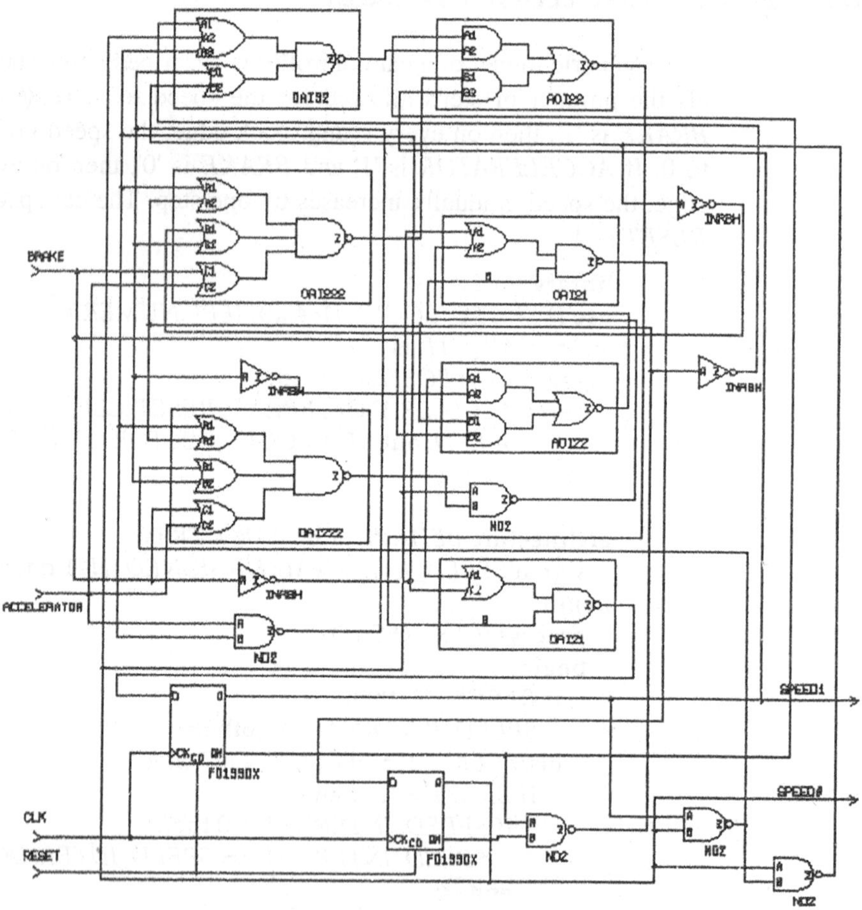

Figure 6-41 A car controller circuit.

6.27 A UART Model

Here is a model of a complete UART circuit that can be synthesized. This circuit converts RS-232 serial input data into parallel data out, and the parallel input data into RS-232 serial data out. The data byte is 8 bits in length. There are four major blocks in this UART model, as shown in Figure 6-42: *RX*, the receiver block, *TX*, the transmitter block, *DIV*, the clock divider and *MP*, the microprocessor block.

The first block *DIV* is a frequency divider. This block has 2 modes of operation, the normal mode and the test mode. In the test mode, the UART chip runs 16 times faster than in the normal mode. Also, the transmission data rate of the UART chip is 16 times faster than the receiving rate. Each block is initialized by setting the reset line low by applying a '0' to port *MR*. The *TX* block accepts 8-bit parallel data from the microprocessor interface (*MP*) block and transmits it serially to the RS-232 port through port *DOUT*. Conversely, the *RX* block receives serial data input, and sends it in 8-bit parallel format to the *MP* block. Again, the transmitter runs at 16 times the speed of the receiver. The microprocessor interface (*MP*) block asynchronously controls the parallel data flow between the *RX* / *TX* blocks and the microprocessor data bus.

The *UART* top-level model glues all these blocks together using component instantiations. The microprocessor entity, *MP*, is described in the structural style, that is, using components. The remaining three are described using the behavioral style. The UART top-level model follows.

```
library IEEE, SYNTH;
use IEEE.STD_LOGIC_1164.all;
use SYNTH.GENERIC_COMP.all; -- Include component declarations.
entity UART is
  port (DIN, CLK, MR, AS, WRN, RDN, CSN,
        TEST: in STD_LOGIC;
        UDIN: in STD_LOGIC_VECTOR (0 to 7);
        INTQN, DOUT: out STD_LOGIC;
        UDOUT: out STD_LOGIC_VECTOR (0 to 7));
end UART;

architecture TOP_LEVEL of UART is
  -- The major building blocks:
  component DIV
    port (CK, RESET, TSN: in STD_LOGIC;
```

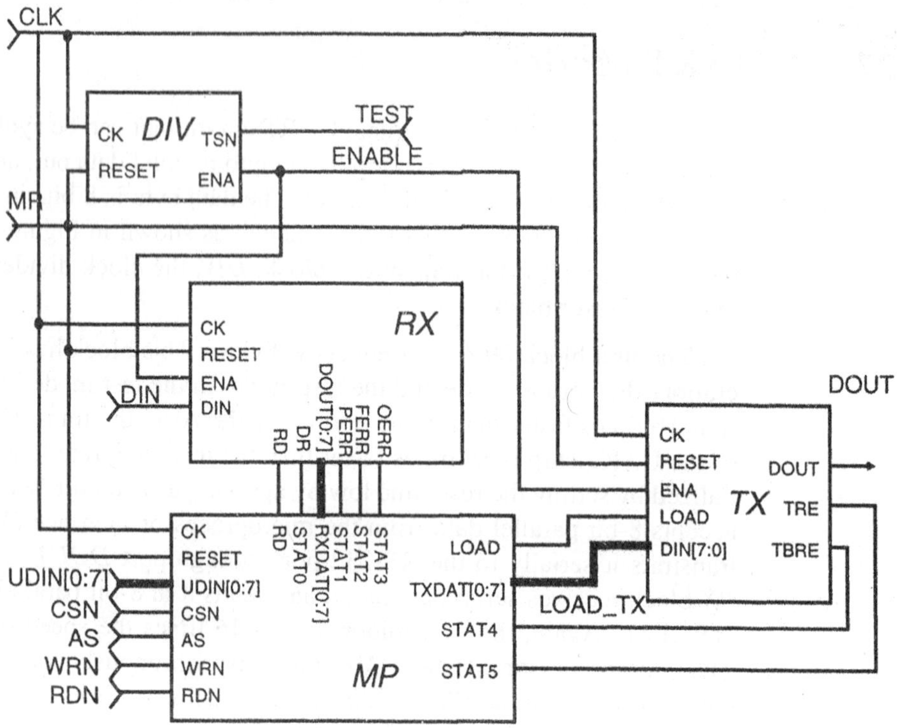

Figure 6-42 The UART circuit.

```
        ENA: out STD_LOGIC);
end component;
component RX
   port (CK, RESET, ENA, DIN, RD: in STD_LOGIC;
        DOUTO: out STD_LOGIC_VECTOR (0 to 7);
        DRO, PERRO, FERRO, OERRO: out STD_LOGIC);
end component;
component TX
   port (CK, RESET, ENABLE, TLOAD: in STD_LOGIC;
        DIN: in STD_LOGIC_VECTOR (0 to 7);
        DOUT, TRE, TBRE: out STD_LOGIC);
end component;
component MP
   port (CK, RESET, CSN, AS, WRN, RDN: in STD_LOGIC;
        UDIN, RXDAT: in STD_LOGIC_VECTOR(0 to 7);
        STAT: in STD_LOGIC_VECTOR(0 to 5);
        LOADVE: inout STD_LOGIC;
```

```
        TXDAT: out STD_LOGIC_VECTOR(0 to 7);
        RD: inout STD_LOGIC;
        INTQN: out STD_LOGIC;
        UDOUT: out STD_LOGIC_VECTOR (0 to 7));
end component;

for all: DIV use entity WORK.DIV(DIV_BEH);
for all: RX use entity WORK.RX(RX_BEH);
for all: TX use entity WORK.TX(TX_BEH);
for all: MP use entity WORK.MP;
for all: BUF use entity SYNTH.BUF;
for all: INRB use entity SYNTH.INRB;

signal CKI, LINE_IN, MRIN, TESTBUF, T_DOUT, CK, RESET,
     TESTN, ENABLE, CKIN, MRINN, RX_READY, R_PERR,
     R_FERR, R_OERR, T_TBRE, TX_BUSYN, LOAD_TX,
     READ_RX: STD_LOGIC;
signal R_DOUT, M_TXDAT: STD_LOGIC_VECTOR(0 to 7);
signal STAT: STD_LOGIC_VECTOR(0 to 5);
begin
  LCLKBUF: BUF port map (CLK, CKI);
  LDINBUF: BUF port map (DIN, LINE_IN);
  LMRBUF: BUF port map (MR, MRIN);
  LTESTBUF: BUF port map (TEST, TESTBUF);
  LDOUT: BUF port map (T_DOUT, DOUT);
  LD: DIV port map (CK, RESET, TESTN, ENABLE);
  LCK: INRB port map (CKIN, CK);
  LRESET: INRB port map (MRINN, RESET);
  LCKG1: INRB port map (CKI, CKIN);
  LMRG1: INRB port map (MRIN, MRINN);
  LTESTN: INRB port map (TESTBUF, TESTN);
  LM: MP port map (CK => CK, RESET => RESET, CSN => CSN,
      AS => AS, WRN => WRN, RDN => RDN, UDIN => UDIN,
      RXDAT => R_DOUT, STAT(0) => RX_READY,
      STAT(1) => R_PERR,
      STAT(2) => R_FERR, STAT(3) => R_OERR, STAT(4) => T_TBRE,
      STAT(5) => TX_BUSYN, LOADVE => LOAD_TX,
      TXDAT => M_TXDAT, RD => READ_RX, INTQN => INTQN,
      UDOUT => UDOUT);
  LR: RX port map (CK, RESET, ENABLE, LINE_IN, READ_RX,
      R_DOUT, RX_READY, R_PERR, R_FERR, R_OERR);
  LT: TX port map (CK, RESET, ENABLE, LOAD_TX,
```

```
        M_TXDAT, T_DOUT, TX_BUSYN, T_TBRE);
end TOP_LEVEL;
```

The microprocessor block *MP* is described next. This is a block described entirely using components, that is, it is described at the structural level.

```
library IEEE;
use IEEE.STD_LOGIC_1164.all;
entity MP is
  port (CK, RESET, CSN, AS, WRN, RDN: in STD_LOGIC;
        UDIN, RXDAT: in STD_LOGIC_VECTOR (0 to 7);
        STAT: in STD_LOGIC_VECTOR (0 to 5);
        LOADVE: inout STD_LOGIC;
        TXDAT: out STD_LOGIC_VECTOR (0 to 7);
        RD: inout STD_LOGIC;
        INTQN: out STD_LOGIC;
        UDOUT: out STD_LOGIC_VECTOR (0 to 7));
end MP;

library SYNTH;
use SYNTH.GENERIC_COMP.all;
architecture MP_STR of MP is
  for all: AND2 use entity SYNTH.AND2;
  for all: BN20T20D use entity SYNTH.BN20T20D;
  for all: FD1P3AX use entity SYNTH.FD1P3AX;
  for all: FD1S1A use entity SYNTH.FD1S1A;
  for all: FD1S3EX use entity SYNTH.FD1S3EX;
  for all: FS0S1D use entity SYNTH.FS0S1D;
  for all: INRB use entity SYNTH.INRB;
  for all: ND2 use entity SYNTH.ND2;
  for all: NR2 use entity SYNTH.NR2;
  for all: NR3 use entity SYNTH.NR3;
  for all: XOR2Z use entity SYNTH.XOR2Z;
  for all: BUF use entity SYNTH.BUF;
  for all: OR2 use entity SYNTH.OR2;
  for all: AOI22 use entity SYNTH.AOI22;

  signal QB_Q, QA_QN, ENAFFO, QA_Q, RESLOG, WRT, ENA42,
      SETLOG, ENA40, RDT, STADRI, ASBUF, CSBUF, RDBUF,
      WRBUF, RDTE, XOLD_Z, UC_LOAD_QN, PRELOAD_Q,
      UC_PRELOAD_QN, LOG_Q, UC_QB_QN, RESETN,
      UC_LOG_QN, UC_XOLD_Z1, QC, QD, RDSYNFB, ENA41,
      RDTLOG, RXDRI, INTN, ORINT, UC_INTFF_Q, RDSYN,
      UC_QC_QN, UC_QD_QN, XORD_Z, UC_QE_QN,
```

```
        UC_RDSYN_QN, UC_XORD_Z1
          : STD_LOGIC;
    signal BUSOUT, INVOUT, DATIN, UPD_Q, RXG, UC_UPD_QN,
        UC_A_QN, A, UC_DAT_QN: STD_LOGIC_VECTOR (0 to 7);
    signal SG: STD_LOGIC_VECTOR(0 to 5);
    signal DEC: STD_LOGIC_VECTOR (0 to 9);
begin
    LENAFFO: AND2 port map (QB_Q, QA_QN, ENAFFO);
    LRESLOG: AND2 port map (QB_Q, QA_Q, RESLOG);
    LSETLOG: AND2 port map (WRT, ENA42, SETLOG);
    LSTADRI: AND2 port map (ENA40, RDT, STADRI);
    LASBUF: BUF port map (AS, ASBUF);
    LCSBUF: BUF port map (CSN, CSBUF);
    LRDBUF: BUF port map (RDN, RDBUF);
    LWRBUF: BUF port map (WRN, WRBUF);

    G0: for J in 0 to 7 generate
      LADBUF: BN20T20D port map (BUSOUT(J), RDTE, INVOUT(J),
              UDIN(J), DATIN(7–J), UDOUT(J));
      LDAT: FD1P3AX port map (UPD_Q(J), ENAFFO, CK,
            TXDAT(J), UC_DAT_QN(J));
      LA: FD1S1A port map (DATIN(7–J), ASBUF, A(J), UC_A_QN(J));
      LUPD: FD1S1A port map (DATIN(7–J), WRT, UPD_Q(J),
            UC_UPD_QN(J));
      LINVOUT: INRB port map (RDTE, INVOUT(J));
      LRXG: INRB port map (RXDAT(J), RXG(J));
    end generate G0;

    LLOAD: FD1S3EX port map (XOLD_Z, CK, RESET, LOADVE,
            UC_LOAD_QN);
    LPRELOAD: FD1S3EX port map (QB_Q, CK, RESET, PRELOAD_Q,
              UC_PRELOAD_QN);
    LQA: FD1S3EX port map (LOG_Q, CK, RESET, QA_Q, QA_QN);
    LQB: FD1S3EX port map (QA_Q, CK, RESET, QB_Q, UC_QB_QN);
    LLOG: FS0S1D port map (SETLOG, RESLOG, RESETN,
          LOG_Q, UC_LOG_QN);
    LDEC3: INRB port map (DEC(1), DEC(3));
    LDEC4: ND2 port map (DEC(1), A(1), DEC(4));
    LDEC5: ND2 port map (DEC(2), A(6), DEC(5));
    LDEC7: NR2 port map (DEC(4), DEC(5), ENA42);
    LWRT: NR2 port map (CSBUF, WRBUF, WRT);
    LRDT1: NR2 port map (CSBUF, RDBUF, RDT);
    LRDT2: NR2 port map (CSBUF, RDBUF, RDTE);
```

```
LDEC1: NR3 port map (A(0), A(2), A(3), DEC(1));
LDEC2: NR3 port map (A(4), A(5), A(7), DEC(2));
LDEC6: NR3 port map (DEC(5), DEC(3), A(1), ENA40);
LXOLD: XOR2Z port map (LOADVE, PRELOAD_Q, XOLD_Z,
        UC_XOLD_Z1);
LRDSUNFB: AND2 port map (QC, QD, RDSYNFB);
LRDTLOG: AND2 port map (RDT, ENA41, RDTLOG);
LRXDRI: AND2 port map (ENA41, RDT, RXDRI);
LINTQ: BUF port map (INTN, INTQN);
LINTFF: FD1S3EX port map (ORINT, CK, RESET, UC_INTFF_Q,
        INTN);
LQC: FD1S3EX port map (RDSYN, CK, RESET, QC, UC_QC_QN);
LQD: FD1S3EX port map (QC, CK, RESET, QD, UC_QD_QN);
LQE: FD1S3EX port map (XORD_Z, CK, RESET, RD, UC_QE_QN);
LRDSYN: FS0S1D port map (RDTLOG, RDSYNFB, RESETN,
        RDSYN, UC_RDSYN_QN);
LRESETN: INRB port map (RESET, RESETN);

G1: for J in 0 to 5 generate
  LSG: INRB port map (STAT(J), SG(J));
  LMUX: AOI22 port map (RXG(J), RXDRI, SG(J), STADRI,
        BUSOUT(J));
end generate G1;

LDEC9: ND2 port map (DEC(8), A(0), DEC(9));
LDEC10: NR2 port map (DEC(5), DEC(9), ENA41);
LDEC8: NR3 port map (A(1), A(2), A(3), DEC(8));
LORINT: OR2 port map (STAT(0), STAT(4), ORINT);
LMUX6: ND2 port map (RXG(6), RXDRI, BUSOUT(6));
LMUX7: ND2 port map (RXG(7), RXDRI, BUSOUT(7));
LXORD: XOR2Z port map (RD, QD, XORD_Z, UC_XORD_Z1);
end MP_STR;
```

Here is the behavioral model for the transmitter block *TX*. This model is a synthesizable model. Rising-edge-triggered flip-flops are inferred for signals *TBR*, *TR*, *STRE*, *STBRE*, *DOUT*, *CBIT* and *PA*; this is because these signals are assigned values under the control of clock *CK*.

```
library IEEE;
use IEEE.STD_LOGIC_1164.all, IEEE.NUMERIC_STD.all;
entity TX is
  port (CK, RESET, ENABLE, TLOAD: in STD_LOGIC;
      DIN: in STD_LOGIC_VECTOR(7 downto 0);
      DOUT,
```

```
      TRE,    -- Tx reg empty.
      TBRE    -- Tx buf empty.
        : out STD_LOGIC);
end TX;

architecture TX_BEH of TX is
  signal TBR, TR: STD_LOGIC_VECTOR(7 downto 0);
  signal CBIT: UNSIGNED(3 downto 0);
  signal PA: STD_LOGIC;
  signal STBRE: STD_LOGIC;
  signal STRE: STD_LOGIC;
begin
  process (CK, RESET, ENABLE, TLOAD, DIN, TBR, TR, CBIT,
           PA, STBRE, STRE)
    variable TEMP_TRE: STD_LOGIC;
    constant CONE: UNSIGNED(3 downto 0) := "0001";
  begin
    if RISING_EDGE(CK) then
      if RESET = '0' then
        STRE <= '1';
        STBRE <= '1';
        DOUT <= '1';
        CBIT <= "0000";
        PA <= '0';
      else
        if TLOAD = '1' then
          TBR <= DIN;
          STBRE <= '0';
        else
          if ENABLE = '1' then
            if (STBRE = '0') and (STRE = '1') then
              TR <= TBR;
              STRE <= '0';
              TEMP_TRE := '0';
              STBRE <= '1';
            else
              TEMP_TRE := STRE;
            end if;

            if TEMP_TRE = '0' then
              case CBIT is
                when "0000" =>
                  DOUT <= '0';
```

```
                    CBIT <= CBIT + CONE;
                  when "0001" | "0010" | "0011" |
                      "0100" | "0101" | "0110" |
                      "0111" | "1000" =>
                    DOUT <= TR(0);
                    PA <= PA xor TR(0);
                    TR <= '1' & TR(7 downto 1);
                    CBIT <= CBIT + CONE;
                  when "1001" =>
                    DOUT <= PA;
                    PA <= '0';
                    TR <= '1' & TR(7 downto 1);
                    CBIT <= CBIT + CONE;
                  when "1010" =>
                    DOUT <= TR(0);
                    TR <= '1' & TR(7 downto 1);
                    CBIT <= CBIT + CONE;
                  when "1011" =>
                    DOUT <= TR(0);
                    STRE <= '1';
                    TR <= '1' & TR(7 downto 1);
                    CBIT <= "0000";
                  when others =>
                    null;
                end case;
              end if;
            end if;
          end if;
        end if;
      end if;
    end process;

    TRE <= STRE;
    TBRE <= STBRE;
  end TX_BEH;
```

Here is the behavioral model for the receiver block *RX*. This model is also synthesizable. Flip-flops are inferred for signals *START*, *CBIT*, *CSAM*, *DI*, *PI*, *SR*, *DR*, *DOUT*, *PERR*, *FERR* and *OERR*.

```
library IEEE;
use IEEE.STD_LOGIC_1164.all;
use IEEE.NUMERIC_STD.all;
entity RX is
  port (CK, RESET, ENA, DIN, RD: in STD_LOGIC;
        DOUTO: out STD_LOGIC_VECTOR (7 downto 0);
        DRO, PERRO, FERRO, OERRO: out STD_LOGIC);
end RX;

architecture RX_BEH of RX is
  signal START: STD_LOGIC;
  signal CBIT, CSAM: UNSIGNED(3 downto 0);
  signal DI, PI: STD_LOGIC;
  signal SR: STD_LOGIC_VECTOR (7 downto 0);
  signal DR: STD_LOGIC;
  signal DOUT: STD_LOGIC_VECTOR(7 downto 0);
  signal PERR, FERR, OERR: STD_LOGIC;
begin
  process (CK, RESET, ENA, DIN, RD, START, CBIT, CSAM,
           DI, PI, SR, DR, DOUT, PERR, FERR, OERR)
    variable TCBIT, TCSAM: INTEGER range 0 to 15;
    constant CONE: UNSIGNED(3 downto 0) := "0001";
  begin
    if RISING_EDGE(CK) then
      TCBIT := TO_INTEGER (CBIT);
      TCSAM := TO_INTEGER (CSAM);

      if RESET = '0' then  -- Reset.
        CBIT <= "0000";
        CSAM <= "0000";
        START <= '0';
        PI <= '0';
        DR <= '0';
        PERR <= '0';
        FERR <= '0';
        OERR <= '0';
      else
        if RD = '1' then
          DR <= '0';
        end if;

        if ENA = '1' then
          if START = '0' then
```

```
          if DIN = '0' then
            CSAM <= CSAM + CONE;
            START <= '1';
          end if;
        else
          if TCSAM = 8 then
            DI <= DIN;
            CSAM <= CSAM + CONE;
          else
            if TCSAM = 15 then
              case TCBIT is
                when 0 =>
                  if DI = '1' then
                    START <= '0';
                  else
                    CBIT <= CBIT + CONE;
                  end if;
                  CSAM <= CSAM + CONE;
                when 1 | 2 | 3 | 4 | 5 | 6 | 7 | 8 =>
                  CBIT <= CBIT + CONE;
                  CSAM <= CSAM + CONE;
                  PI <= PI xor DI;
                  SR <= DI & SR(7 downto 1);
                when 9 =>
                  CBIT <= CBIT + CONE;
                  CSAM <= CSAM + CONE;
                  PI <= PI xor DI;
                when 10 =>
                  PERR <= PI;
                  PI <= '0';

                  if DI = '0' then
                    FERR <= '1';
                  else
                    FERR <= '0';
                  end if;

                  if DR = '1' then
                    OERR <= '1';
                  else
                    OERR <= '0';
                  end if;
```

```
                DR <= '1';
                DOUT <= SR;
                CBIT <= "0000";
                START <= '0';
              when others =>
                null;
            end case;
          else
            CSAM <= CSAM + CONE;
          end if;
        end if;
      end if;
    end if;
  end if;
 end if;
end process;

DRO <= DR;
DOUTO <= DOUT;
PERRO <= PERR;
FERRO <= FERR;
OERRO <= OERR;
end RX_BEH;
```

Here is a synthesizable model for the divider block *DIV*. This circuit produces a pulse every sixteen clock cycles. If signal *TESTN* is '0', it operates in the fast mode, that is, a pulse is produced for every clock cycle. Signal *COUNTER* is inferred as flip-flops.

```
library IEEE;
use IEEE.STD_LOGIC_1164.all;
use IEEE.NUMERIC_STD.all;
entity DIV is
  port (CK, RESET, TESTN: in STD_LOGIC;
       ENA: out STD_LOGIC);
end DIV;

architecture DIV_BEH of DIV is
  signal COUNTER: UNSIGNED(3 downto 0);
begin
  -- Synchronous section:
  process (CK, RESET, TESTN, COUNTER)
    constant CONE: UNSIGNED (3 downto 0) := "0001";
  begin
```

```
      if RISING_EDGE (CK) then
        if RESET = '0' then
          COUNTER <= "0000";
        else
          if TESTN = '0' then
            COUNTER <= "1111";
          else
            COUNTER <= COUNTER + CONE;
          end if;
        end if;
      end if;
    end process;

    -- Combinational section:
    ENA <= '1' when COUNTER = "1111" else '0';
  end DIV_BEH;
```

6.28 A Blackjack Model

Here is a synthesizable model of a blackjack program. This program is played with a deck of cards. Cards 2 to 10 have values equal to their face value, and an ace has a value of either 1 or 11. The object of the game is to accept a number of random cards such that the total score (sum of values of all cards) is as close as possible to 21 without exceeding 21.

The signal *INSERT_CARD* indicates when the program is ready to accept a new card. A card is accepted at the rising edge of *CLOCK* if *INSERT_CARD* is true. Signal *CARD_VALUE* has the value of the card. If a sequence of cards is accepted such that the total falls between 17 and 21, then signal *WON* is set to true, indicating that the game has been won. If total exceeds 21, then the program checks to see if an ace was accepted as a 1 or a 10; if it was accepted as a 10, the value of ace is changed to 1 and the program gets ready to accept a new card; if not, signal *LOST* is set to true indicating that it has lost. If either signal *WON* or *LOST* is set, no more cards are accepted. The game can be reset by setting *NEW_GAME* to true.

```
entity BLACKJACK is
  port (CARD_VALUE: in INTEGER range 0 to 11;
        CLOCK: in BIT;
        INSERT_CARD: in BOOLEAN;
        NEW_GAME: in BOOLEAN;                  -- Resets game.
        TOTAL_POINTS: out INTEGER range 0 to 31;
        WON, LOST: buffer BOOLEAN);
end BLACKJACK;


architecture BEHAVIOR of BLACKJACK is
begin
  process (NEW_GAME, CLOCK)
    variable ACE_AVAILABLE: BOOLEAN;
    variable ACE_VALUE_IS_11: BOOLEAN;
      -- ACE_VALUE_IS_11 is valid only if ACE_AVAILABLE is true.
    variable TOT_PTS: INTEGER range 0 to 31;
  begin
    if NEW_GAME then
      WON <= FALSE;
      LOST <= FALSE;
      ACE_AVAILABLE := FALSE;
      ACE_VALUE_IS_11 := FALSE;
      TOT_PTS := 0;
    elsif CLOCK = '1' and CLOCK'EVENT then
      if INSERT_CARD and (not WON) and (not LOST) then
        if CARD_VALUE = 11 then
          ACE_AVAILABLE := TRUE;
          ACE_VALUE_IS_11 := TRUE;
        end if;

        TOT_PTS := TOT_PTS + CARD_VALUE;

        case TOT_PTS is
          when 0 to 16 =>
            null;
          when 17 to 21 =>
            WON <= TRUE;
          when 22 to 31 =>
            if ACE_AVAILABLE and ACE_VALUE_IS_11 then
              ACE_VALUE_IS_11 := FALSE;
              TOT_PTS := TOT_PTS - 10;
            else
```

```
              LOST <= TRUE;
            end if;
          end case;
        end if;
      end if;

      TOTAL_POINTS <= TOT_PTS;
    end process;
  end BEHAVIOR;
```

❑

Appendix A

Synthesizable Constructs

To give an idea of what VHDL constructs are synthesizable by a synthesis tool, this appendix gives a listing of the synthesizable VHDL constructs that are recognized by the ArchSyn synthesis system, v14.0. The material is organized to reflect the contents of the IEEE Standard VHDL Language Reference Manual, IEEE Std 1076-1993.

Constructs that have relevance only to simulation are identified as "ignored constructs" and constructs that are not synthesizable are marked as "not supported". The constructs are categorized as follows:

i. *Supported*: Constructs that get synthesized into hardware.
ii. *Not supported*: Synthesis terminates when such a construct is present in the input file.
iii. *Ignored*: Warning messages are issued during synthesis, except for declarations and specifications.

In the following tables, the first column mentions the VHDL feature, the second column indicates whether the feature is supported or not, and the third column is for comments and exceptions.

Design Entities and Configurations		
Entity Declarations		
Entity Header	Supported	Generics are also supported. Default values for ports are ignored.
Entity Declarative Part	Supported	
Entity Statements	Ignored	
Architecture Bodies	Supported	Multiple architecture bodies are allowed.
Configurations	Ignored	

Subprograms and Packages		
Subprogram Declarations	Supported	Recursion is not supported. Default values for formal parameters not supported.
Subprogram Bodies	Supported	
Subprogram Overloading	Supported	
Operator Overloading	Supported	

Subprograms and Packages		
Resolution Functions	Ignored	Signals are connected together, based on a global option specified: *wired-and*: drivers are and'ed together. *wired-or*: drivers are or'ed together. *tri-state*: drivers connected to each other.
Package Declarations	Supported	
Package Bodies	Supported	

Types		
Scalar Types		
Enumeration Types	Supported	Null ranges are not supported.
Integer Types	Supported	Null ranges are not supported. Integers allowed in range $-(2^{31}-1)$ to $+(2^{31}-1)$.
Physical Types	Ignored	Use of physical types are not supported. Physical type literals are ignored.
Floating Point Types	Ignored	Use of floating point types and literals are not supported.
Composite Types		
Array Types	Supported	More than two dimension not supported. Null arrays are not supported.
Record Types	Supported	
Access Types	Ignored	Use of access types is not supported.

Types		
File Types	Ignored	Use of file types is not supported.
Incomplete Type Declarations	Ignored	

Declarations		
Type Declarations	Supported	
Subtype declarations	Supported	
Object Declarations		
Constant Declarations	Supported	
Signal Declarations	Supported	Register and bus declarations are not supported. Resolution functions are ignored. Initial values are ignored.
Variable Declarations	Supported	Initial values are ignored.
File Declarations	Ignored	
Interface Declarations	Supported	Linkage mode is not supported.
Alias Declarations	Ignored	
Attribute Declarations	Supported	
Component Declarations	Supported	

Specifications		
Attribute Specifications	Supported	
Configuration Specifications	Ignored	
Disconnection Specifications	Ignored	

Names		
Simple Names	Supported	
Selected Names	Supported	
Indexed Names	Supported	
Slice Names	Supported	Null slices are not supported.
Attribute Names		
Predefined array attributes	Supported	The supported ones are: *'BASE*, *'LEFT*, *'RIGHT*, *'HIGH*, *'LOW*, *'RANGE*, *'REVERSE_RANGE*, *'LENGTH*, *'EVENT*, and *'STABLE*. Attributes *'EVENT* and *'STABLE* are supported only in `wait` and `if` statements to specify events on clocks.
User-defined attributes	Supported	The attribute *ENUM_ENCODING* is the only one supported.

Expressions		
Operators		
Logical operators	Supported	

Expressions		
Relational operators	Supported	
Adding operators	Supported	
Multiplying operators	Supported	`mod` and `rem` supported only for positive numbers.
Miscellaneous operators	Supported	Exponentiation supported only if both operands are constants or if left operand is a power of two.
Operands		
Integer literals	Supported	
Floating point literals	Not supported	
Based literals	Supported	
Physical literals	Ignored	
Enumeration literals	Supported	
String literals	Supported	Only under the condition that each character has a single bit encoded value.
Bit-string literals	Supported	
Null literals	Not supported	
Aggregates	Supported	
Function Calls	Supported	
Qualified Expressions	Supported	
Type Conversions	Supported	
Allocators	Not supported	

Expressions		
Static Expressions	Supported	
Universal Expressions	Supported	

Sequential Statements		
Wait Statement	Supported	Only the "**wait until**" form is supported and it can only be used to specify clock-related events. The `wait` statement has the form: **wait until** *clock_expression* ; The `wait` statement, if present, must be the first statement in a process.
Assertion Statement	Ignored	
Signal Assignment Statement	Supported	`guarded` option not supported. `transport` option is ignored. `after` clause is ignored. Multiple waveform elements are not supported.
Variable Assignment Statement	Supported	
Procedure call Statement	Supported	Type conversion on formal parameters is not supported.
If Statement	Supported	
Case Statement	Supported	
Loop Statement		
For-iteration scheme	Supported	Ranges must be globally static.

Sequential Statements		
While-iteration scheme	Not supported	
No-iteration scheme	Not supported	
Next Statement	Supported	
Exit Statement	Supported	
Return Statement	Supported	
Null Statement	Supported	

Concurrent Statements		
Block Statement	Supported	Guards are not supported. Ports and generics are not supported.
Process Statement	Supported	Sensitivity list is ignored.
Concurrent Procedure call	Supported	
Concurrent Assertion Statement	Ignored	
Concurrent Signal Assignment Statement	Supported	`guarded` option not supported. `transport` option is ignored. `after` clause is ignored. Multiple waveform elements are not supported. `unaffected` not supported.
Conditional Signal Assignment	Supported	
Selected Signal Assignment	Supported	

Concurrent Statements		
Component Instantiation Statement	Supported	Type conversion on a formal port is not supported.
Generate Statement	Supported	

Design Units and Analysis		
Design Units	Supported	Separate compilation allowed.
Design Libraries	Supported	
Context Clauses	Supported	

Pre-defined Language Environment		
Predefined Attributes	Supported	The only supported ones are: *'BASE*, *'LEFT*, *'RIGHT*, *'HIGH*, *'LOW*, *'RANGE*, *'REVERSE_RANGE*, *'LENGTH*, *'EVENT*, and *'STABLE*. Attributes *'EVENT* and *'STABLE* are supported only in `wait` and `if` statements to specify events on clocks.
STANDARD package	Supported	Type *STRING* is not supported. Type *TIME* is ignored. Function *NOW* is ignored.
TEXTIO package	Not supported	

❑

Appendix B

An Arithmetic Package

This appendix describes an arithmetic package based on the IEEE standard *STD_LOGIC_1164* package that is part of the ArchSyn synthesis system. Many examples in the first edition of the book used this package.

Package STD_LOGIC_ARITH

This package defines two array types *UNSIGNED* and *SIGNED* of element type *STD_LOGIC*. The type *SIGNED* represents a signed number in two's complement form, while the type *UNSIGNED* represents unsigned numbers. The package also contains overloaded operator functions that operate on these types. Conversion functions are also defined in this package.

```
-- This package resides in library SYNTH.
library IEEE;
use IEEE.STD_LOGIC_1164 all;
package STD_LOGIC_ARITH is
  -- The types UNSIGNED and SIGNED:
  type UNSIGNED is array (NATURAL range <>) of STD_LOGIC;
  type SIGNED is array (NATURAL range <>) of STD_LOGIC;

  -- Conversion functions:
  function TO_INTEGER (U: UNSIGNED) return INTEGER;
  function TO_INTEGER (S: SIGNED) return INTEGER;

  function TO_STDLOGICVECTOR (U: UNSIGNED;
             SIZE : INTEGER) return STD_LOGIC_VECTOR;
  subtype LONG is STD_LOGIC_VECTOR (31 downto 0);
  function TO_STDLOGICVECTOR (I : INTEGER) return LONG;
  function TO_STDLOGICVECTOR (I, SIZE : INTEGER)
             return STD_LOGIC_VECTOR;

  function TO_UNSIGNED (I, SIZE : INTEGER) return UNSIGNED;
  function TO_UNSIGNED (S: SIGNED; SIZE: INTEGER)
             return UNSIGNED;
  function TO_UNSIGNED (U: UNSIGNED; SIZE: INTEGER)
             return UNSIGNED;

  function TO_SIGNED (I, SIZE : INTEGER) return SIGNED;
  function TO_SIGNED (U : UNSIGNED; SIZE : INTEGER)
             return SIGNED;
  function TO_SIGNED (S: SIGNED; SIZE: INTEGER)
             return SIGNED;

  function TO_STDULOGIC (C: CHARACTER)
             return STD_ULOGIC;
  function TO_CHARACTER (S: STD_ULOGIC)
             return CHARACTER;

  -- Binary arithmetic functions:
  function "+" (L: UNSIGNED; R: UNSIGNED) return UNSIGNED;
  function "+" (L: SIGNED; R: SIGNED) return SIGNED;
  function "+" (L: SIGNED; R: INTEGER) return SIGNED;
  function "+" (L: INTEGER; R: SIGNED) return SIGNED;
  function "+" (L: UNSIGNED; R: INTEGER) return UNSIGNED;
  function "+" (L: INTEGER; R: UNSIGNED) return UNSIGNED;
```

```
function "-" (L: UNSIGNED; R: UNSIGNED) return UNSIGNED;
function "-" (L: SIGNED; R: SIGNED) return SIGNED;
function "-" (L: SIGNED; R: INTEGER) return SIGNED;
function "-" (L: INTEGER; R: SIGNED) return SIGNED;
function "-" (L: UNSIGNED; R: INTEGER) return UNSIGNED;
function "-" (L: INTEGER; R: UNSIGNED) return UNSIGNED;

function "*" (L: UNSIGNED; R: UNSIGNED) return UNSIGNED;
function "*" (L: SIGNED; R: SIGNED) return SIGNED;

function "/" (L: UNSIGNED; R: UNSIGNED) return UNSIGNED;
function "/" (L: SIGNED; R: SIGNED) return SIGNED;

function "mod" (L: UNSIGNED; R: UNSIGNED)
        return UNSIGNED;
function "mod" (L: SIGNED; R: SIGNED) return SIGNED;

function "rem" (L: UNSIGNED; R: UNSIGNED)
        return UNSIGNED;
function "rem" (L: SIGNED; R: SIGNED) return SIGNED;

-- Unary arithmetic functions:
function "-" (L: SIGNED) return SIGNED;
function "abs" (L: SIGNED) return SIGNED;

-- Comparison functions:
function "<" (L: UNSIGNED; R: UNSIGNED) return BOOLEAN;
function "<" (L: UNSIGNED; R: INTEGER) return BOOLEAN;
function "<" (L: INTEGER; R: UNSIGNED) return BOOLEAN;
function "<" (L: INTEGER; R: SIGNED) return BOOLEAN;
function "<" (L: SIGNED; R: SIGNED) return BOOLEAN;
function "<" (L: SIGNED; R: INTEGER) return BOOLEAN;

function "<=" (L: UNSIGNED; R: UNSIGNED) return BOOLEAN;
function "<=" (L: UNSIGNED; R: INTEGER) return BOOLEAN;
function "<=" (L: INTEGER; R: UNSIGNED) return BOOLEAN;
function "<=" (L: INTEGER; R: SIGNED) return BOOLEAN;
function "<=" (L: SIGNED; R: SIGNED) return BOOLEAN;
function "<=" (L: SIGNED; R: INTEGER) return BOOLEAN;

function ">=" (L: UNSIGNED; R: UNSIGNED) return BOOLEAN;
function ">=" (L: UNSIGNED; R: INTEGER) return BOOLEAN;
```

```
function ">=" (L: INTEGER; R: UNSIGNED) return BOOLEAN;
function ">=" (L: INTEGER; R: SIGNED) return BOOLEAN;
function ">=" (L: SIGNED; R: SIGNED) return BOOLEAN;
function ">=" (L: SIGNED; R: INTEGER) return BOOLEAN;

function ">" (L: UNSIGNED; R: UNSIGNED) return BOOLEAN;
function ">" (L: UNSIGNED; R: INTEGER) return BOOLEAN;
function ">" (L: INTEGER; R: UNSIGNED) return BOOLEAN;
function ">" (L: INTEGER; R: SIGNED) return BOOLEAN;
function ">" (L: SIGNED; R: SIGNED) return BOOLEAN;
function ">" (L: SIGNED; R: INTEGER) return BOOLEAN;


function "=" (L: UNSIGNED; R: UNSIGNED) return BOOLEAN;
function "=" (L: UNSIGNED; R: INTEGER) return BOOLEAN;
function "=" (L: INTEGER; R: UNSIGNED) return BOOLEAN;
function "=" (L: INTEGER; R: SIGNED) return BOOLEAN;
function "=" (L: SIGNED; R: SIGNED) return BOOLEAN;
function "=" (L: SIGNED; R: INTEGER) return BOOLEAN;

function "/=" (L: UNSIGNED; R: UNSIGNED) return BOOLEAN;
function "/=" (L: UNSIGNED; R: INTEGER) return BOOLEAN;
function "/=" (L: INTEGER; R: UNSIGNED) return BOOLEAN;
function "/=" (L: INTEGER; R: SIGNED) return BOOLEAN;
function "/=" (L: SIGNED; R: SIGNED) return BOOLEAN;
function "/=" (L: SIGNED; R: INTEGER) return BOOLEAN;

-- Logical operations:
function "and" (L, R: UNSIGNED) return UNSIGNED;
function "nand" (L, R: UNSIGNED) return UNSIGNED;
function "or" (L, R: UNSIGNED) return UNSIGNED;
function "nor" (L, R: UNSIGNED) return UNSIGNED;
function "xor" (L, R: UNSIGNED) return UNSIGNED;
function "not" (L: UNSIGNED) return UNSIGNED;

function "and" (L, R: SIGNED) return SIGNED;
function "nand" (L, R: SIGNED) return SIGNED;
function "or" (L, R: SIGNED) return SIGNED;
function "nor" (L, R: SIGNED) return SIGNED;
function "xor" (L, R: SIGNED) return SIGNED;
function "not" (L: SIGNED) return SIGNED;
```

```
-- Shift functions:
function SHIFT_LEFT (U : UNSIGNED; SIZE : NATURAL)
        return UNSIGNED;
function SHIFT_LEFT (S: SIGNED; SIZE : NATURAL)
        return SIGNED;
function SHIFT_RIGHT (U: UNSIGNED; SIZE : NATURAL)
        return UNSIGNED;
function SHIFT_RIGHT (S: SIGNED; SIZE : NATURAL)
        return SIGNED;

-- Preset / clear procedure:
procedure PRESET_CLEAR (signal FF: out UNSIGNED;
        PC_VALUE: UNSIGNED);
procedure PRESET_CLEAR (signal FF: out SIGNED;
        PC_VALUE: SIGNED);
procedure PRESET_CLEAR (signal FF: out INTEGER;
        PC_VALUE: INTEGER);

-- Clock-level functions:
function HIGH_LEVEL (CLK: STD_ULOGIC) return BOOLEAN;
function LOW_LEVEL (CLK: STD_ULOGIC) return BOOLEAN;

-- Utility function used in test benches:
function NOT_EQUALS (OBSERVED, EXPECTED :
        STD_ULOGIC) return BOOLEAN;

end package STD_LOGIC_ARITH;
```

❑

Appendix C

A Generic Library

This appendix describes a package *GENERIC_COMP* that contains a list of generic component declarations. These components are used in the synthesized netlists shown or described in this text. Functionality of each component is described using comments.

```
-- This package resides in library SYNTH.
--
library IEEE;
use IEEE.STD_LOGIC_1164.all;
package GENERIC_COMP is
   component AND2
        -- Z <= A and B;
      port (A, B: in STD_ULOGIC;
           Z: out STD_ULOGIC);
   end component;
```

```
component AOI21
    -- Z <= not ((A1 and A2) or B);
  port (A1, A2, B: in STD_ULOGIC;
      Z: out STD_ULOGIC);
end component;
component AOI211
    -- Z <= not ((A1 and A2) or B1 or B2);
  port (A1, A2, B1, B2: in STD_ULOGIC;
      Z: out STD_ULOGIC);
end component;
component AOI22
    -- Z <= not ((A1 and A2) or (B1 and B2));
  port (A1, A2, B1, B2: in STD_ULOGIC;
      Z: out STD_ULOGIC);
end component;
component BN20T20D
    -- Bidirectional buffer.
    -- Z <= PADI;
    -- PADO <= '0' when A='0' and STN='0' else
    --          '1' when A='1' and ST='1' else
    --          'Z';
  port (A, ST, STN, PADI: in STD_ULOGIC;
      Z, PADO: out STD_ULOGIC);
end component;
component BUF
    -- Z <= A;
  port (A: in STD_ULOGIC;
      Z: out STD_ULOGIC);
end component;
component FD1P3AX
    -- Positive edge-triggered, positive-level sample,
    -- static D-type FF.
  port (D, SP, CK: in STD_ULOGIC;
      Q, QN: out STD_ULOGIC);
end component;
component FD1S1A
    -- Positive-level sense static D-type FF (latch).
  port (D, CK: in STD_ULOGIC;
      Q, QN: out STD_ULOGIC);
end component;
```

```
component FD1S1B
    -- Positive-level sense, positive asynchronous preset,
    -- static D-type FF (latch).
  port (D, CK, PD: in STD_ULOGIC;
        Q, QN: out STD_ULOGIC);
end component;
component FD1S1D
    -- Positive-level sense, positive asynchronous clear,
    -- static D-type FF (latch).
  port (D, CK, CD: in STD_ULOGIC;
        Q, QN: out STD_ULOGIC);
end component;
component FD1S1F
    -- Positive-level sense, negative asynchronous clear,
    -- positive asynchronous preset, static D-type FF (latch).
  port (D, CK, PD, CDN: in STD_ULOGIC;
        Q, QN: out STD_ULOGIC);
end component;
component FD1S2AX
    -- Negative edge-triggered, static D-type FF.
  port (D, CK: in STD_ULOGIC;
        Q, QN: out STD_ULOGIC);
end component;
component FD1S2BX
    -- Negative edge-triggered, positive asynchronous preset,
    -- static D-type FF.
  port (D, CK, PD: in STD_ULOGIC;
        Q, QN: out STD_ULOGIC);
end component;
component FD1S2CX
    -- Negative edge-triggered, positive asynchronous preset,
    -- positive asynchronous clear, static D-type FF.
  port (D, CK, PD: in STD_ULOGIC;
        Q, QN: out STD_ULOGIC);
end component;
component FD1S2DX
    -- Negative edge-triggered, positive asynchronous clear,
    -- static D-type FF.
  port (D, CK, CD: in STD_ULOGIC;
        Q, QN: out STD_ULOGIC);
end component;
```

```
component FD1S2EX
    -- Negative edge-triggered, negative asynchronous clear,
    -- static D-type FF.
  port (D, CK, CDN: in STD_ULOGIC;
      Q, QN: out STD_ULOGIC);
end component;
component FD1S2FX
    -- Negative edge-triggered, negative asynchronous clear,
    -- positive asynchronous preset, static D-type FF.
  port (D, CK, PD, CDN: in STD_ULOGIC;
      Q, QN: out STD_ULOGIC);
end component;
component FD1S2GX
    -- Negative edge-triggered, negative asynchronous preset,
    -- static D-type FF.
  port (D, CK, PD, CDN: in STD_ULOGIC;
      Q, QN: out STD_ULOGIC);
end component;
component FD1S2IX
    -- Negative edge-triggered, positive synchronous clear,
    -- static D-type FF.
  port (D, CK, CD: in STD_ULOGIC;
      Q, QN: out STD_ULOGIC);
end component;
component FD1S2JX
    -- Negative edge-triggered, positive synchronous preset,
    -- static D-type FF.
  port (D, CK, PD: in STD_ULOGIC;
      Q, QN: out STD_ULOGIC);
end component;
component FD1S2NX
    -- Negative edge-triggered, positive asynchronous clear,
    -- negative asynchronous preset, static D-type FF.
  port (D, CK, PDN, CD: in STD_ULOGIC;
      Q, QN: out STD_ULOGIC);
end component;
component FD1S2OX
    -- Negative edge-triggered, positive synchronous clear,
    -- positive synchronous preset, static D-type FF.
  port (D, CK, PD, CD: in STD_ULOGIC;
      Q, QN: out STD_ULOGIC);
end component;
```

```
component FD1S3AX
    -- Positive edge-triggered, static D-type FF.
  port (D, CK: in STD_ULOGIC;
      Q, QN: out STD_ULOGIC);
end component;
component FD1S3BX
    -- Positive edge-triggered, positive asynchronous preset,
    -- static D-type FF.
  port (D, CK: in STD_ULOGIC;
      Q, QN: out STD_ULOGIC);
end component;
component FD1S3CX
    -- Positive edge-triggered, positive asynchronous clear,
    -- positive asynchronous preset, static D-type FF.
  port (D, CK: in STD_ULOGIC;
      Q, QN: out STD_ULOGIC);
end component;
component FD1S3EX
    -- Positive edge-triggered, negative synchronous clear,
    -- static D-type FF.
  port (D, CK, CDN: in STD_ULOGIC;
      Q, QN: out STD_ULOGIC);
end component;
component FL1S2AX
    -- Negative edge-triggered, data select front end, scan FF.
  port (D0, D1, CK, SD: in STD_ULOGIC;
      Q, QN: out STD_ULOGIC);
end component;
component FL1S2EX
    -- Negative edge-triggered, data select front end,
    -- negative asynchronous clear, scan FF.
  port (D0, D1, CK, SD, CDN: in STD_ULOGIC;
      Q, QN: out STD_ULOGIC);
end component;
component FL1S3AX
    -- Positive edge-triggered, data select front end, scan FF.
  port (D0, D1, CK, SD: in STD_ULOGIC;
      Q, QN: out STD_ULOGIC);
end component;
component FL1S3CX
    -- Positive edge-triggered, data select front end, positive
    -- asynchronous clear, positive asynchronous preset, scan FF.
  port (D0, D1, CK, SD: in STD_ULOGIC;
```

```
        Q, QN: out STD_ULOGIC);
end component;
component FL1S3EX
      -- Positive edge-triggered, data select front end,
      -- negative asynchronous clear, scan FF.
  port (D0, D1, CK, SD, CDN: in STD_ULOGIC;
        Q, QN: out STD_ULOGIC);
end component;
component FS0S1D
      -- Positive-level S input, positive-level R input,
      -- positive asynchronous clear, R-S FF (latch).
  port (S, R, CD: in STD_ULOGIC;
        Q, QN: out STD_ULOGIC);
end component;
component INRB
      -- Z <= not A;
  port (A: in STD_ULOGIC;
        Z: out STD_ULOGIC);
end component;
component INRBH
      -- Z <= not A;
  port (A: in STD_ULOGIC;
        Z: out STD_ULOGIC);
end component;
component ND2
      -- Z <= A nand B;
  port (A, B: in STD_ULOGIC;
        Z: out STD_ULOGIC);
end component;
component ND3
      -- Z <= not (A and B and C);
  port (A, B, C: in STD_ULOGIC;
        Z: out STD_ULOGIC);
end component;
component ND4
      -- Z <= not (A and B and C and D);
  port (A, B, C, D: in STD_ULOGIC;
        Z: out STD_ULOGIC);
end component;
component NR2
      -- Z <= not (A or B);
  port (A, B: in STD_ULOGIC;
        Z: out STD_ULOGIC);
```

```
end component;
component NR3
    -- Z <= not (A or B or C);
  port (A, B, C: in STD_ULOGIC;
       Z: out STD_ULOGIC);
end component;
component NR4
    -- Z <= not (A or B or C or D);
  port (A, B, C, D: in STD_ULOGIC;
       Z: out STD_ULOGIC);
end component;
component OAI21
    -- Z <= not ((A1 or A2) and B);
  port (A1, A2, B: in STD_ULOGIC;
       Z: out STD_ULOGIC);
end component;
component OAI22
    -- Z <= not ((A1 or A2) and (B1 or B2));
  port (A1, A2, B1, B2: in STD_ULOGIC;
       Z: out STD_ULOGIC);
end component;
component OAI4321
    -- Z <= not ((A1 or A2 or A3 or A4) and (B1 or B2 or B3)
    --    and (C1 and C2) and D);
  port (A1, A2, A3, A4, B1, B2, B3, C1, C2, D: in STD_ULOGIC;
       Z: out STD_ULOGIC);
end component;
component OR2
    -- Z <= A or B;
  port (A, B: in STD_ULOGIC;
       Z: out STD_ULOGIC);
end component;
component OR4
    -- Z <= A or B or C or D;
  port (A, B, C, D: in STD_ULOGIC;
       Z: out STD_ULOGIC);
end component;
component TBUS
    -- Q <= 'Z' when CK = '0' and CKN = '1',
    --       '0' when CK = '1' and D = '0',
    --       '1' when CKN = '0' and D = '1';
  port (D, CK, CKN: in STD_ULOGIC;
       Q: out STD_ULOGIC);
```

```
    end component;
    component XNOR2
        -- Z <= not (A xor B);
      port (A, B: in STD_ULOGIC;
            Z: out STD_ULOGIC);
    end component;
    component XOR2
        -- Z <= A xor B;
      port (A, B: in STD_ULOGIC;
            Z: out STD_ULOGIC);
    end component;
    component XOR2Z
        -- Z <= A xor B; Z1 <= not (A or B);
      port (A, B: in STD_ULOGIC;
            Z, Z1: out STD_ULOGIC);
    end component;
  end GENERIC_COMP;
```

Appendix D

IEEE Standard Arithmetic Packages

This appendix provides a listing of the IEEE Std 1076.3-1997 VHDL synthesis arithmetic packages, *NUMERIC_BIT* and *NUMERIC_STD*[1]. Many examples in this book are based on these standard packages. A summary of the two packages is described in a tabular form in the first section.

D.1 Summary of Packages

Function Id(s)	*NUMERIC_BIT*	*NUMERIC_STD*
A.1	**abs**	**abs**
A.2	unary -	unary -
A.3-8	binary +	binary +
A.9-14	binary -	binary -
A.15-20	*	*
A.21-26	/	/
A.27-32	**rem**	**rem**
A.33-38	**mod**	**mod**
C.1-6	>	>
C.7-12	<	<
C.13-18	<=	<=
C.19-24	>=	>=
C.25-30	=	=
C.31-36	/=	/=
S.1, S.3	*SHIFT_LEFT*	*SHIFT_LEFT*
S.2, S.4	*SHIFT_RIGHT*	*SHIFT_RIGHT*
S.5, S.7	*ROTATE_LEFT*	*ROTATE_LEFT*
S.6, S.8	*ROTATE_RIGHT*	*ROTATE_RIGHT*
S.9, S.10	(predefined in VHDL)	**sll**
S.11, S.12		**srl**
S.13, S.14		**rol**
S.15, S.16		**ror**
R.1-2	*RESIZE*	*RESIZE*
D.1-2	*TO_INTEGER*	*TO_INTEGER*
D.3	*TO_UNSIGNED*	*TO_UNSIGNED*
D.4	*TO_SIGNED*	*TO_SIGNED*
E.1	*RISING_EDGE*	(defined by package
E.2	*FALLING_EDGE*	*STD_LOGIC_1164*)
L.1, L.8	**not**	**not**
L.2, L.9	**and**	**and**
L.3, L.10	**or**	**or**
L.4, L.11	**nand**	**nand**
L.5, L.12	**nor**	**nor**
L.6, L.13	**xor**	**xor**
L.7, L.14	**xnor**	**xnor**
M.1-M.5		*STD_MATCH*
T.1-2		*TO_01*

D.2 Package NUMERIC_BIT

```
-- Copyright © 1997 by IEEE. All rights reserved.
--
-- This source file is an essential part of IEEE Standard P1076.3, Standard VHDL
-- Synthesis Packages.
--
-- This source file represents a portion of IEEE Standard P1076.3.
--
-- This package may be modified to include additional data required by tools, but it
-- must in no way change the external interfaces or simulation behavior of the
-- description. It is permissible to add comments and/or attributes to the package
-- declarations, but not to change or delete any original lines of the package
-- declaration. The package body may be changed only in accordance with the terms of
-- 7.1 and 7.2 of this standard.
--
-- Title : Standard VHDL Synthesis Packages (1076.3, NUMERIC_BIT)
--
-- Library    : This package shall be compiled into a library symbolically named IEEE.
--
-- Developers : IEEE DASC Synthesis Working Group, PAR 1076.3
--
-- Purpose    : This package defines numeric types and arithmetic functions for use
-- with synthesis tools. Two numeric types are define:
--    UNSIGNED: represents an UNSIGNED number in vector form
--    SIGNED: represents a SIGNED number in vector form.
-- The base element type is type BIT. The leftmost bit is treated as the most significant
-- bit. Signed vectors are represented in two's complement form. This package contains
-- overloaded arithmetic operators on the SIGNED and UNSIGNED types. The
-- package also contains useful type conversions functions, clock detection functions,
-- and other utility functions. If any argument to a function is a null array, a null array
-- is returned (exceptions, if any, are noted individually).
--
-- Note : No declarations or definitions shall be included in, or excluded from this
-- package. The "package declaration" defines the types, subtypes and declarations of
-- NUMERIC_BIT. The NUMERIC_BIT package body shall be considered the formal
-- definition of the semantics of this package. Tool developers may choose to
-- implement the package body in the most efficient manner available to them.
--
-- Version    : 2.4
-- Date       : 12 April 1995

package NUMERIC_BIT is
constant CopyRightNotice: STRING := "Copyright © 1997 IEEE. All rights reserved.";
```

```
-- Numeric array type definitions
type UNSIGNED is array (NATURAL range <> ) of BIT;
type SIGNED is array (NATURAL range <> ) of BIT;

-- Arithmetic Operators:
-- Id: A.1
function "abs" (ARG: SIGNED) return SIGNED;
-- Result subtype: SIGNED(ARG'LENGTH-1 downto 0).
-- Result: Returns the absolute value of a SIGNED vector ARG.
-- Id: A.2
function "-" (ARG: SIGNED) return SIGNED;
-- Result subtype: SIGNED(ARG'LENGTH-1 downto 0).
-- Result: Returns the value of the unary minus operation on a SIGNED vector ARG.

-- Id: A.3
function "+" (L, R: UNSIGNED) return UNSIGNED;
-- Result subtype: UNSIGNED(MAX(L'LENGTH, R'LENGTH)-1 downto 0).
-- Result: Adds two UNSIGNED vectors that may be of different lengths.
-- Id: A.4
function "+" (L, R: SIGNED) return SIGNED;
-- Result subtype: SIGNED(MAX(L'LENGTH, R'LENGTH)-1 downto 0).
-- Result: Adds two SIGNED vectors that may be of different lengths.
-- Id: A.5
function "+" (L: UNSIGNED; R: NATURAL) return UNSIGNED;
-- Result subtype: UNSIGNED(L'LENGTH-1 downto 0).
-- Result: Adds an UNSIGNED vector, L, with a non-negative INTEGER, R.
-- Id: A.6
function "+" (L: NATURAL; R: UNSIGNED) return UNSIGNED;
-- Result subtype: UNSIGNED(R'LENGTH-1 downto 0).
-- Result: Adds a non-negative INTEGER, L, with an UNSIGNED vector, R.
-- Id: A.7
function "+" (L: INTEGER; R: SIGNED) return SIGNED;
-- Result subtype: SIGNED(R'LENGTH-1 downto 0).
-- Result: Adds an INTEGER, L(may be positive or negative), to a SIGNED vector, R.
-- Id: A.8
function "+" (L: SIGNED; R: INTEGER) return SIGNED;
-- Result subtype: SIGNED(L'LENGTH-1 downto 0).
-- Result: Adds a SIGNED vector, L, to an INTEGER, R.

-- Id: A.9
function "-" (L, R: UNSIGNED) return UNSIGNED;
-- Result subtype: UNSIGNED(MAX(L'LENGTH, R'LENGTH)-1 downto 0).
-- Result: Subtracts two UNSIGNED vectors that may be of different lengths.
-- Id: A.10
function "-" (L, R: SIGNED) return SIGNED;
-- Result subtype: SIGNED(MAX(L'LENGTH, R'LENGTH)-1 downto 0).
-- Result: Subtracts a SIGNED vector, R, from another SIGNED vector, L,
```

-- that may possibly be of different lengths.
-- Id: A.11
function "–" (*L*: *UNSIGNED*; *R*: *NATURAL*) **return** *UNSIGNED*;
-- Result subtype: *UNSIGNED*(*L'LENGTH*–1 **downto** 0).
-- Result: Subtracts a non-negative *INTEGER*, *R*, from an *UNSIGNED* vector, *L*.
-- Id: A.12
function "–" (*L*: *NATURAL*; *R*: *UNSIGNED*) **return** *UNSIGNED*;
-- Result subtype: *UNSIGNED*(*R'LENGTH*–1 **downto** 0).
-- Result: Subtracts an *UNSIGNED* vector, *R*, from a non-negative *INTEGER*, *L*.
-- Id: A.13
function "–" (*L*: *SIGNED*; *R*: *INTEGER*) **return** *SIGNED*;
-- Result subtype: *SIGNED*(*L'LENGTH*–1 **downto** 0).
-- Result: Subtracts an *INTEGER*, *R*, from a *SIGNED* vector, *L*.
-- Id: A.14
function "–" (*L*: *INTEGER*; *R*: *SIGNED*) **return** *SIGNED*;
-- Result subtype: *SIGNED*(*R'LENGTH*–1 **downto** 0).
-- Result: Subtracts a *SIGNED* vector, *R*, from an *INTEGER*, *L*.

-- Id: A.15
function "*" (*L*, *R*: *UNSIGNED*) **return** *UNSIGNED*;
-- Result subtype: *UNSIGNED*((*L'LENGTH*+*R'LENGTH*–1) **downto** 0).
-- Result: Performs the multiplication operation on two *UNSIGNED*
-- vectors that may possibly be of different lengths.
-- Id: A.16
function "*" (*L*, *R*: *SIGNED*) **return** *SIGNED*;
-- Result subtype: *SIGNED*((*L'LENGTH*+*R'LENGTH*–1) **downto** 0)
-- Result: Multiplies two *SIGNED* vectors that may possibly be of different lengths.
-- Id: A.17
function "*" (*L*: *UNSIGNED*; *R*: *NATURAL*) **return** *UNSIGNED*;
-- Result subtype: *UNSIGNED*((*L'LENGTH*+*L'LENGTH*–1) **downto** 0).
-- Result: Multiplies an *UNSIGNED* vector, *L*, with a non-negative *INTEGER*, *R*.
-- *R* is converted to an *UNSIGNED* vector of size *L'LENGTH* before multiplication.
-- Id: A.18
function "*" (*L*: *NATURAL*; *R*: *UNSIGNED*) **return** *UNSIGNED*;
-- Result subtype: *UNSIGNED*((*R'LENGTH*+*R'LENGTH*–1) **downto** 0).
-- Result: Multiplies an *UNSIGNED* vector, *R*, with a non-negative *INTEGER*, *L*.
-- *L* is converted to an *UNSIGNED* vector of size *R'LENGTH* before multiplication.
-- Id: A.19
function "*" (*L*: *SIGNED*; *R*: *INTEGER*) **return** *SIGNED*;
-- Result subtype: *SIGNED*((*L'LENGTH*+*L'LENGTH*–1) **downto** 0)
-- Result: Multiplies a *SIGNED* vector, *L*, with an *INTEGER*, *R*. *R* is
-- converted to a *SIGNED* vector of size *L'LENGTH* before multiplication.
-- Id: A.20
function "*" (*L*: *INTEGER*; *R*: *SIGNED*) **return** *SIGNED*;
-- Result subtype: *SIGNED*((*R'LENGTH*+*R'LENGTH*–1) **downto** 0)
-- Result: Multiplies a *SIGNED* vector, *R*, with an *INTEGER*, *L*. *L* is
-- converted to a *SIGNED* vector of size *R'LENGTH* before multiplication.

```
-- NOTE: If second argument is zero for "/" operator, a severity level of ERROR
-- is issued.
-- Id: A.21
function "/" (L, R: UNSIGNED) return UNSIGNED;
-- Result subtype: UNSIGNED(L'LENGTH-1 downto 0)
-- Result: Divides an UNSIGNED vector, L, by another UNSIGNED vector, R.
-- Id: A.22
function "/" (L, R: SIGNED) return SIGNED;
-- Result subtype: SIGNED(L'LENGTH-1 downto 0)
-- Result: Divides an SIGNED vector, L, by another SIGNED vector, R.
-- Id: A.23
function "/" (L: UNSIGNED; R: NATURAL) return UNSIGNED;
-- Result subtype: UNSIGNED(L'LENGTH-1 downto 0)
-- Result: Divides an UNSIGNED vector, L, by a non-negative INTEGER, R.
--    If NO_OF_BITS(R) > L'LENGTH, result is truncated to L'LENGTH.
-- Id: A.24
function "/" (L: NATURAL; R: UNSIGNED) return UNSIGNED;
-- Result subtype: UNSIGNED(R'LENGTH-1 downto 0)
-- Result: Divides a non-negative INTEGER, L, by an UNSIGNED vector, R.
--    If NO_OF_BITS(L) > R'LENGTH, result is truncated to R'LENGTH.
-- Id: A.25
function "/" (L: SIGNED; R: INTEGER) return SIGNED;
-- Result subtype: SIGNED(L'LENGTH-1 downto 0)
-- Result: Divides a SIGNED vector, L, by an INTEGER, R.
-- If NO_OF_BITS(R) > L'LENGTH, result is truncated to L'LENGTH.
-- Id: A.26
function "/" (L: INTEGER; R: SIGNED) return SIGNED;
-- Result subtype: SIGNED(R'LENGTH-1 downto 0)
-- Result: Divides an INTEGER, L, by a SIGNED vector, R.
-- If NO_OF_BITS(L) > R'LENGTH, result is truncated to R'LENGTH.

-- NOTE: If second argument is zero for "rem" operator, a severity
--       level of ERROR is issued.
-- Id: A.27
function "rem" (L, R: UNSIGNED) return UNSIGNED;
-- Result subtype: UNSIGNED(R'LENGTH-1 downto 0)
-- Result: Computes "L rem R" where L and R are UNSIGNED vectors.
-- Id: A.28
function "rem" (L, R: SIGNED) return SIGNED;
-- Result subtype: SIGNED(R'LENGTH-1 downto 0)
-- Result: Computes "L rem R" where L and R are SIGNED vectors.
-- Id: A.29
function "rem" (L: UNSIGNED; R: NATURAL) return UNSIGNED;
-- Result subtype: UNSIGNED(L'LENGTH-1 downto 0)
```

```
-- Result: Computes "L rem R" where L is an UNSIGNED vector and R is a
-- non-negative INTEGER. If NO_OF_BITS(R) > L'LENGTH, result is truncated
-- to L'LENGTH.
-- Id: A.30
function "rem" (L: NATURAL; R: UNSIGNED) return UNSIGNED;
-- Result subtype: UNSIGNED(R'LENGTH-1 downto 0)
-- Result: Computes "L rem R" where R is an UNSIGNED vector and
--    L is a non-negative INTEGER.
--    If NO_OF_BITS(L) > R'LENGTH, result is truncated to R'LENGTH.
-- Id: A.31
function "rem" (L: SIGNED; R: INTEGER) return SIGNED;
-- Result subtype: SIGNED(L'LENGTH-1 downto 0)
-- Result: Computes "L rem R" where L is SIGNED vector and R is an INTEGER.
--    If NO_OF_BITS(R) > L'LENGTH, result is truncated to L'LENGTH.
-- Id: A.32
function "rem" (L: INTEGER; R: SIGNED) return SIGNED;
-- Result subtype: SIGNED(R'LENGTH-1 downto 0)
-- Result: Computes "L rem R" where R is SIGNED vector and L is an INTEGER.
--    If NO_OF_BITS(L) > R'LENGTH, result is truncated to R'LENGTH.

-- NOTE: If second argument is zero for "mod" operator, a severity
--    level of ERROR is issued.
-- Id: A.33
function "mod" (L, R: UNSIGNED) return UNSIGNED;
-- Result subtype: UNSIGNED(R'LENGTH-1 downto 0)
-- Result: Computes "L mod R" where L and R are UNSIGNED vectors.
-- Id: A.34
function "mod" (L, R: SIGNED) return SIGNED;
-- Result subtype: SIGNED(R'LENGTH-1 downto 0)
-- Result: Computes "L mod R" where L and R are SIGNED vectors.
-- Id: A.35
function "mod" (L: UNSIGNED; R: NATURAL) return UNSIGNED;
-- Result subtype: UNSIGNED(L'LENGTH-1 downto 0)
-- Result: Computes "L mod R" where L is an UNSIGNED vector
--      and R is a non-negative INTEGER.
--      If NO_OF_BITS(R) > L'LENGTH, result is truncated to L'LENGTH.
-- Id: A.36
function "mod" (L: NATURAL; R: UNSIGNED) return UNSIGNED;
-- Result subtype: UNSIGNED(R'LENGTH-1 downto 0)
-- Result: Computes "L mod R" where R is an UNSIGNED vector
--      and L is a non-negative INTEGER.
--      If NO_OF_BITS(L) > R'LENGTH, result is truncated to R'LENGTH.
-- Id: A.37
function "mod" (L: SIGNED; R: INTEGER) return SIGNED;
-- Result subtype: SIGNED(L'LENGTH-1 downto 0)
-- Result: Computes "L mod R" where L is a SIGNED vector and R is an INTEGER.
--      If NO_OF_BITS(R) > L'LENGTH, result is truncated to L'LENGTH.
```

-- Id: A.38
function "mod" (*L*: *INTEGER*; *R*: *SIGNED*) **return** *SIGNED*;
-- Result subtype: *SIGNED*(*R'LENGTH*–1 **downto** 0)
-- Result: Computes "*L* **mod** *R*" where *L* is an *INTEGER* and *R* is a *SIGNED* vector.
-- If *NO_OF_BITS*(*L*) > *R'LENGTH*, result is truncated to *R'LENGTH*.

-- Comparison Operators
-- Id: C.1
function ">" (*L*, *R*: *UNSIGNED*) **return** *BOOLEAN*;
-- Result subtype: *BOOLEAN*
-- Result: Computes "*L* > *R*" where *L* and *R* are *UNSIGNED* vectors possibly of
-- different lengths.
-- Id: C.2
function ">" (*L*, *R*: *SIGNED*) **return** *BOOLEAN*;
-- Result subtype: *BOOLEAN*
-- Result: Computes "*L* > *R*" where *L* and *R* are *SIGNED* vectors possibly of different
-- lengths.
-- Id: C.3
function ">" (*L*: *NATURAL*; *R*: *UNSIGNED*) **return** *BOOLEAN*;
-- Result subtype: *BOOLEAN*
-- Result: Computes "*L* > *R*" where *L* is a non-negative *INTEGER* and *R* is an
-- *UNSIGNED* vector.
-- Id: C.4
function ">" (*L*: *INTEGER*; *R*: *SIGNED*) **return** *BOOLEAN*;
-- Result subtype: *BOOLEAN*
-- Result: Computes "*L* > *R*" where *L* is a *INTEGER* and *R* is a *SIGNED* vector.
-- Id: C.5
function ">" (*L*: *UNSIGNED*; *R*: *NATURAL*) **return** *BOOLEAN*;
-- Result subtype: *BOOLEAN*
-- Result: Computes "*L* > *R*" where *L* is an *UNSIGNED* vector and
-- *R* is a non-negative *INTEGER*.
-- Id: C.6
function ">" (*L*: *SIGNED*; *R*: *INTEGER*) **return** *BOOLEAN*;
-- Result subtype: *BOOLEAN*
-- Result: Computes "*L* > *R*" where *L* is a *SIGNED* vector and *R* is a *INTEGER*.

-- Id: C.7
function "<" (*L*, *R*: *UNSIGNED*) **return** *BOOLEAN*;
-- Result subtype: *BOOLEAN*
-- Result: Computes "*L* < *R*" where *L* and *R* are *UNSIGNED* vectors
-- possibly of different lengths.
-- Id: C.8
function "<" (*L*, *R*: *SIGNED*) **return** *BOOLEAN*;
-- Result subtype: *BOOLEAN*
-- Result: Computes "*L* < *R*" where *L* and *R* are *SIGNED* vectors possibly of different
-- lengths.

```
-- Id: C.9
function "<" (L: NATURAL; R: UNSIGNED) return BOOLEAN
-- Result subtype: BOOLEAN
-- Result: Computes "L < R" where L is a non-negative INTEGER and R is an
-- UNSIGNED vector.
-- Id: C.10
function "<" (L: INTEGER; R: SIGNED) return BOOLEAN;
-- Result subtype: BOOLEAN
-- Result: Computes "L < R" where L is an INTEGER and R is a SIGNED vector.
-- Id: C.11
function "<" (L: UNSIGNED; R: NATURAL) return BOOLEAN;
-- Result subtype: BOOLEAN
-- Result: Computes "L < R" where L is an UNSIGNED vector and
--        R is a non-negative INTEGER.
-- Id: C.12
function "<" (L: SIGNED; R: INTEGER) return BOOLEAN;
-- Result subtype: BOOLEAN
-- Result: Computes "L < R" where L is a SIGNED vector and R is an INTEGER.

-- Id: C.13
function "<=" (L, R: UNSIGNED) return BOOLEAN;
-- Result subtype: BOOLEAN
-- Result: Computes "L <= R" where L and R are UNSIGNED vectors
--        possibly of different lengths.
-- Id: C.14
function "<=" (L, R: SIGNED) return BOOLEAN;
-- Result subtype: BOOLEAN
-- Result: Computes "L <= R" where L and R are SIGNED vectors
--        possibly of different lengths.
-- Id: C.15
function "<=" (L: NATURAL; R: UNSIGNED) return BOOLEAN;
-- Result subtype: BOOLEAN
-- Result: Computes "L <= R" where L is a non-negative INTEGER
--        and R is an UNSIGNED vector.
-- Id: C.16
function "<=" (L: INTEGER; R: SIGNED) return BOOLEAN;
-- Result subtype: BOOLEAN
-- Result: Computes "L <= R" where L is an INTEGER and R is a SIGNED vector.
-- Id: C.17
function "<=" (L: UNSIGNED; R: NATURAL) return BOOLEAN;
-- Result subtype: BOOLEAN
-- Result: Computes "L <= R" where L is an UNSIGNED vector and
--        R is a non-negative INTEGER.
-- Id: C.18
function "<=" (L: SIGNED; R: INTEGER) return BOOLEAN;
-- Result subtype: BOOLEAN
```

-- Result: Computes "*L* <= *R*" where *L* is a *SIGNED* vector and *R* is an *INTEGER*.

-- Id: C.19
function ">=" (*L, R*: *UNSIGNED*) **return** *BOOLEAN*;
-- Result subtype: *BOOLEAN*
-- Result: Computes "*L* >= *R*" where *L* and *R* are *UNSIGNED* vectors
-- possibly of different lengths.
-- Id: C.20
function ">=" (*L, R*: *SIGNED*) **return** *BOOLEAN*;
-- Result subtype: *BOOLEAN*
-- Result: Computes "*L* >= *R*" where *L* and *R* are *SIGNED* vectors
-- possibly of different lengths.
-- Id: C.21
function ">=" (*L*: *NATURAL*; *R*: *UNSIGNED*) **return** *BOOLEAN*;
-- Result subtype: *BOOLEAN*
-- Result: Computes "*L* >= *R*" where *L* is a non-negative *INTEGER*
-- and *R* is an *UNSIGNED* vector.
-- Id: C.22
function ">=" (*L*: *INTEGER*; *R*: *SIGNED*) **return** *BOOLEAN*;
-- Result subtype: *BOOLEAN*
-- Result: Computes "*L* >= *R*" where *L* is an *INTEGER* and *R* is a *SIGNED* vector.
-- Id: C.23
function ">=" (*L*: *UNSIGNED*; *R*: *NATURAL*) **return** *BOOLEAN*;
-- Result subtype: *BOOLEAN*
-- Result: Computes "*L* >= *R*" where *L* is an *UNSIGNED* vector and
-- *R* is a non-negative *INTEGER*.
-- Id: C.24
function ">=" (*L*: *SIGNED*; *R*: *INTEGER*) **return** *BOOLEAN*;
-- Result subtype: *BOOLEAN*
-- Result: Computes "*L* >= *R*" where *L* is a *SIGNED* vector and *R* is an *INTEGER*.

-- Id: C.25
function "=" (*L, R*: *UNSIGNED*) **return** *BOOLEAN*;
-- Result subtype: *BOOLEAN*
-- Result: Computes "*L* = *R*" where *L* and *R* are *UNSIGNED* vectors
-- possibly of different lengths.
-- Id: C.26
function "=" (*L, R*: *SIGNED*) **return** *BOOLEAN*;
-- Result subtype: *BOOLEAN*
-- Result: Computes "*L* = *R*" where *L* and *R* are *SIGNED* vectors
-- possibly of different lengths.
-- Id: C.27
function "=" (*L*: *NATURAL*; *R*: *UNSIGNED*) **return** *BOOLEAN*;
-- Result subtype: *BOOLEAN*
-- Result: Computes "*L* = *R*" where *L* is a non-negative *INTEGER*
-- and *R* is an *UNSIGNED* vector.

```
-- Id: C.28
function "=" (L: INTEGER; R: SIGNED) return BOOLEAN;
-- Result subtype: BOOLEAN
-- Result: Computes "L = R" where L is an INTEGER and R is a SIGNED vector.
-- Id: C.29
function "=" (L: UNSIGNED; R: NATURAL) return BOOLEAN;
-- Result subtype: BOOLEAN
-- Result: Computes "L = R" where L is an UNSIGNED vector and
--       R is a non-negative INTEGER.
-- Id: C.30
function "=" (L: SIGNED; R: INTEGER) return BOOLEAN;
-- Result subtype: BOOLEAN
-- Result: Computes "L = R" where L is a SIGNED vector and R is an INTEGER.

-- Id: C.31
function "/=" (L, R: UNSIGNED) return BOOLEAN;
-- Result subtype: BOOLEAN
-- Result: Computes "L /= R" where L and R are UNSIGNED vectors
--       possibly of different lengths.
-- Id: C.32
function "/=" (L, R: SIGNED) return BOOLEAN;
-- Result subtype: BOOLEAN
-- Result: Computes "L /= R" where L and R are SIGNED vectors
--       possibly of different lengths.
-- Id: C.33
function "/=" (L: NATURAL; R: UNSIGNED) return BOOLEAN;
-- Result subtype: BOOLEAN
-- Result: Computes "L /= R" where L is a non-negative INTEGER
--       and R is an UNSIGNED vector.
-- Id: C.34
function "/=" (L: INTEGER; R: SIGNED) return BOOLEAN;
-- Result subtype: BOOLEAN
-- Result: Computes "L /= R" where L is an INTEGER and R is a SIGNED vector.
-- Id: C.35
function "/=" (L: UNSIGNED; R: NATURAL) return BOOLEAN;
-- Result subtype: BOOLEAN
-- Result: Computes "L /= R" where L is an UNSIGNED vector and
--       R is a non-negative INTEGER.
-- Id: C.36
function "/=" (L: SIGNED; R: INTEGER) return BOOLEAN;
-- Result subtype: BOOLEAN
-- Result: Computes "L /= R" where L is a SIGNED vector and R is an INTEGER.

-- Shift and Rotate Functions
-- Id: S.1
function SHIFT_LEFT (ARG: UNSIGNED; COUNT: NATURAL) return UNSIGNED;
```

-- Result subtype: *UNSIGNED(ARG'LENGTH–1* **downto** 0)
-- Result: Performs a shift-left on an *UNSIGNED* vector *COUNT* times. The vacated
-- positions are filled with Bit '0'. The *COUNT* leftmost bits are lost.
-- Id: S.2
function *SHIFT_RIGHT* (*ARG*: *UNSIGNED*; *COUNT*: *NATURAL*) **return** *UNSIGNED*;
-- Result subtype: *UNSIGNED(ARG'LENGTH–1* **downto** 0)
-- Result: Performs a shift-right on an *UNSIGNED* vector *COUNT* times. The vacated
-- positions are filled with Bit '0'. The *COUNT* rightmost bits are lost.
-- Id: S.3
function *SHIFT_LEFT* (*ARG*: *SIGNED*; *COUNT*: *NATURAL*) **return** *SIGNED*;
-- Result subtype: *SIGNED(ARG'LENGTH–1* **downto** 0)
-- Result: Performs a shift-left on a *SIGNED* vector *COUNT* times. The vacated
-- positions are filled with Bit '0'. The *COUNT* leftmost bits are lost.
-- Id: S.4
function *SHIFT_RIGHT* (*ARG*: *SIGNED*; *COUNT*: *NATURAL*) **return** *SIGNED*;
-- Result subtype: *SIGNED(ARG'LENGTH–1* **downto** 0)
-- Result: Performs a shift-right on a *SIGNED* vector *COUNT* times. The vacated
-- positions are filled with the leftmost bit, *ARG'LEFT*. The *COUNT* rightmost bits
-- are lost.

-- Id: S.5
function *ROTATE_LEFT* (*ARG*: *UNSIGNED*; *COUNT*: *NATURAL*) **return** *UNSIGNED*;
-- Result subtype: *UNSIGNED(ARG'LENGTH–1* **downto** 0)
-- Result: Performs a rotate-left of an *UNSIGNED* vector *COUNT* times.
-- Id: S.6
function *ROTATE_RIGHT* (*ARG*: *UNSIGNED*; *COUNT*: *NATURAL*)
  return *UNSIGNED*;
-- Result subtype: *UNSIGNED(ARG'LENGTH–1* **downto** 0)
-- Result: Performs a rotate-right of an *UNSIGNED* vector *COUNT* times.
-- Id: S.7
function *ROTATE_LEFT* (*ARG*: *SIGNED*; *COUNT*: *NATURAL*) **return** *SIGNED*;
-- Result subtype: *SIGNED(ARG'LENGTH–1* **downto** 0)
-- Result: Performs a logical rotate-left of a *SIGNED* vector *COUNT* times.
-- Id: S.8
function *ROTATE_RIGHT* (*ARG*: *SIGNED*; *COUNT*: *NATURAL*) **return** *SIGNED*;
-- Result subtype: *SIGNED(ARG'LENGTH–1* **downto** 0)
-- Result: Performs a logical rotate-right of a *SIGNED* vector *COUNT* times.

-- Note: Functions S.9 through S.16 are not compatible with VHDL 1076-1987. Com-
-- ment out the function (declaration and body) for VHDL 1076-1987 compatibility.

-- Id: S.9
function "**sll**" (*ARG*: *UNSIGNED*; *COUNT*: *INTEGER*) **return** *UNSIGNED*;
-- Result subtype: *UNSIGNED(ARG'LENGTH–1* **downto** 0)
-- Result: *SHIFT_LEFT(ARG, COUNT)*

-- Id: S.10
function **"sll"** (*ARG*: *SIGNED*; *COUNT*: *INTEGER*) **return** *SIGNED*;
-- Result subtype: *SIGNED*(*ARG'LENGTH*–1 **downto** 0)
-- Result: *SHIFT_LEFT*(*ARG*, *COUNT*)
-- Id: S.11
function **"srl"** (*ARG*: *UNSIGNED*; *COUNT*: *INTEGER*) **return** *UNSIGNED*;
-- Result subtype: *UNSIGNED*(*ARG'LENGTH*–1 **downto** 0)
-- Result: *SHIFT_RIGHT*(*ARG*, *COUNT*)
-- Id: S.12
function **"srl"** (*ARG*: *SIGNED*; *COUNT*: *INTEGER*) **return** *SIGNED*;
-- Result subtype: *SIGNED*(*ARG'LENGTH*–1 **downto** 0)
-- Result: *SIGNED*(*SHIFT_RIGHT*(*UNSIGNED*(*ARG*), *COUNT*))
-- Id: S.13
function **"rol"** (*ARG*: *UNSIGNED*; *COUNT*: *INTEGER*) **return** *UNSIGNED*;
-- Result subtype: *UNSIGNED*(*ARG'LENGTH*–1 **downto** 0)
-- Result: *ROTATE_LEFT*(*ARG*, *COUNT*)
-- Id: S.14
function **"rol"** (*ARG*: *SIGNED*; *COUNT*: *INTEGER*) **return** *SIGNED*;
-- Result subtype: *SIGNED*(*ARG'LENGTH*–1 **downto** 0)
-- Result: *ROTATE_LEFT*(*ARG*, *COUNT*)
-- Id: S.15
function **"ror"** (*ARG*: *UNSIGNED*; *COUNT*: *INTEGER*) **return** *UNSIGNED*;
-- Result subtype: *UNSIGNED*(*ARG'LENGTH*–1 **downto** 0)
-- Result: *ROTATE_RIGHT*(*ARG*, *COUNT*)
-- Id: S.16
function **"ror"** (*ARG*: *SIGNED*; *COUNT*: *INTEGER*) **return** *SIGNED*;
-- Result subtype: *SIGNED*(*ARG'LENGTH*–1 **downto** 0)
-- Result: *ROTATE_RIGHT*(*ARG*, *COUNT*)

-- *RESIZE* Functions
-- Id: R.1
function *RESIZE* (*ARG*: *SIGNED*; *NEW_SIZE*: *NATURAL*) **return** *SIGNED*;
-- Result subtype: *SIGNED*(*NEW_SIZE*–1 **downto** 0)
-- Result: Resizes the *SIGNED* vector *ARG* to the specified size. To create a larger
-- vector, the new [leftmost] bit positions are filled with the sign bit (*ARG'LEFT*). When
-- truncating, the sign bit is retained along with the rightmost part.
-- Id: R.2
function *RESIZE* (*ARG*: *UNSIGNED*; *NEW_SIZE*: *NATURAL*) **return** *UNSIGNED*;
-- Result subtype: *UNSIGNED*(*NEW_SIZE*–1 **downto** 0)
-- Result: Resizes the *UNSIGNED* vector *ARG* to the specified size. To create
-- a larger vector, the new [leftmost] bit positions are filled with '0'. When
-- truncating, the leftmost bits are dropped.

-- Conversion Functions
-- Id: D.1
function *TO_INTEGER* (*ARG*: *UNSIGNED*) **return** *NATURAL*;

```
-- Result subtype: NATURAL. Value cannot be negative since
--    parameter is an UNSIGNED vector.
-- Result: Converts the UNSIGNED vector to an INTEGER.
-- Id: D.2
function TO_INTEGER (ARG: SIGNED) return INTEGER;
-- Result subtype: INTEGER
-- Result: Converts a SIGNED vector to an INTEGER.
-- Id: D.3
function TO_UNSIGNED (ARG, SIZE: NATURAL) return UNSIGNED;
-- Result subtype: UNSIGNED(SIZE-1 downto 0)
-- Result: Converts a non-negative INTEGER to an UNSIGNED
--    vector with the specified size.
-- Id: D.4
function TO_SIGNED (ARG: INTEGER; SIZE: NATURAL) return SIGNED;
-- Result subtype: SIGNED(SIZE-1 downto 0)
-- Result: Converts an INTEGER to a SIGNED vector of the specified size.

-- Logical Operators
-- Id: L.1
function "not" (L: UNSIGNED) return UNSIGNED;
-- Result subtype: UNSIGNED(L'LENGTH-1 downto 0)
-- Result: Termwise inversion
-- Id: L.2
function "and" (L, R: UNSIGNED) return UNSIGNED;
-- Result subtype: UNSIGNED(L'LENGTH-1 downto 0)
-- Result: Vector AND operation
-- Id: L.3
function "or" (L, R: UNSIGNED) return UNSIGNED;
-- Result subtype: UNSIGNED(L'LENGTH-1 downto 0)
-- Result: Vector OR operation
-- Id: L.4
function "nand" (L, R: UNSIGNED) return UNSIGNED;
-- Result subtype: UNSIGNED(L'LENGTH-1 downto 0)
-- Result: Vector NAND operation
-- Id: L.5
function "nor" (L, R: UNSIGNED) return UNSIGNED;
-- Result subtype: UNSIGNED(L'LENGTH-1 downto 0)
-- Result: Vector NOR operation
-- Id: L.6
function "xor" (L, R: UNSIGNED) return UNSIGNED;
-- Result subtype: UNSIGNED(L'LENGTH-1 downto 0)
-- Result: Vector XOR operation
---------------------------------------------------------------------------
-- Note : Functions L.7 and L.14 are not compatible with VHDL 1076-1987. Comment
-- out the function (declaration and body) for VHDL 1076-1987 compatibility.
---------------------------------------------------------------------------
```

-- Id: L.7
function "**xnor**" (*L*, *R*: *UNSIGNED*) **return** *UNSIGNED*;
-- Result subtype: *UNSIGNED*(*L'LENGTH*–1 **downto** 0)
-- Result: Vector *XNOR* operation
-- Id: L.8
function "**not**" (*L*: *SIGNED*) **return** *SIGNED*;
-- Result subtype: *SIGNED*(*L'LENGTH*–1 **downto** 0)
-- Result: Termwise inversion
-- Id: L.9
function "**and**" (*L*, *R*: *SIGNED*) **return** *SIGNED*;
-- Result subtype: *SIGNED*(*L'LENGTH*–1 **downto** 0)
-- Result: Vector AND operation
-- Id: L.10
function "**or**" (*L*, *R*: *SIGNED*) **return** *SIGNED*;
-- Result subtype: *SIGNED*(*L'LENGTH*–1 **downto** 0)
-- Result: Vector OR operation
-- Id: L.11
function "**nand**" (*L*, *R*: *SIGNED*) **return** *SIGNED*;
-- Result subtype: *SIGNED*(*L'LENGTH*–1 **downto** 0)
-- Result: Vector NAND operation
-- Id: L.12
function "**nor**" (*L*, *R*: *SIGNED*) **return** *SIGNED*;
-- Result subtype: *SIGNED*(*L'LENGTH*–1 **downto** 0)
-- Result: Vector NOR operation
-- Id: L.13
function "**xor**" (*L*, *R*: *SIGNED*) **return** *SIGNED*;
-- Result subtype: *SIGNED*(*L'LENGTH*–1 **downto** 0)
-- Result: Vector XOR operation
-- Id: L.14
function "**xnor**" (*L*, *R*: *SIGNED*) **return** *SIGNED*;
-- Result subtype: *SIGNED*(*L'LENGTH*–1 **downto** 0)
-- Result: Vector XNOR operation

-- Edge Detection Functions
-- Id: E.1
function *RISING_EDGE* (**signal** *S*: *BIT*) **return** *BOOLEAN*;
-- Result subtype: *BOOLEAN*
-- Result: Returns TRUE if an event is detected on signal *S* and the
-- value changed from a '0' to a '1'.
-- Id: E.2
function *FALLING_EDGE* (**signal** *S*: *BIT*) **return** *BOOLEAN*;
-- Result subtype: *BOOLEAN*
-- Result: Returns TRUE if an event is detected on signal *S* and the
-- value changed from a '1' to a '0'.
end *NUMERIC_BIT*;

D.3 Package NUMERIC_STD


```
--
-- This source file is an essential part of IEEE Standard P1076.3,
-- Standard VHDL Synthesis Packages.
--
-- This source file represents a portion of IEEE Standard P1076.3.
--
-- This package may be modified to include additional data required by tools, but it
-- must in no way change the external interfaces or simulation behavior of the
-- description. It is permissible to add comments and/or attributes to the package
-- declarations, but not to change or delete any original lines of the package
-- declaration. The package body may be changed only in accordance with the terms of
-- 7.1 and 7.2 of this draft standard.
--
-- Title : Standard VHDL Synthesis Packages (1076.3, NUMERIC_STD)
--
-- Library    : This package shall be compiled into a library symbolically named IEEE.
--
-- Developers : IEEE DASC Synthesis Working Group, PAR 1076.3
--
-- Purpose    : This package defines numeric types and arithmetic functions for use
-- with synthesis tools. Two numeric types are defined:
-- > UNSIGNED: represents UNSIGNED number in vector form
-- > SIGNED: represents a SIGNED number in vector form
-- The base element type is type STD_LOGIC. The leftmost bit is treated as the most
-- significant bit. Signed vectors are represented in two's complement form. This
-- package contains overloaded arithmetic operators on the SIGNED and UNSIGNED
-- types. The package also contains useful type conversions functions. If any argument
-- to a function is a null array, a null array is returned (exceptions, if any, are noted
-- individually).
--
-- Note : No declarations or definitions shall be included in, or excluded from this
-- package. The "package declaration" defines the types, subtypes and declarations of
-- NUMERIC_STD. The NUMERIC_STD package body shall be considered the formal
-- definition of the semantics of this package. Tool developers may choose to
-- implement the package body in the most efficient manner available to them.
--
-- Modification history :
-- ---------------------------------------------------------------
--  Version    : 2.4
--  Date       : 12 April 1995
-- -----------------------------------------------------------------------
library IEEE;
use IEEE.STD_LOGIC_1164.all;
```

```
package NUMERIC_STD is
constant CopyRightNotice: STRING := "Copyright © 1997 IEEE. All rights reserved.";

-- Numeric array type definitions
type UNSIGNED is array (NATURAL range <>) of STD_LOGIC;
type SIGNED is array (NATURAL range <>) of STD_LOGIC;

-- Arithmetic Operators:
-- Id: A.1
function "abs" (ARG: SIGNED) return SIGNED;
-- Result subtype: SIGNED(ARG'LENGTH–1 downto 0).
-- Result: Returns the absolute value of a SIGNED vector ARG.
-- Id: A.2
function "–" (ARG: SIGNED) return SIGNED;
-- Result subtype: SIGNED(ARG'LENGTH–1 downto 0).
-- Result: Returns the value of the unary minus operation on a SIGNED vector ARG.

-- Id: A.3
function "+" (L, R: UNSIGNED) return UNSIGNED;
-- Result subtype: UNSIGNED(MAX(L'LENGTH, R'LENGTH)–1 downto 0).
-- Result: Adds two UNSIGNED vectors that may be of different lengths.
-- Id: A.4
function "+" (L, R: SIGNED) return SIGNED;
-- Result subtype: SIGNED(MAX(L'LENGTH, R'LENGTH)–1 downto 0).
-- Result: Adds two SIGNED vectors that may be of different lengths.
-- Id: A.5
function "+" (L: UNSIGNED; R: NATURAL) return UNSIGNED;
-- Result subtype: UNSIGNED(L'LENGTH–1 downto 0).
-- Result: Adds an UNSIGNED vector, L, with a non-negative INTEGER, R.
-- Id: A.6
function "+" (L: NATURAL; R: UNSIGNED) return UNSIGNED;
-- Result subtype: UNSIGNED(R'LENGTH–1 downto 0).
-- Result: Adds a non-negative INTEGER, L, with an UNSIGNED vector, R.
-- Id: A.7
function "+" (L: INTEGER; R: SIGNED) return SIGNED;
-- Result subtype: SIGNED(R'LENGTH–1 downto 0).
-- Result: Adds an INTEGER, L(may be positive or negative), to a SIGNED vector, R.
-- Id: A.8
function "+" (L: SIGNED; R: INTEGER) return SIGNED;
-- Result subtype: SIGNED(L'LENGTH–1 downto 0).
-- Result: Adds a SIGNED vector, L, to an INTEGER, R.

-- Id: A.9
function "–" (L, R: UNSIGNED) return UNSIGNED;
-- Result subtype: UNSIGNED(MAX(L'LENGTH, R'LENGTH)–1 downto 0).
-- Result: Subtracts two UNSIGNED vectors that may be of different lengths.
```

```
-- Id: A.10
function "–" (L, R: SIGNED) return SIGNED;
-- Result subtype: SIGNED(MAX(L'LENGTH, R'LENGTH)–1 downto 0).
-- Result: Subtracts a SIGNED vector, R, from another SIGNED
--      vector, L, that may possibly be of different lengths.
-- Id: A.11
function "–" (L: UNSIGNED;R: NATURAL) return UNSIGNED;
-- Result subtype: UNSIGNED(L'LENGTH–1 downto 0).
-- Result: Subtracts a non-negative INTEGER, R, from an UNSIGNED vector, L.
-- Id: A.12
function "–" (L: NATURAL; R: UNSIGNED) return UNSIGNED;
-- Result subtype: UNSIGNED(R'LENGTH–1 downto 0).
-- Result: Subtracts an UNSIGNED vector, R, from a non-negative INTEGER, L.
-- Id: A.13
function "–" (L: SIGNED; R: INTEGER) return SIGNED;
-- Result subtype: SIGNED(L'LENGTH–1 downto 0).
-- Result: Subtracts an INTEGER, R, from a SIGNED vector, L.
-- Id: A.14
function "–" (L: INTEGER; R: SIGNED) return SIGNED;
-- Result subtype: SIGNED(R'LENGTH–1 downto 0).
-- Result: Subtracts a SIGNED vector, R, from an INTEGER, L.

-- Id: A.15
function "*" (L, R: UNSIGNED) return UNSIGNED;
-- Result subtype: UNSIGNED((L'LENGTH+R'LENGTH–1) downto 0).
-- Result: Performs the multiplication operation on two UNSIGNED
--      vectors that may possibly be of different lengths.
-- Id: A.16
function "*" (L, R: SIGNED) return SIGNED;
-- Result subtype: SIGNED((L'LENGTH+R'LENGTH–1) downto 0)
-- Result: Multiplies two SIGNED vectors that may possibly be of different lengths.
-- Id: A.17
function "*" (L: UNSIGNED; R: NATURAL) return UNSIGNED;
-- Result subtype: UNSIGNED((L'LENGTH+L'LENGTH–1) downto 0).
-- Result: Multiplies an UNSIGNED vector, L, with a non-negative INTEGER, R. R is
-- converted to an UNSIGNED vector of size L'LENGTH before multiplication.
-- Id: A.18
function "*" (L: NATURAL; R: UNSIGNED) return UNSIGNED;
-- Result subtype: UNSIGNED((R'LENGTH+R'LENGTH–1) downto 0).
-- Result: Multiplies an UNSIGNED vector, R, with a non-negative INTEGER, L. L is
-- converted to an UNSIGNED vector of size R'LENGTH before multiplication.
-- Id: A.19
function "*" (L: SIGNED; R: INTEGER) return SIGNED;
-- Result subtype: SIGNED((L'LENGTH+L'LENGTH–1) downto 0)
-- Result: Multiplies a SIGNED vector, L, with an INTEGER, R. R is
-- converted to a SIGNED vector of size L'LENGTH before multiplication.
```

-- Id: A.20
function "*" (*L*: *INTEGER*; *R*: *SIGNED*) **return** *SIGNED*;
-- Result subtype: *SIGNED*((*R'LENGTH*+*R'LENGTH*–1) **downto** 0)
-- Result: Multiplies a *SIGNED* vector, *R*, with an *INTEGER*, *L*. *L* is
-- converted to a *SIGNED* vector of size *R'LENGTH* before multiplication.

-- NOTE: If second argument is zero for "/" operator, a severity level
-- of ERROR is issued.
-- Id: A.21
function "/" (*L*, *R*: *UNSIGNED*) **return** *UNSIGNED*;
-- Result subtype: *UNSIGNED*(*L'LENGTH*–1 **downto** 0)
-- Result: Divides an *UNSIGNED* vector, *L*, by another *UNSIGNED* vector, *R*.
-- Id: A.22
function "/" (*L*, *R*: *SIGNED*) **return** *SIGNED*;
-- Result subtype: *SIGNED*(*L'LENGTH*–1 **downto** 0)
-- Result: Divides an *SIGNED* vector, *L*, by another *SIGNED* vector, *R*.
-- Id: A.23
function "/" (*L*: *UNSIGNED*; *R*: *NATURAL*) **return** *UNSIGNED*;
-- Result subtype: *UNSIGNED*(*L'LENGTH*–1 **downto** 0)
-- Result: Divides an *UNSIGNED* vector, *L*, by a non-negative *INTEGER*, *R*.
-- If *NO_OF_BITS*(*R*) > *L'LENGTH*, result is truncated to *L'LENGTH*.
-- Id: A.24
function "/" (*L*: *NATURAL*; *R*: *UNSIGNED*) **return** *UNSIGNED*;
-- Result subtype: *UNSIGNED*(*R'LENGTH*–1 **downto** 0)
-- Result: Divides a non-negative *INTEGER*, *L*, by an *UNSIGNED* vector, *R*.
-- If *NO_OF_BITS*(*L*) > *R'LENGTH*, result is truncated to *R'LENGTH*.
-- Id: A.25
function "/" (*L*: *SIGNED*; *R*: *INTEGER*) **return** *SIGNED*;
-- Result subtype: *SIGNED*(*L'LENGTH*–1 **downto** 0)
-- Result: Divides a *SIGNED* vector, *L*, by an *INTEGER*, *R*.
-- If *NO_OF_BITS*(*R*) > *L'LENGTH*, result is truncated to *L'LENGTH*.
-- Id: A.26
function "/" (*L*: *INTEGER*; *R*: *SIGNED*) **return** *SIGNED*;
-- Result subtype: *SIGNED*(*R'LENGTH*–1 **downto** 0)
-- Result: Divides an *INTEGER*, *L*, by a *SIGNED* vector, *R*.
-- If *NO_OF_BITS*(*L*) > *R'LENGTH*, result is truncated to *R'LENGTH*.

-- NOTE: If second argument is zero for "**rem**" operator, a severity
-- level of ERROR is issued.
-- Id: A.27
function "**rem**" (*L*, *R*: *UNSIGNED*) **return** *UNSIGNED*;
-- Result subtype: *UNSIGNED*(*R'LENGTH*–1 **downto** 0)
-- Result: Computes "*L* **rem** *R*" where *L* and *R* are *UNSIGNED* vectors.
-- Id: A.28
function "**rem**" (*L*, *R*: *SIGNED*) **return** *SIGNED*;
-- Result subtype: *SIGNED*(*R'LENGTH*–1 **downto** 0)
-- Result: Computes "*L* **rem** *R*" where *L* and *R* are *SIGNED* vectors.

-- Id: A.29
function "**rem**" (*L*: *UNSIGNED*; *R*: *NATURAL*) **return** *UNSIGNED*;
-- Result subtype: *UNSIGNED*(*L'LENGTH*–1 **downto** 0)
-- Result: Computes "*L* **rem** *R*" where *L* is an *UNSIGNED* vector and *R* is a non-
-- negative *INTEGER*. If *NO_OF_BITS*(*R*) > *L'LENGTH*, result is truncated
-- to *L'LENGTH*.
-- Id: A.30
function "**rem**" (*L*: *NATURAL*; *R*: *UNSIGNED*) **return** *UNSIGNED*;
-- Result subtype: *UNSIGNED*(*R'LENGTH*–1 **downto** 0)
-- Result: Computes "*L* **rem** *R*" where *R* is an *UNSIGNED* vector and
--   *L* is a non-negative *INTEGER*.
--   If *NO_OF_BITS*(*L*) > *R'LENGTH*, result is truncated to *R'LENGTH*.
-- Id: A.31
function "**rem**" (*L*: *SIGNED*; *R*: *INTEGER*) **return** *SIGNED*;
-- Result subtype: *SIGNED*(*L'LENGTH*–1 **downto** 0)
-- Result: Computes "*L* **rem** *R*" where *L* is *SIGNED* vector and *R* is an *INTEGER*.
--   If *NO_OF_BITS*(*R*) > *L'LENGTH*, result is truncated to *L'LENGTH*.
-- Id: A.32
function "**rem**" (*L*: *INTEGER*; *R*: *SIGNED*) **return** *SIGNED*;
-- Result subtype: *SIGNED*(*R'LENGTH*–1 **downto** 0)
-- Result: Computes "*L* **rem** *R*" where *R* is *SIGNED* vector and *L* is an *INTEGER*.
--   If *NO_OF_BITS*(*L*) > *R'LENGTH*, result is truncated to *R'LENGTH*.

-- NOTE: If second argument is zero for "**mod**" operator, a severity
--   level of ERROR is issued.
-- Id: A.33
function "**mod**" (*L*, *R*: *UNSIGNED*) **return** *UNSIGNED*;
-- Result subtype: *UNSIGNED*(*R'LENGTH*–1 **downto** 0)
-- Result: Computes "*L* **mod** *R*" where *L* and *R* are *UNSIGNED* vectors.
-- Id: A.34
function "**mod**" (*L*, *R*: *SIGNED*) **return** *SIGNED*;
-- Result subtype: *SIGNED*(*R'LENGTH*–1 **downto** 0)
-- Result: Computes "*L* **mod** *R*" where *L* and *R* are *SIGNED* vectors.
-- Id: A.35
function "**mod**" (*L*: *UNSIGNED*; *R*: *NATURAL*) **return** *UNSIGNED*;
-- Result subtype: *UNSIGNED*(*L'LENGTH*–1 **downto** 0)
-- Result: Computes "*L* **mod** *R*" where *L* is an *UNSIGNED* vector
--   and *R* is a non-negative *INTEGER*.
--   If *NO_OF_BITS*(*R*) > *L'LENGTH*, result is truncated to *L'LENGTH*.
-- Id: A.36
function "**mod**" (*L*: *NATURAL*; *R*: *UNSIGNED*) **return** *UNSIGNED*;
-- Result subtype: *UNSIGNED*(*R'LENGTH*–1 **downto** 0)
-- Result: Computes "*L* **mod** *R*" where *R* is an *UNSIGNED* vector
--   and *L* is a non-negative *INTEGER*.
--   If *NO_OF_BITS*(*L*) > *R'LENGTH*, result is truncated to *R'LENGTH*.
-- Id: A.37
function "**mod**" (*L*: *SIGNED*; *R*: *INTEGER*) **return** *SIGNED*;

```
-- Result subtype: SIGNED(L'LENGTH-1 downto 0)
-- Result: Computes "L mod R" where L is a SIGNED vector and R is an INTEGER.
--        If NO_OF_BITS(R) > L'LENGTH, result is truncated to L'LENGTH.
-- Id: A.38
function "mod" (L: INTEGER; R: SIGNED) return SIGNED;
-- Result subtype: SIGNED(R'LENGTH-1 downto 0)
-- Result: Computes "L mod R" where L is an INTEGER and R is a SIGNED vector.
--        If NO_OF_BITS(L) > R'LENGTH, result is truncated to R'LENGTH.

-- Comparison Operators
-- Id: C.1
function ">" (L, R: UNSIGNED) return BOOLEAN;
-- Result subtype: BOOLEAN
-- Result: Computes "L > R" where L and R are UNSIGNED vectors
--        possibly of different lengths.
-- Id: C.2
function ">" (L, R: SIGNED) return BOOLEAN;
-- Result subtype: BOOLEAN
-- Result: Computes "L > R" where L and R are SIGNED vectors
--        possibly of different lengths.
-- Id: C.3
function ">" (L: NATURAL; R: UNSIGNED) return BOOLEAN;
-- Result subtype: BOOLEAN
-- Result: Computes "L > R" where L is a non-negative INTEGER
--        and R is an UNSIGNED vector.
-- Id: C.4
function ">" (L: INTEGER; R: SIGNED) return BOOLEAN;
-- Result subtype: BOOLEAN
-- Result: Computes "L > R" where L is a INTEGER and R is a SIGNED vector.
-- Id: C.5
function ">" (L: UNSIGNED; R: NATURAL) return BOOLEAN;
-- Result subtype: BOOLEAN
-- Result: Computes "L > R" where L is an UNSIGNED vector and
--        R is a non-negative INTEGER.
-- Id: C.6
function ">" (L: SIGNED; R: INTEGER) return BOOLEAN;
-- Result subtype: BOOLEAN
-- Result: Computes "L > R" where L is a SIGNED vector and R is a INTEGER.

-- Id: C.7
function "<" (L, R: UNSIGNED) return BOOLEAN;
-- Result subtype: BOOLEAN
-- Result: Computes "L < R" where L and R are UNSIGNED vectors
--        possibly of different lengths.
-- Id: C.8
function "<" (L, R: SIGNED) return BOOLEAN;
-- Result subtype: BOOLEAN
```

```
-- Result: Computes "L < R" where L and R are SIGNED vectors
--      possibly of different lengths.
-- Id: C.9
function "<" (L: NATURAL; R: UNSIGNED) return BOOLEAN;
-- Result subtype: BOOLEAN
-- Result: Computes "L < R" where L is a non-negative INTEGER
--      and R is an UNSIGNED vector.
-- Id: C.10
function "<" (L: INTEGER; R: SIGNED) return BOOLEAN;
-- Result subtype: BOOLEAN
-- Result: Computes "L < R" where L is an INTEGER and R is a SIGNED vector.
-- Id: C.11
function "<" (L: UNSIGNED; R: NATURAL) return BOOLEAN;
-- Result subtype: BOOLEAN
-- Result: Computes "L < R" where L is an UNSIGNED vector and
--      R is a non-negative INTEGER.
-- Id: C.12
function "<" (L: SIGNED; R: INTEGER) return BOOLEAN;
-- Result subtype: BOOLEAN
-- Result: Computes "L < R" where L is a SIGNED vector and R is an INTEGER.

-- Id: C.13
function "<=" (L, R: UNSIGNED) return BOOLEAN;
-- Result subtype: BOOLEAN
-- Result: Computes "L <= R" where L and R are UNSIGNED vectors
--      possibly of different lengths.
-- Id: C.14
function "<=" (L, R: SIGNED) return BOOLEAN;
-- Result subtype: BOOLEAN
-- Result: Computes "L <= R" where L and R are SIGNED vectors
--      possibly of different lengths.
-- Id: C.15
function "<=" (L: NATURAL; R: UNSIGNED) return BOOLEAN;
-- Result subtype: BOOLEAN
-- Result: Computes "L <= R" where L is a non-negative INTEGER
--      and R is an UNSIGNED vector.
-- Id: C.16
function "<=" (L: INTEGER; R: SIGNED) return BOOLEAN;
-- Result subtype: BOOLEAN
-- Result: Computes "L <= R" where L is an INTEGER and R is a SIGNED vector.
-- Id: C.17
function "<=" (L: UNSIGNED; R: NATURAL) return BOOLEAN;
-- Result subtype: BOOLEAN
-- Result: Computes "L <= R" where L is an UNSIGNED vector and
--      R is a non-negative INTEGER.
-- Id: C.18
function "<=" (L: SIGNED; R: INTEGER) return BOOLEAN;
```

```
-- Result subtype: BOOLEAN
-- Result: Computes "L <= R" where L is a SIGNED vector and R is an INTEGER.

-- Id: C.19
function ">=" (L, R: UNSIGNED) return BOOLEAN;
-- Result subtype: BOOLEAN
-- Result: Computes "L >= R" where L and R are UNSIGNED vectors
--      possibly of different lengths.
-- Id: C.20
function ">=" (L, R: SIGNED) return BOOLEAN;
-- Result subtype: BOOLEAN
-- Result: Computes "L >= R" where L and R are SIGNED vectors
--      possibly of different lengths.
-- Id: C.21
function ">=" (L: NATURAL; R: UNSIGNED) return BOOLEAN;
-- Result subtype: BOOLEAN
-- Result: Computes "L >= R" where L is a non-negative INTEGER
--      and R is an UNSIGNED vector.
-- Id: C.22
function ">=" (L: INTEGER; R: SIGNED) return BOOLEAN;
-- Result subtype: BOOLEAN
-- Result: Computes "L >= R" where L is an INTEGER and R is a SIGNED vector.
-- Id: C.23
function ">=" (L: UNSIGNED; R: NATURAL) return BOOLEAN;
-- Result subtype: BOOLEAN
-- Result: Computes "L >= R" where L is an UNSIGNED vector and
--      R is a non-negative INTEGER.
-- Id: C.24
function ">=" (L: SIGNED; R: INTEGER) return BOOLEAN;
-- Result subtype: BOOLEAN
-- Result: Computes "L >= R" where L is a SIGNED vector and R is an INTEGER.

-- Id: C.25
function "=" (L, R: UNSIGNED) return BOOLEAN;
-- Result subtype: BOOLEAN
-- Result: Computes "L = R" where L and R are UNSIGNED vectors
--      possibly of different lengths.
-- Id: C.26
function "=" (L, R: SIGNED) return BOOLEAN;
-- Result subtype: BOOLEAN
-- Result: Computes "L = R" where L and R are SIGNED vectors
--      possibly of different lengths.
-- Id: C.27
function "=" (L: NATURAL; R: UNSIGNED) return BOOLEAN;
-- Result subtype: BOOLEAN
-- Result: Computes "L = R" where L is a non-negative INTEGER
--      and R is an UNSIGNED vector.
```

```
-- Id: C.28
function "=" (L: INTEGER; R: SIGNED) return BOOLEAN;
-- Result subtype: BOOLEAN
-- Result: Computes "L = R" where L is an INTEGER and R is a SIGNED vector.
-- Id: C.29
function "=" (L: UNSIGNED; R: NATURAL) return BOOLEAN;
-- Result subtype: BOOLEAN
-- Result: Computes "L = R" where L is an UNSIGNED vector and
--       R is a non-negative INTEGER.
-- Id: C.30
function "=" (L: SIGNED; R: INTEGER) return BOOLEAN;
-- Result subtype: BOOLEAN
-- Result: Computes "L = R" where L is a SIGNED vector and R is an INTEGER.

-- Id: C.31
function "/=" (L, R: UNSIGNED) return BOOLEAN;
-- Result subtype: BOOLEAN
-- Result: Computes "L /= R" where L and R are UNSIGNED vectors
--       possibly of different lengths.
-- Id: C.32
function "/=" (L, R: SIGNED) return BOOLEAN;
-- Result subtype: BOOLEAN
-- Result: Computes "L /= R" where L and R are SIGNED vectors
--       possibly of different lengths.
-- Id: C.33
function "/=" (L: NATURAL; R: UNSIGNED) return BOOLEAN;
-- Result subtype: BOOLEAN
-- Result: Computes "L /= R" where L is a non-negative INTEGER
--       and R is an UNSIGNED vector.
-- Id: C.34
function "/=" (L: INTEGER; R: SIGNED) return BOOLEAN;
-- Result subtype: BOOLEAN
-- Result: Computes "L /= R" where L is an INTEGER and R is a SIGNED vector.
-- Id: C.35
function "/=" (L: UNSIGNED; R: NATURAL) return BOOLEAN;
-- Result subtype: BOOLEAN
-- Result: Computes "L /= R" where L is an UNSIGNED vector and
--       R is a non-negative INTEGER.
-- Id: C.36
function "/=" (L: SIGNED; R: INTEGER) return BOOLEAN;
-- Result subtype: BOOLEAN
-- Result: Computes "L /= R" where L is a SIGNED vector and R is an INTEGER.

-- Shift and Rotate Functions
-- Id: S.1
function SHIFT_LEFT (ARG: UNSIGNED; COUNT: NATURAL) return UNSIGNED;
-- Result subtype: UNSIGNED(ARG'LENGTH-1 downto 0)
```

```
-- Result: Performs a shift-left on an UNSIGNED vector COUNT times. The vacated
-- positions are filled with '0'. The COUNT leftmost elements are lost.
-- Id: S.2
function SHIFT_RIGHT (ARG: UNSIGNED; COUNT: NATURAL) return UNSIGNED;
-- Result subtype: UNSIGNED(ARG'LENGTH-1 downto 0)
-- Result: Performs a shift-right on an UNSIGNED vector COUNT times. The vacated
-- positions are filled with '0'. The COUNT rightmost elements are lost.
-- Id: S.3
function SHIFT_LEFT (ARG: SIGNED; COUNT: NATURAL) return SIGNED;
-- Result subtype: SIGNED(ARG'LENGTH-1 downto 0)
-- Result: Performs a shift-left on a SIGNED vector COUNT times. The vacated
-- positions are filled with '0'. The COUNT leftmost elements are lost.
-- Id: S.4
function SHIFT_RIGHT (ARG: SIGNED; COUNT: NATURAL) return SIGNED;
-- Result subtype: SIGNED(ARG'LENGTH-1 downto 0)
-- Result: Performs a shift-right on a SIGNED vector COUNT times. The vacated
-- positions are filled with the leftmost element, ARG'LEFT. The COUNT rightmost
-- elements are lost.

-- Id: S.5
function ROTATE_LEFT (ARG: UNSIGNED; COUNT: NATURAL) return UNSIGNED;
-- Result subtype: UNSIGNED(ARG'LENGTH-1 downto 0)
-- Result: Performs a rotate-left of an UNSIGNED vector COUNT times.
-- Id: S.6
function ROTATE_RIGHT (ARG: UNSIGNED; COUNT: NATURAL)
        return UNSIGNED;
-- Result subtype: UNSIGNED(ARG'LENGTH-1 downto 0)
-- Result: Performs a rotate-right of an UNSIGNED vector COUNT times.
-- Id: S.7
function ROTATE_LEFT (ARG: SIGNED; COUNT: NATURAL) return SIGNED;
-- Result subtype: SIGNED(ARG'LENGTH-1 downto 0)
-- Result: Performs a logical rotate-left of a SIGNED vector COUNT times.
-- Id: S.8
function ROTATE_RIGHT (ARG: SIGNED; COUNT: NATURAL) return SIGNED;
-- Result subtype: SIGNED(ARG'LENGTH-1 downto 0)
-- Result: Performs a logical rotate-right of a SIGNED vector COUNT times.

------------------------------------------------------------------------
-- Note : Functions S.9 to S.16 are not compatible with VHDL 1076-1987. Comment
-- out the function (declaration and body) for VHDL 1076-1987 compatibility.
------------------------------------------------------------------------
-- Id: S.9
function "sll" (ARG: UNSIGNED; COUNT: INTEGER) return UNSIGNED;
-- Result subtype: UNSIGNED(ARG'LENGTH-1 downto 0)
-- Result: SHIFT_LEFT(ARG, COUNT)
-- Id: S.10
function "sll" (ARG: SIGNED; COUNT: INTEGER) return SIGNED;
```

-- Result subtype: *SIGNED(ARG'LENGTH*–1 **downto** 0)
-- Result: *SHIFT_LEFT(ARG, COUNT)*
-- Id: S.11
function "**srl**" (*ARG*: *UNSIGNED*; *COUNT*: *INTEGER*) **return** *UNSIGNED*;
-- Result subtype: *UNSIGNED(ARG'LENGTH*–1 **downto** 0)
-- Result: *SHIFT_RIGHT(ARG, COUNT)*
-- Id: S.12
function "**srl**" (*ARG*: *SIGNED*; *COUNT*: *INTEGER*) **return** *SIGNED*;
-- Result subtype: *SIGNED(ARG'LENGTH*–1 **downto** 0)
-- Result: *SIGNED(SHIFT_RIGHT(UNSIGNED(ARG), COUNT))*
-- Id: S.13
function "**rol**" (*ARG*: *UNSIGNED*; *COUNT*: *INTEGER*) **return** *UNSIGNED*;
-- Result subtype: *UNSIGNED(ARG'LENGTH*–1 **downto** 0)
-- Result: *ROTATE_LEFT(ARG, COUNT)*
-- Id: S.14
function "**rol**" (*ARG*: *SIGNED*; *COUNT*: *INTEGER*) **return** *SIGNED*;
-- Result subtype: *SIGNED(ARG'LENGTH*–1 **downto** 0)
-- Result: *ROTATE_LEFT(ARG, COUNT)*
-- Id: S.15
function "**ror**" (*ARG*: *UNSIGNED*; *COUNT*: *INTEGER*) **return** *UNSIGNED*;
-- Result subtype: *UNSIGNED(ARG'LENGTH*–1 **downto** 0)
-- Result: *ROTATE_RIGHT(ARG, COUNT)*
-- Id: S.16
function "**ror**" (*ARG*: *SIGNED*; *COUNT*: *INTEGER*) **return** *SIGNED*;
-- Result subtype: *SIGNED(ARG'LENGTH*–1 **downto** 0)
-- Result: *ROTATE_RIGHT(ARG, COUNT)*

-- *RESIZE* Functions
-- Id: R.1
function *RESIZE* (*ARG*: *SIGNED*; *NEW_SIZE*: *NATURAL*) **return** *SIGNED*;
-- Result subtype: *SIGNED(NEW_SIZE*–1 **downto** 0)
-- Result: Resizes the *SIGNED* vector *ARG* to the specified size. To create a larger
-- vector, the new [leftmost] bit positions are filled with the sign bit (*ARG'LEFT*). When
-- truncating, the sign bit is retained along with the rightmost part.
-- Id: R.2
function *RESIZE* (*ARG*: *UNSIGNED*; *NEW_SIZE*: *NATURAL*) **return** *UNSIGNED*;
-- Result subtype: *UNSIGNED(NEW_SIZE*–1 **downto** 0)
-- Result: Resizes the *SIGNED* vector *ARG* to the specified size. To create a
-- larger vector, the new [leftmost] bit positions are filled with '0'. When
-- truncating, the leftmost bits are dropped.

-- Conversion Functions
-- Id: D.1
function *TO_INTEGER* (*ARG*: *UNSIGNED*) **return** *NATURAL*;
-- Result subtype: *NATURAL*. Value cannot be negative since
-- parameter is an *UNSIGNED* vector.
-- Result: Converts the *UNSIGNED* vector to an *INTEGER*.

```
-- Id: D.2
function TO_INTEGER (ARG: SIGNED) return INTEGER;
-- Result subtype: INTEGER
-- Result: Converts a SIGNED vector to an INTEGER.
-- Id: D.3
function TO_UNSIGNED (ARG, SIZE: NATURAL) return UNSIGNED;
-- Result subtype: UNSIGNED(SIZE-1 downto 0)
-- Result: Converts a non-negative INTEGER to an UNSIGNED
-- vector with the specified SIZE.
-- Id: D.4
function TO_SIGNED (ARG: INTEGER; SIZE: NATURAL) return SIGNED;
-- Result subtype: SIGNED(SIZE-1 downto 0)
-- Result: Converts an INTEGER to a SIGNED vector of the specified SIZE.

-- Logical Operators
-- Id: L.1
function "not" (L: UNSIGNED) return UNSIGNED;
-- Result subtype: UNSIGNED(L'LENGTH-1 downto 0)
-- Result: Termwise inversion
-- Id: L.2
function "and" (L, R: UNSIGNED) return UNSIGNED;
-- Result subtype: UNSIGNED(L'LENGTH-1 downto 0)
-- Result: Vector AND operation
-- Id: L.3
function "or" (L, R: UNSIGNED) return UNSIGNED;
-- Result subtype: UNSIGNED(L'LENGTH-1 downto 0)
-- Result: Vector OR operation
-- Id: L.4
function "nand" (L, R: UNSIGNED) return UNSIGNED;
-- Result subtype: UNSIGNED(L'LENGTH-1 downto 0)
-- Result: Vector NAND operation
-- Id: L.5
function "nor" (L, R: UNSIGNED) return UNSIGNED;
-- Result subtype: UNSIGNED(L'LENGTH-1 downto 0)
-- Result: Vector NOR operation
-- Id: L.6
function "xor" (L, R: UNSIGNED) return UNSIGNED;
-- Result subtype: UNSIGNED(L'LENGTH-1 downto 0)
-- Result: Vector XOR operation

-- ---------------------------------------------------------------------------
-- Note : Functions L.7 and L.14 are not compatible with VHDL 1076-1987. Comment
-- out the function (declaration and body) for VHDL 1076-1987 compatibility.
-- ---------------------------------------------------------------------------
-- Id: L.7
function "xnor" (L, R: UNSIGNED) return UNSIGNED;
-- Result subtype: UNSIGNED(L'LENGTH-1 downto 0)
```

-- Result: Vector XNOR operation
-- Id: L.8
function "**not**" (*L*: *SIGNED*) **return** *SIGNED*;
-- Result subtype: *SIGNED*(*L*'*LENGTH*–1 **downto** 0)
-- Result: Termwise inversion
-- Id: L.9
function "**and**" (*L*, *R*: *SIGNED*) **return** *SIGNED*;
-- Result subtype: *SIGNED*(*L*'*LENGTH*–1 **downto** 0)
-- Result: Vector AND operation
-- Id: L.10
function "**or**" (*L*, *R*: *SIGNED*) **return** *SIGNED*;
-- Result subtype: *SIGNED*(*L*'*LENGTH*–1 **downto** 0)
-- Result: Vector OR operation
-- Id: L.11
function "**nand**" (*L*, *R*: *SIGNED*) **return** *SIGNED*;
-- Result subtype: *SIGNED*(*L*'*LENGTH*–1 **downto** 0)
-- Result: Vector NAND operation
-- Id: L.12
function "**nor**" (*L*, *R*: *SIGNED*) **return** *SIGNED*;
-- Result subtype: *SIGNED*(*L*'*LENGTH*–1 **downto** 0)
-- Result: Vector NOR operation
-- Id: L.13
function "**xor**" (*L*, *R*: *SIGNED*) **return** *SIGNED*;
-- Result subtype: *SIGNED*(*L*'*LENGTH*–1 **downto** 0)
-- Result: Vector XOR operation
-- Id: L.14
function "**xnor**" (*L*, *R*: *SIGNED*) **return** *SIGNED*;
-- Result subtype: *SIGNED*(*L*'*LENGTH*–1 **downto** 0)
-- Result: Vector XNOR operation

-- Match Functions
-- Id: M.1
function *STD_MATCH* (*L*, *R*: *STD_ULOGIC*) **return** *BOOLEAN*;
-- Result subtype: *BOOLEAN*
-- Result: terms compared per *STD_LOGIC_1164* intent
-- Id: M.2
function *STD_MATCH* (*L*, *R*: *UNSIGNED*) **return** *BOOLEAN*;
-- Result subtype: *BOOLEAN*
-- Result: terms compared per *STD_LOGIC_1164* intent
-- Id: M.3
function *STD_MATCH* (*L*, *R*: *SIGNED*) **return** *BOOLEAN*;
-- Result subtype: *BOOLEAN*
-- Result: terms compared per *STD_LOGIC_1164* intent
-- Id: M.4
function *STD_MATCH* (*L*, *R*: *STD_LOGIC_VECTOR*) **return** *BOOLEAN*;
-- Result subtype: *BOOLEAN*
-- Result: terms compared per *STD_LOGIC_1164* intent

-- Id: M.5
function *STD_MATCH* (*L, R*: *STD_ULOGIC_VECTOR*) **return** *BOOLEAN;*
-- Result subtype: *BOOLEAN*
-- Result: terms compared per *STD_LOGIC_1164* intent

-- Translation Functions
-- Id: T.1
function *TO_01* (*S*: *UNSIGNED; XMAP*: *STD_LOGIC* := '0') **return** *UNSIGNED;*
-- Result subtype: *UNSIGNED(S'RANGE)*
-- Result: Termwise, 'H' is translated to '1', and 'L' is translated to '0'. If a value other
-- than '0' | '1' | 'H' | 'L' is found, the array is set to (**others** => *XMAP*), and a warning is
-- issued.
-- Id: T.2
function *TO_01* (*S*: *SIGNED; XMAP*: *STD_LOGIC* := '0') **return** *SIGNED;*
-- Result subtype: *SIGNED(S'RANGE)*
-- Result: Termwise, 'H' is translated to '1', and 'L' is translated to '0'. If a value other
-- than '0' | '1' | 'H' | 'L' is found, the array is set to (**others** => *XMAP*), and a warning is
-- issued.

end *NUMERIC_STD;*

❑

Bibliography

Here is a select list of suggested readings and books on the VHDL language and on VHDL synthesis.

1. Airiau R., et. al., *Circuit Synthesis with VHDL*, Boston: Kluwer Academic, 1994.
2. Armstrong, J. R., *Chip-level Modeling with VHDL*, Englewood Cliffs, NJ: Prentice Hall, 1988.
3. Ashenden, P.J., *The Designers Guide to VHDL*, Morgan Kaufmann, 1995.
4. Ashenden, P.J., *The VHDL Cookbook*, The University of Adelaide, Australia, 1990.
5. Baker, L., *VHDL Programming with Advanced Topics*, John Wiley and Sons, Inc., 1993.
6. Berge, J-M., et al., *VHDL Designer's Reference*, Kluwer Academic, 1992.
7. Berge, J-M., et al., *VHDL'92*, Kluwer Academic, 1993.
8. Bhasker, J., *A VHDL Primer*, Englewood Cliffs, NJ: Prentice Hall, 1992.

9. Bhasker, J., *A VHDL Primer: Revised edition*, Englewood Cliffs, NJ: Prentice Hall, 1995.

10. Bhasker, J., *A Guide to VHDL Syntax*, Englewood Cliffs, NJ: Prentice Hall, 1995.

11. Bhasker, J., *VHDL: Features and Applications*, A self-study course, IEEE, 1995.

12. Bhasker, J., *Process-Graph Analyzer: A Front-end Tool for VHDL Behavioral Synthesis*, Software Practice and Experience, vol. 18, no. 5, May 1988.

13. Bhasker, J., *An Algorithm for Microcode Compaction of VHDL Behavioral Descriptions*, Proc. 20th Microprogramming Workshop, December 1987.

14. Coelho, D., *The VHDL Handbook*, Boston: Kluwer Academic, 1988.

15. Cohen, Ben, *VHDL Coding Styles and Methodologies*, Boston: Kluwer Academic, 1995.

16. De Micheli, G., R.K. Brayton and A. Sangiovanni Vincentelli, *Optimal State Assignment for Finite State Machines*, IEEE Transactions on CAD, CAD-4(3), pp269-284, July 1985.

17. Harr, R., and A. Stanculescu (eds.), *Applications of VHDL to Circuit Design*, Boston: Kluwer Academic, 1991.

18. Hsu, Y-C., et. al., *VHDL Modeling for Digital Design Synthesis*, Boston: Kluwer Academic, 1995.

19. *IEEE Standard VHDL Language Reference Manual, Std 1076-1993*, IEEE, NY, 1993.

20. *IEEE Standard Multivalue Logic System for VHDL Model Interoperability (Std_Logic_1164)*, Std 1164-1993, IEEE, 1993.

21. Kurup, Pran and T. Abbasi, *Logic Synthesis Using Synopsys*, Boston: Kluwer Academic, 1995.

22. Lipsett, R., et. al., *VHDL: Hardware Description and Design*, Boston: Kluwer Academic, 1989.

23. Navabi, Z., *VHDL Analysis and Modeling of Digital Systems*, McGraw Hill, 1993.

24. Ott, D.E. and T.J. Wilderotter, *A Designer's Guide to VHDL Synthesis*, Boston: Kluwer Academic, 1994.

25. Perry, D., *VHDL*, New York: McGraw Hill, 1991.

26. Schoen, J.M., *Performance and Fault Modeling with VHDL*, Englewood Cliffs, NJ: Prentice Hall, 1992.

27. Smith, Doug, *HDL Chip Design*, Doone Publications, 1996.

❑

Index